Playing for Power

the MODERN SOUTH

PLAYING FOR POWER

Black Resistance in Amateur Basketball and Football in Jim Crow Virginia

MARVIN T. CHILES

THE UNIVERSITY OF ALABAMA PRESS
TUSCALOOSA

The University of Alabama Press
Tuscaloosa, Alabama 35487-0380
uapress.ua.edu

Typeface: Minion Pro

Cover image: (*Top*) VIAA 1951 state basketball game between Peabody High School of Petersburg (winner) and Lawrence Dunbar High School of Lynchburg and (*bottom*) a live shot of a VIA football game, circa 1951; both images courtesy of Virginia Union University Archives and Special Collections

Cover design: Sandy Turner Jr.

Cataloging-in-Publication data is available from the Library of Congress.
ISBN: 978-0-8173-2238-0 (cloth)
ISBN: 978-0-8173-6210-2 (paper)
E-ISBN: 978-0-8173-9565-0

Contents

Figures

Illustrations are courtesy of Virginia Union University Archives and Special Collections.

Acknowledgments

THIS BOOK COMBINES my passion for sports with my vocation of historical writing. To do this, I needed much encouragement, patience, and a publisher willing to see the value in a project of this magnitude. The encouragement and patience came from my loving wife, Alia Quinn Chiles. She is my everything, and this book is just another testament to how real her commitment has been to me as a man, husband, father, and scholar. I also thank my mentors Robert A. Pratt of the University of Georgia, Steven Reich of James Madison University, Julian Maxwell Hayter of the University of Richmond, and Abner "Woody" Holton III of the University of South Carolina. It was these men who encouraged me that pivoting toward my passion of sport history would better unpack my ideas about race and culture.

Even the dead deserve reverence, so I thank the men and women whose names and efforts are discussed in this book. They created what I call "the bygone world of sport"—a realm where Black people resisted segregation by exercising their commitment to racial equality with athletic exercise. It is because of them that sports are not just recreational games to Black people. Rather, athletics is a pillar of Black American life, culture, and full citizenship. Last but certainly not least, I thank Claire Lewis Evans and Kristen Hop of the University of Alabama Press. Claire saw the promise of this project well before a word was ever written. Kristen facilitated this manuscript from its original form to its final product. To call Claire and Kristen class acts would be an understatement given their commitment to me as a scholar and the bygone world as a subject of inquiry.

Playing for Power

INTRODUCTION

Representatives of the Virginia Interscholastic Heritage Association (VIHA) and Virginia State University (VSU) met in fall 2017 to create a public history website and archive with oral histories, photos, and other materials for Black Jim Crow–era high school sports.[1] In archiving this history, VIHA and Virginia State set out to accomplish three things. First, they created a memento honoring the importance of this chapter in the commonwealth's past. Second, they set out to create an archive for living alumni who were integral to this story. And third, both institutions wanted to provide a space where those who remained could congregate annually in remembrance of this increasingly forgotten history. Local media took immediate notice, as for some, segregated athletics was as much a lived experience as it is now a history to be remembered by those who never experienced legal segregation. Moreover, a Newport News–based newspaper found in their coverage of a VIHA event that Jim Crow–era sport still "lives on in the memories of its participants" despite many of them fighting for racial integration during the Civil Rights era.[2]

The VIHA is one of many alumni organizations around the nation that have more recently remembered, commemorated, and generated public awareness about the legacy of segregated sports.[3] These groups do not just celebrate Jim Crow athletics as an extension of the Civil Rights Movement, in that their importance is linked to the long fight for racial integration. In fact, their efforts do just the opposite. These groups celebrate segregated athletics because the games represented an oppressed race cultivating community in defiance of societal oppression. Jim Crow sports helped turn spaces occupied by Black people into communities where Black boys learned life lessons from Black men; Black men overcame discrimination in becoming community leaders; educational institutions served the needs of their race; and individual efforts coalesced into a collective striving for social equality. Segregated games were training grounds for personhood, masculinity, citizenship, and community. On a personal, interpersonal, and communal level, segregated games generated racial uplift and moral formation in a way that modern-day amateur sports, while being integrated, professionalized, and nationally consumed, are not geared to do. This is the memory that alumni organizations are pushing into public discourse. This became clear to me when I took interest in VIHA's work with Virginia State in 2017, while I was still a graduate student nearly eight hours (by car) away at the University of Georgia.

Few people, with the exception of early American scholars, think of the Commonwealth of Virginia and its history with sports in mind.[4] After all, Virginia is nationally recognized as the birthplace of America because of the Jamestown settlement, the seedbed for American racism with the arrival of African slaves in 1619, the "Mother of Presidents" for being the birthplace of eight occupants of the Oval Office, the cultural and political seat of the Confederate States of America during the Civil War; ground zero for massive resistance to the *Brown v. Board of Education* (1954) decision; and the place where Confederate memorialization was called into serious question. No state better represents a long-standing American dilemma—the juxtaposition of freedom for some and unfreedom for others—than Virginia. It was here where Black people helped redefine freedom as a right for all Americans through resistance to slavery and segregation. Hence, Virginia's history of Black sports during Jim Crow represents an under-told chapter of this tome of racial history—where African Americans used athletics to redefine freedom and, in the process, also redefined the meaning and exercise of sport.

VIHA's and Virginia State's efforts reveal that Virginia has contributed much more to the nation than previously given credit for. I grew up in the commonwealth when it pumped out a litany of iconic Black athletes, the most notable being NBA hall of famers Alonzo Mourning, Grant Hill, and Allen Iverson, as well as NFL greats Bruce Smith, Lawrence Taylor, Michael Vick, and Tiki and Ronde Barber, just to name a few. It was not until recently that I discovered that these men stood on the shoulders of giants. The integrated amateur athletic world that allowed Mourning, Hill, Iverson, the Barbers, Taylor, Smith, and Vick to follow those such as Willie Lanier, Moses Malone, Ralph Sampson, Charles Haley, and others to become American sports icons evolved from a lesser-known period where Black high schools and colleges helped improve the race through community solidarity and masculine attainment. Had the above athletes been born just a few decades prior, they would have been a part of this insular world where football and basketball games made race leaders, not professional athletes, whose play embodied the resilience Black people had in the face of segregation and disenfranchisement. This book reconstructs this almost forgotten world, attempts to understand it, and even celebrates the culture of segregated athletics. This effort, in the end, is written in homage to an era of segregation that has been long ignored by scholars and, until recently, forgotten by the public.

Playing for Power is a chronologically organized, thematic narrative analysis of Black high school and college football and basketball culture in Virginia and the South between emancipation and integration. I argue that basketball and football coalesced into key cultural institutions that sustained Black people's collective sense of community, achievement, and purpose during Jim Crow. From the 1890s to the 1970s, amateur football and basketball strengthened education, neutralized class divisions, groomed male leadership, cultivated race pride, and expressed collective desires for racial modernity and equality. This bygone world developed the Black human capital that was supposed to be suppressed by second-class citizenship. This development happened in stages, as amateur athletics evolved from an institution builder at the turn of the century, to a shaper of Black manhood by the 1920s, a flashpoint for educational activism in the 1930s, and a metric of proper Black achievement in the World War II era. At the outset of the modern Civil Rights Movement of the 1960s, all-Black amateur sport, while resilient and ever changing with the needs of Black people, succumbed to the inevitability of integration.

This sports history provides a crucial way to understand how Black people developed and nurtured a cultural resistance to white supremacy during segregation. White people created and used Jim Crow as a political and social weapon to limit Black ambition and progress. Black Virginians reshaped those boundaries to create a free world amid societal unfreedom. Living as free people in their own segregated communities allowed Black Americans to create an athletic world that pushed for racial progress through objective, meritocratic achievement anchored by masculine leadership and institutional competency. Moreover, the freedom of sports allowed Black Virginians to shape their athletic culture to fit the multifaceted needs of a downtrodden race. The autonomy and achievement found in sports sustained collective beliefs in racial equality, beliefs that Black people later expressed in the modern Civil Rights Movement after World War II. Furthermore, I claim that to better understand Black resistance to white supremacy after slavery, one must have intimate knowledge of Black life outside of workspaces, churches, and Civil Rights organizations, where the gridiron and hardwood often took center stage.

While Black Virginians played many amateur sports, this book focuses on men's football and basketball in high schools and historically Black colleges and universities (HBCUs). This decision is source based. Archival records demonstrate that Black Virginians and Southerners played, organized, and consumed more amateur football and men's basketball than any other sports during segregation. These sports were important foundations for racial uplift because unlike baseball, a sport dominated by the professional ranks, basketball's and football's popularity rested within the amateur world. The concept of amateurism—play without pay—allowed these sports to become ethical mechanisms for teaching physical education, manhood, community, and institution building in ways that baseball could not. Black leaders widely acknowledged this fact during Jim Crow.[5] Track and field were also a popular amateur sport during segregation. However, as I show, HBCU and Black high school sports were built on the popularity of football, first, and basketball, second. Track and field's international appeal assured that the highest feat was representing one's country in the Olympics, whereas the national and regional popularity of professional football and basketball before World War II made representing one's race institution the highest honor for footballers and basketballers. In sum: track and field simply thrived in the Black athletic world created and shaped by football and basketball.

It is also important to note that my focus on men's sports does not imply that Black women did not also contribute to the bygone world as well. Black women did in fact play sports at the high school and college level, but the number of sports they played and the number of women playing them was demonstrably lower than their male counterparts. Their contribution made for a fuller athletic culture, as both sexes participated in uplifting the race beyond the psychological and literal confines of segregation. Yet, the athletic and scientific worlds did not, until very recently, believe that women had the capacity for intense athletic exertion. Until the passage of Title IX legislation in the 1970s, white and Black athletic leadership (mostly male) of both races treated women's athletics as recreational and physical education for "traditional" Victorian womanhood. Women's sports were to train female bodies and minds for marriage and motherhood, as many considered competitive glory a masculine virtue. Women's sports were so isolated from the orbit of racial advancement via competition that HBCUs and Black high schools rarely published material about them prior to the passage and implementation of Title IX. My focus on men's basketball and football is not intended to ignore Black women's contribution to Black sport. Rather, I seek to analyze the sports that buttressed Black advancement during Jim Crow through the realm of athletics.[6]

This book makes a needed intervention into the literature on Jim Crow Virginia. Political histories of Virginia collectively define the commonwealth's seventy-five years between Reconstruction and the modern Civil Rights Movement by its oppressive oligarchic regime, which used politics, law, and custom to maintain the feudal social order of white elites and Black peasants.[7] Histories about Black life in Jim Crow Virginia apply the same framework as previous scholarship, seeing race relations strictly through the binary prism of segregation and the activist fight to end it.[8] Sports histories do an even bigger disservice to the Black athletic legacy in the commonwealth. With the exception of the scholarship about tennis legend Arthur Ashe, the few academic monographs and articles about Virginia sports history published in the *Journal of Sports History*, *Virginia Magazine of History and Biography*, and *International Journal of the History of Sport* focus almost exclusively on white athletics.[9] While the prevailing scholarship explains why Black Virginians engaged in full-scale legal and social rebellion in the 1960s, it is wholly uninterested in the cultural means by which Black people pushed for racial equality decades prior.

I use sport history to argue that Black people thrived under Jim Crow Virginia by turning segregation into congregation—a theoretical framework popularized by historian Earl Lewis.[10] Moreover, Black resistance to inequality was more cultural than political, as Black people used everyday actions within their communities to oppose the premise of inherent Black inferiority that undergirded segregation and disenfranchisement. Athletics became a sphere where Black people exerted tremendous influence by imparting and expressing moral lessons that held they were equal to whites due to their cultural refinement, masculinity, race pride, religiosity, and adherence to objective meritocracy. It was in the world of sport where Black Virginians made their most fervent and continual bids for racial equality. With metrics of success being unquestionable in athletics, Black Virginians always knew that they were equal to white people even when law and custom said otherwise.[11]

Playing for Power also interweaves Virginia with current sports literature. Sport historians currently focus on the development of amateur sports becoming favorite American spectacles and definers of Southern identity in the early twentieth century. In doing so, they often neglect the institutional bonds between college and high school sports.[12] My focus on Virginia reveals that sports connected high schools and colleges more than previous scholars acknowledge. It is in the Black sports world where this is most true, as high schools and HBCUs used competitive athletics as a cultural battleground in their war for racial equality.[13]

Lastly, I join recent efforts to use sports as a lens to better understand Black life writ large.[14] Historians of Black sport define athletics during segregation as another theater of the modern Civil Rights Movement (integration into white society) or Black Power Movement (liberation from white society).[15] The Virginia story shows that Black sports largely operated outside of this paradigm. In the bygone world of sport, Black people focused less on overt calls for integration and liberation than they did on congregation. Athletics was not a bullhorn for the "Long Civil Rights" or Black Power Movements.

Rather, it fostered the multigenerational culture of resilience against white supremacist beliefs that the latter movements relied upon. Hence, this book furthers a more recent wave of history that sees Black sports as a medium for congregation and uplift through meritocratic athletic exercise.[16]

This book sandwiches five chapters between an introduction and a coda. Chapter 1 discusses how Black educational institutions seized control of amateur athletic culture to subvert notions of racial inferiority in New South Virginia. Between the 1880s and 1920s, Black people migrated to high schools and colleges in urban centers and created thriving amateur football and basketball clubs. Educational leaders saw these games as platforms to uplift the race physically, mentally, and communally, and thus they formed the Colored Intercollegiate Athletic Association (CIAA) in 1912, the Virginia Interscholastic Athletic Association (VIAA) in 1927, and the Southern Interscholastic Athletic Association (SIAA) and Western Division of the Virginia State High School Athletic Association (W-VSHAA) by 1934. These amateur athletic leagues were Progressive creations that solidified, organized, and gave higher purpose to Black athletics. Chapter 1 puts this development into conversation with the scholarship on Black organizationalism in the New South age. New South historians claim that Black Southerners endured the earliest days of segregation by formalizing existing community ties through churches, mutual aid societies, schools, fraternities/sororities, business leagues, labor unions, and civic clubs. However, they ignore the creation and organization of amateur sports. Thus, chapter 1 argues that the institutionalization of amateur sports was a function of New South organizationalism, as Black athletic leaders exuded commitments to the self-help ideals prevalent in other Black institutions of the era.

Chapter 2 shows how Black athletics in Virginia shaped racial manhood during the New Negro era of the 1920s. Media outlets such as the *Norfolk Journal and Guide*, *Richmond Planet*, and CIAA Bulletin treated Black football and basketball as purpose-driven spectacles that uplifted the race through fostering a rugged form of masculinity I define as *Black athletic manhood*. This manhood, as articulated by players and coaches, was a process by which Black boys became male leaders through learning, playing, and teaching life lessons through football and basketball. Chapter 2 fills a historiographical gap left by historians who have not mentioned the conceptual and rhetorical development of racial manhood and modernity through sport as a New Negro creation. Moreover, I argue that Black Virginians connected amateur sports with the New Negro movement through intellectualizing athletic participation.

Chapter 3 shows that Black activists used high school football and basketball to argue for more public-sector investment in Black education during the 1930s. This reversed a more solidified cultural dynamism in which Black people did not expect local, state, or federal agencies to help fund their own institutions. Public education funding through sports did not make Black institutions solely reliant on the state. Rather, it provided the money necessary to strengthen Black control of their own institutions during the nation's darkest economic hour. This chapter places high school and college sports at the center of Black New Deal activism. Black Virginians took part in teacher salary equalization campaigns, the desegregation of Southern graduate schools, the integration of New Deal labor programs, and open access to housing. Less talked about is how they used athletics to infiltrate the New Deal to improve their condition. Black people used sports to argue for more school funding because it was an avenue of racial success that garnered white respect; thus they did not mind ceding financial assistance without requiring direct control. Sports, while seemingly harmless to white supremacy, was critical for the Black educational progress needed to maintain cultural resistance to prevailing beliefs in Black inferiority. This dynamic reveals the subversive nature of Black sports, as Black citizens used a seemingly neutral cultural product to garner white funding for their own racial advancement.

Chapter 4 discusses how Virginia HBCUs led the Black college world in overcoming mid-twentieth-century crises that threatened to undermine amateur sports across the nation. Between 1932 and 1945, CIAA leadership attacked corrupt practices within their most successful football and basketball programs. This gave them the moral and institutional authority to compel other HBCUs and local high schools to continue playing sports despite World War II mobilization. This chapter integrates HBCUs within the historiography about college sports corruption and reform, a topic that is mostly discussed among white colleges. Historians broadly argue that college sports are defined by their ability to overcome crises that threatened to end them. HBCU sports fits well within this scholarly consensus. Furthermore, I argue that CIAA leadership—filled with Black Virginians—grew their organizational power to seize control of Black sports when commercialism stressed its moral fabric to the point that it could no longer remain the ethical pillar of racial uplift. This ensured that basketball and football games continued amid controversy and maintained their ethos just as the sports world became more tolerant of interracial competition.

Chapter 5 unpacks Black Virginia's athletic resistance to the uncomfortable age of integration. While everyday Black people protested segregation in the courts, city halls, and streets, athletic leaders worked behind the scenes to maintain all-Black sports. For the CIAA, this meant maintaining their control over blue-chip Black athletes who desired to play at integrated schools. Thus, they changed their name from the *Colored* Intercollegiate

Athletic Association to the *Central* Intercollegiate Athletic Association, and they encouraged member institutions to award scholarships to compete with white universities. Black Virginia high schools, under the direction of the reorganized Virginia Interscholastic Association (VIA), went in the opposite direction. Instead of trying to compete with the all-white Virginia High School League, VIA convinced the segregationist Virginia Legislature to underwrite the only statewide Black high school sports league. The CIAA and VIA differed in their approach, but they aligned on maintaining Black administrative control over the winds of change brought about by the modern Civil Rights Movement while not detracting from the larger Black freedom struggle in the commonwealth, South, and nation. Integration coupled with internal issues to assure that, by the 1970s, Virginia HBCUs and Black high school officials could not stem the tide of Black athletes toward white-run institutions.

The coda explains the current state of Black amateur football and basketball in Virginia, the South, and the nation. Since integration, HBCUs have lost their place atop Black amateur athletics. Black high schools and grassroots organizations filled this void and have, since the mid-1980s, become the trendsetters of Black athletic expression and administration. Much of this paradigm shift took place with the rise of grassroots basketball organizations, most notably that of the Boo Williams Summer League and AAU organization in Hampton, Virginia. What began as a community-run summer basketball league in 1982 had evolved by the 1990s and 2000s into the nation's most popular grassroots basketball brand. With their urban bravado, fast-paced style of play, and Nike sponsorship, Boo Williams made Virginia's Tidewater a known hub for some of the nation's best Black athletic talent. They did this with urban Black coaches at a time when star Black athletes were increasingly being taught by white coaches in white institutions. Moreover, they did this at a time when white institutions incorporated Black athletes for commercialization, which directly opposed the bygone world where Black amateur sports were pillars of racial uplift. If the bygone spirit of Black athletics lives anywhere today, it resides with Boo Williams and the grassroots basketball world. While the impact of Boo Williams will be touched on in this section, the intricacies and broader impact of his work will be further developed in a separate book I am writing with the blessing and exclusive source access given to me by Marcellus "Boo" Williams Jr., himself.

Finding enough sources to write this history was difficult but not impossible. Due to the COVID-19 pandemic, I was unable to gain access to Hampton University Archives. This was a significant burden given that Hampton is one of the handful of Black colleges that have had the resources to collect and archive their sports history before the 1960s. Thus, this book is like others in its genre in relying heavily on newspaper accounts. I include many Black-owned newspapers from across the nation, but I lean most on the *Norfolk Journal and Guide*. The *Journal and Guide* was founded by Norfolk native Plummer Bernard Young Sr. as, among other things, the quintessential Black sports platform in Virginia and much of the South during Jim Crow. Few newspapers followed Black amateur football and basketball as closely as Young's *Journal and Guide*; hence I treat it as both a factual record and a historical actor in shaping Black sports culture.

Thanks to Virginia Union University, this book also includes heavy analysis of CIAA records and bulletins. Founded in 1912, the CIAA was the first ever all-Black intercollegiate conference, and it was once home to every Virginia HBCU. These bulletins recorded factoids like rosters and statistics while also compiling many speeches, articles, histories, and meeting minutes held by the CIAA since 1923. This collection was an invaluable resource for reconstructing the Black amateur athletic world through the lens of its administrative and executive taskmasters. Virginia State University also provided me with access to the only existing record of Virginia's Black high school sports league—the Virginia Interscholastic Association (formally the Virginia Interscholastic Athletic Association). This was the final installment of Virginia's all-Black high school sports league, as its predecessors, which will be discussed in the book, do not have any surviving records outside of newspaper articles. I also used the few high school and college yearbooks I could locate to help write this history as well. This book extracts much from limited source material to help reconstruct the bygone world of sport and legitimize Virginia's Black sports history as a topic for further academic inquiry.

1

THE INSTITUTIONS, 1865–1927

Two highly touted amateur football teams took center stage in Virginia's Tidewater region on a mild fall day in November 1895. At Suffolk's Peanut Park, the sky was clear, the air was crisp, the fans were raving, and the rival elevens kicked off what was to be a masterful display of New South modernity. On one end sat the hometown boys of Suffolk High School. Across from them on the opposing sideline were the rival elevens of Norfolk's Brambleton Athletic Club. The port town of Norfolk was Virginia's largest city and the site of New South industrialism. Suffolk was reminiscent of the Old South, where open lots of land were filled with more farm animals than people. This gridiron clash was a site of the old world versus the new, where Virginia boys used organized violence to debate the social and political merits of progress versus tradition.[1]

There was one thing missing from this festive event that was prevalent in most aspects of New South Virginia, and that was Black people. While there is little documentary evidence of this event outside of the *Norfolk Virginia-Pilot* newspaper account, it is safe to assume that there were no Black people at the Suffolk High versus Brambleton football game. Yet, an all-Black football game took place miles away at Norfolk's League Park a week later between Shaw University and the Norfolk-based Columbia Athletic Club (CAC). The white-owned *Virginia-Pilot* surprisingly took interest in this all-Black urban game. They implored white locals to support the CAC as they did the Brambleton boys against Suffolk. For a CAC victory over Shaw would restore the commonwealth's place atop the region's gridiron altar by avenging the University of Virginia's loss to the University of North Carolina at Chapel Hill, a game that had taken place just a week earlier on that very same field.[2]

Amateur athletics in New South Virginia was filled with notions of sectional reconciliation, collective identity, and the Black cultural dynamism that unintendedly sprang forth as a result. At the outset of the twentieth century, Southerners embraced organized sports such as football and basketball to help them culturally reconnect with the nation after the Civil War. Yet, white people viewed sports as a canvas of social norms and not as an agent of social change. Football games in Virginia, for example, were segregated by race, and white urban and rural dwellers used them to settle sociopolitical debates between urbanity and rural life. Black people played football, too. But their games took place in urban spaces almost exclusively. The spatial dichotomy of Black and white football games reflected a different reality between the races, as inner cities were places where Black residents psychologically advanced past the days of slavery. Urban spaces along with the athletic culture they fostered were catalyzing for Black Southerners, who were shut out of white society with segregation and disenfranchisement, in that they allowed for the display of Black progress in such a way that white culture would not oppose their efforts. Moreover, this context reveals why the *Virginia-Pilot*'s coverage of the all-white Suffolk versus Brambleton game differed from the contest between CAC and Shaw. While white and Black players technically shared the same game, they did so in different spaces and with different understandings of what those games meant.

Jim Crow segregation and disenfranchisement blinded white people to Black cultural developments and collective ambition that was often in plain sight. Some white people viewed segregation as a system in which the two races operated in separate worlds that hindered Black cultural progress. But some white people knew better. "The Negro," once said white man Fred Alexander, Virginia's Superintendent of Negro Education, "is so definitely isolated that there is a minimum contact between the two groups." This minimal contact assured that "the white group is unaware of the thinking and desire of the Negro and knows almost nothing about his progress and potentiality for contributing to community improvement."[3] Thus, the CAC and Shaw game was not, as white people would believe, just a battle in white Virginia's regional war for football supremacy. It was a cultural movement where Black resistance to white supremacy could thrive in a segregated world. Black Virginians formed vibrant neighborhoods, churches, schools, and business districts that white people were always suspicious of.[4] This suspicion often went away when Black people took to the gridiron or gymnasium. There, Black boys and men displayed their beliefs in racial equality with little-to-no white suspicion at all. This Black athletic resistance was so covert that white spectators, as seen in the *Virginia-Pilot*'s coverage of the CAC and Shaw game, cheered them on and assigned their own meaning to what they witnessed. White people considered Black players to be "just playing games." However, football and basketball were much more than that. Opposing Black teams never played *against* one another when they took to the gridiron and hardwood; they played *with* one another in a larger athletic community whose goal was to undermine beliefs that Black people were inherently inferior to white people.

Black Virginians used amateur football and basketball to promote racial equality through institutional solidarity at the turn of the twentieth century. Between the 1880s and 1920s, Black Virginians migrated to high schools and colleges in urban centers and played amateur football and basketball. Black educators saw these games as a platform to improve the race physically, mentally, and communally. Thus, they placed these games under organizations such as the Colored Intercollegiate Athletic Association (CIAA), a collegiate league, in 1912 and the Virginia Interscholastic Athletic Association (VIAA), a high school league, in 1927. These leagues were the consummation of grassroots activity and middle-class administrative control, as they solidified, organized, and gave higher purpose to activities underway before their creation. What Norfolk-based newspaperman Plummer Bernard Young Sr. once deemed the "unparalleled awakening of interest in school athletics" in early-twentieth-century Virginia was a cultural push to ensure that sports uplifted the race in the age of Jim Crow.[5]

This chapter sees the diffusion and organization of amateur football and basketball in Virginia as a reflection of New South optimism after the Civil War and, a take that accords with Edward Ayers's rejection of C. Vann Woodward's argument that the New South period was a time of Southern misery and cultural regression.[6] By focusing on the development of Black football and basketball, I put amateur athletics into conversation with the scholarship on Black organizationalism in the New South. Historians push athletics to the periphery of discussions about organizationalism, arguing that Black Southerners endured the earliest days of segregation by formalizing and growing existing community ties through churches, mutual aid societies, schools, fraternities/sororities, business leagues, labor unions, and civic clubs that previously operated as underground ventures during slavery.[7] Many Black New South organizations were started and run by Black people who had never been slaves, making them ventures in Black aspirational beliefs that freedom required community commitments to autonomy and achievement when few areas of life presented that opportunity. Virginia's Black sports leagues fit within this scholarly consensus. Furthermore, understanding Black life at the outset of Jim Crow requires cultural analysis of the spaces—both physical and psychological—that Black people created to live as free people amid unfreedom. One of those spaces was the world of sport.

"FOR OUR SAKES, AS WELL AS FOR THEIRS"

Precipitating amateur footballs and basketballs flowering in New South Virginia was Black educators taking more control of the schools that later housed amateur sports. This control was not a linear or preordained process. As historian Adam Fairclough makes clear, "the history of black schools in the South was not one of African American autonomy." In fact, it was "far from it."[8]

In Virginia, Black education was a contested terrain in which white people sought to control its function and meaning to limit Black progress.[9] Free Black Virginians faced little reprisal in creating makeshift schools in their homes and churches prior to the 1830s. However, the Virginia Legislature banned Black schooling outright in 1831 in response to the Nat Turner Rebellion in Southampton County. After the Civil War, Black education was legalized and controlled by white-run groups such as the Freedmen's Bureau, American Missionary Association, and the Virginia Legislature.[10] These groups designed Black education to reinstitutionalize free people into a state of inferiority through underfunding, segregation, and a reliance on white leadership. As a result, Black education was in a porous state throughout the 1860s and 1870s. While the charter generation of Black Virginia educators such as John Oliver, Thomas DeSailles Tucker, and Mary Smith Peake exercised some control over Black schools as early as 1861, the majority of Black communities had white teachers and principals who were mostly Northern transplants who taught elementary-level literacy to children, teens, and adults for less than half a year's time.[11] The post–Civil War educational agenda, as set out by William H. Ruffner, Virginia's first superintendent of education, was to educate Black students well enough to be profitable laborers "for our sakes, as well as for theirs," he once said.[12]

Black education entered an awakening between the late 1870s and 1900s, as Black educators mobilized to better control Black life through schooling. After Reconstruction, Black educators in Virginia and the South became community advocates, demanding that they better control Black schooling by becoming instructors and principals.[13] White Virginians allowed this because the damage they inflicted on Black schools seemed irreparable. By 1880, Virginia had three hundred Black schools in total with nearly twenty thousand students and five thousand teachers statewide. Virginia had no Black public high schools until the Peabody Fund, John F. Slater Fund, Julius Rosenwald Foundation, and most importantly the Anna T. Jeanes Fund built them between 1897 and 1910.[14] Even with white Northern philanthropic aid, Black schools were sparsely funded and poorly organized due to a complete lack of state-level investment.[15] With Black politicians mostly out of positions of political power after Reconstruction, white Virginia leaders felt comfortable hiring Black teachers and principals to lead some Black schools. As Black educators gained footholds in their schools, they formed direct ties to white philanthropic organizations, solidifying their managerial control over Black education throughout the commonwealth.[16]

The Black push for control of Black education was most seen with the rise of historically Black colleges and universities (HBCUs). Virginia's first HBCUs—Virginia Union University (1865), then named Richmond Theological Seminary, and Hampton Institute (now University) (1868)—while not having Black presidents until the twentieth century, both employed Black professors as early as the 1880s. In 1882, the Virginia Legislature chartered the commonwealth's first public HBCU in Virginia Normal and Collegiate Institute, later named Virginia State College (now University). This institution was the hallmark of the Black educational empowerment movement in the 1880s. Between 1879 and 1884, Black Virginians participated in the Readjuster Revolution. This biracial political alliance, where Black Virginians helped white dissident Democrats oust Conservative elites from state, local, and federal offices, produced the gift that was Virginia State—a public college with a Black board of visitors, Black president in John Mercer Langston, and all-Black faculty.[17]

Northern white organizations followed the general feeling among Black Virginians in the 1880s, in that they should have more control of their institutions of higher learning. The American Baptist Home Mission Society helped found Lynchburg Theological Seminary, later named Virginia Seminary and College (now the Virginia University of Lynchburg) in 1886 under the direction of Black president Dr. Phillip F. Morris. Two years later, the Protestant Episcopal Church helped found Saint Paul's Normal and Industrial School—later Saint Paul's College—in 1888 with Black minister James Solomon Russell at the helm. This emphasis on Virginia HBCUs being Black run and controlled extended well into the twentieth century. By the 1930s, Virginia Union (then under the direction of its first Black president, Dr. Samuel DeWitt Proctor), helped found the Norfolk Unit of Virginia Union University—later Norfolk State University—at the behest of Black Norfolk middle-class professionals and educators clamoring for another postsecondary institution in the growing Tidewater area.[18]

The rise of Jim Crow segregation had swamped Black educational gains while buttressing Black control over Black schooling by the new century. The Readjuster Revolution sparked a reactionary wave of state-level disenfranchisement and segregation laws beginning in 1884. This later crystalized into anti-Black voting restrictions being codified in the Virginia Constitution of 1902.[19] This two-decade wave of Negrophobia compelled Lynchburg Seminary's white board to remove Dr. Phillip Morris from his presidency in 1890. The overwhelmingly white Virginia Legislature also removed Virginia State's college status with the 1902 Constitution, and the white-passing James Russell struggled mightily to keep Saint Paul's running as white support for the school nearly vanished by the turn of the century.[20] Black primary and secondary schools felt the pinch as well. White supremacist oligarchs such as lawyer Walter Allen Watson and University of Virginia professors Richard Heath Dabney and Paul B. Barringer, for example, advocated for defunding already underfunded Black schools. Their reasoning was that formal education ruined race relations because the very act of schooling Black children stimulated beliefs in racial equality.[21] Furthermore, state officials severely underpaid Black teachers and professors compared to their white counterparts, and they consolidated and defunded Black secondary schools to the point that many relied exclusively on Northern grant money from the Jeanes Fund for programs and teacher salaries.[22]

White supremacy and niggardly spending on education accompanied a Black uplift ideology that would later be named after the man who embodied it. Born into slavery in Franklin County, Virginia in 1856, and later attending both Virginia Union and Hampton Institute, Booker T. Washington had become the most prominent Black intellectual and educator by the turn of the century. Washington's rise to prominence came in large part because of widespread Black and white acceptance of his racial uplift philosophy. While secretly funding Civil Rights efforts throughout the country, Washington told Black Southerners to "cast down your buckets where you are" and acquire skilled trades, build community-run institutions, divest from electoral politics, and embrace Northern philanthropy for Black education. To Washington, Black activism was to be seen in educational and economic solidarity and not at the ballot box. Black Virginians adhered to Washington's message, leading to a growth of Black churches, businesses, and fraternal and mutual aid societies and contributing to the decline of Black political activism by the turn of the century. Thus, when the Virginia Legislature added a white state supervisor of Negro education in 1910 to oversee Black schools, Black educators worked with him and Northern philanthropies directly to better train Black teachers and administer Black education as a community venture.[23] Black education became a Bookerite pillar alongside industry and religion in creating a world where Black people could express desires to live as free people while under the thumb of white racism.

There was a silver lining for Black education in the age of Jim Crow. Black schooling became an afterthought in the white Virginia mind, a burden of obligation for the state, and an exercise in benevolent patriarchal control by white Northern liberals. While white public officials and Northern philanthropists disagreed on funding Black education, neither would have ever believed that Black people were, or could ever be, equal to white people. Like Black life in general, Black schools operated almost undisturbed by white society unless they flagrantly ran afoul of the color line.[24] Within the confines of segregation, Black Virginians wisely used white ambivalence to create a thriving world of sport where they defined the rules, regulations, and meaning.

"TO PROMOTE CLEAN, MANLY SPORT"

In March 1912, Hampton Institute's athletic director Charles Holston Williams and Virginia Union Dean John W. Barco met with Ernest J. Marshal from Howard University; W. E. Atkins, Charles R. Frazier, and H. P. Hargrave of Shaw University of North Carolina; and George Johnson of Lincoln University of Pennsylvania. These Black professors and athletic directors represented their respective HBCUs in taking the unprecedented step to form the Colored Intercollegiate Athletic Association (CIAA). This began the educational takeover of Black amateur football and basketball world in Jim Crow Virginia and the South.[25] By solidifying existing athletic relations under a governing body run by educators who were "to promote clean, manly sport," the CIAA defied contemporary beliefs that college athletics were solely an exercise of white masculine supremacy.[26] Each participating HBCU had white faculty and administration. Yet not one white person was present at the inaugural CIAA meeting. This reflected that while Black education was overseen by white people, HBCU sports, like Black education writ large, were to be shaped and defined by Black people.

Black basketball founding father Edwin Bancroft Henderson remembered quite correctly that "athletics entered [Black] college life as a foundling. It was not a planned institution" upon its inception.[27] To settle disputes about which intramural clubs, fraternities, and graduating classes held on-campus supremacy, students at Virginia Union, Hampton, Virginia Seminary, Saint Paul's, and Virginia State played evening football games as early as 1892, with basketball becoming a popular intramural sport by 1901.[28] Faculty and administration celebrated these games because they promoted school spirit and pride among students.[29] Hampton, in particular, considered the organization of competitive sports clubs on campus as "the beginnings of citizenship" for Black people.[30] HBCUs could not contain the popularity of the campus games they played. "Each year greater interest and more enthusiasm have grown among the students, so that more men have participated in the games," said Hampton's Charles Williams in 1911.[31] What Williams referred to was by 1900, students, players, faculty, parents, and alumni organized the first set of HBCU intercollegiate contests.[32] Decades later, "athletics," explained the *Norfolk Journal and Guide* in regards to football specifically by the 1920s, "is regarded as a matter of fact . . . in our colleges and social uplift centers" throughout Black America.[33]

HBCUs participated in the rapid growth of organized sports on American college campuses. Just as "King Football" reigned supreme at white colleges, at Black colleges, "the major sport was [also] football. Other sports, for the most part, were lost sight of," a Union school history from the 1920s made clear.[34] A student poll at Virginia State reaffirmed the athletic pecking order in Black Virginia, as they overwhelmingly voted football as their favorite sport. Yet, this same poll showed that basketball was not far behind as the second favorite sport in HBCU life.[35] Football's popularity with the public, as well as the "physical endurance and strength and mental alertness" to win the contest, endeared the game to hardscrabble Southerners, Black and white alike. Moreover, the *Norfolk Journal and Guide* dispelled any suggestion that football competed with other sports for importance in American life, saying that "no better evidence that football is being played to the king's taste today could be found than the fact that never was the sport as popular as now, never was it better played and never did it so strongly compete with baseball for the coveted title of the Great American Game" for Black and white people.[36]

Basketball was not too far behind. The game was brought to the South to be "given to the [urban] poor" by the YMCA's Muscular Christianity Movement, via various churches, just two years after its creation in 1893.[37] Nearly every Virginia city and county had makeshift basketball teams playing games at various YMCAs by 1895.[38] Almost immediately after the final football game ended at places like Hampton on Thanksgiving Day, "the first basket ball match had begun" with "a large gathering" of spectators anticipating the game staking its place in Black athletic life by 1900.[39] It did not take long for men's basketball to become a "favorite game among both [Black] boys and girls," said the Black-owned *Southern Workman* in 1912.[40] The same paper claimed four years later that with "the excitement of the football season being over, basketball immediately took the stage" at HBCUs.[41] CIAA president Thomas Puryear of Virginia State confirmed basketball's popularity in 1927, saying that while "football is the most popular sport on our athletic calendar. . . . no one of us who reads and interprets the athletic signs of the times fails to see basketball as a coming sport."[42] Basketball would later share space with football as a favored game in Black Virginia and the South by the 1940s, much of which had to do with the popularity of Virginia Union's cage exploits—a topic that will be discussed in chapter 4. The *Pittsburgh Courier* all but admitted basketball's rise to prominence in 1940, opining that "down in the Old Dominion state, where Tobacco is King and Cotton is Queen a new sports monarch has ascended the throne. It's Prince Basketball."[43] Hardwood contests sat alongside of gridiron games in transitioning from intramural pastimes and sideshows at Black annual exhibitions to on-campus attractions for prospective students, parents, and alumni.[44]

On the back of football and basketball was the rise of women's sports in the CIAA. Women's sport at HBCUs began with spectating in men's sport. The *Southern Workman* noted with astonishment in January 1901 "the appearance of the girls in their neat gymnasium suits immediately attracted the attention of the crowd," as Hampton basketball fanatics saw the "Lady Seasiders" insist that they be allowed to play for campus visitors after the boys were done. For Hampton, this act "was the first time the girls had taken part of the sports of the day."[45] Since the turn of the twentieth century, women at coed and all-women colleges (both Black and white) have engaged in intramural swimming, racing, rowing, baseball, squash, and basketball. The rise of women's games reflected the larger ideological shift in American womanhood, one where women, particularly the educated middle class, were to strengthen their bodies to develop the mental and ethical commitments to God, marriage, and motherhood.[46] Even the Black press implored Black colleges to support women's sports because "health [is] just as important to the girl and woman as it is to the boy and man." Thus, implored the *Baltimore Afro-American* in 1910: HBCUs had a moral obligation to "give the feminine sex a chance to develop strong healthy bodies" through sport.[47] Some white colleges pushed women's intercollegiate sport to the degree that they recruited Black female student athletes, such as basketball star Ethel M. Cautious Davis of Wellesley College.[48] St. Paul's invested heavily in its women's tennis program.[49] Hampton, by way of Miss Frances E. Weston, used Charles Williams's physical education and interpretative dance program to grow the CIAA's best women's gymnastics team.[50] Yet, HBCU alumni and faculty, like white colleges, were slow to match the investment in men's and women's sports. The reason was that they saw women's sports as a primary function of physical education. More plainly, "parents believe the physical training will make their daughters fine women in a bodily as well as in a mental and moral sense."[51] In some cases, when women asked for their athletic councils (precursor to athletic departments run by faculty and alumni) for intercollegiate clubs, they were flatly rejected.[52]

The growth of HBCU football and basketball was not uncontested. The *Southern Workman* found in 1910 that many Black parents and HBCU faculty were annoyed that "football is occupying much of the . . . student mind these days."[53] Despite some resistance, intercollegiate games remained fixtures at HBCUs, mainly because they operated as celebratory events to commemorate Thanksgiving Day and Emancipation Day—a precursor to Juneteenth, a holiday that was originally celebrated in January.[54] Most importantly, the games became a point of fellowship between HBCUs, leading to historic in-and-out-of-state rivalries such as Union and Hampton, Union and Virginia State, Hampton and Tuskegee, Hampton and Howard, and Saint Paul's and Virginia Seminary.[55] Intercollegiate basketball and football also bolstered the profile of HBCUs among Black people, as "our athletic relations" with "stronger fellowship" between prominent institutions, said the *Southern Workman*, reflected Black New South zeal for cultural modernity.[56]

Black Virginia's athletic culture fit within a larger college sports diaspora, a trend that did not go unnoticed by Southern media. The *Southern Collegian* took note that as of April 1874, "without any warning," students at schools such as Washington and Lee College took to their quads and played football games in their spare time.[57] These quad games later sprouted into intercollegiate spectacles, leading the *Tazewell Church Valley News* to exclaim sixteen years later that "football is not only the autumn game of New England."[58] The *Wheeling Register* agreed, noting in 1890 that "football is the reigning sport with the [Southern] University students."[59] It had become clear by 1895 that football was "more popular than ever in the South," the *Harrisonburg Evening News* opined.[60] Basketball later shared the mantle, as the *Norfolk Virginian* celebrated its arrival in 1896, claiming that in spite of the criticism of being a feminine game, "it permits of quite as much rough play as football."[61] In sum, Virginia HBCUs embraced football and basketball alongside of their white counterparts in the commonwealth and southern region.

After the Confederate South's defeat in April 1865, regional boosters clamored for the South to reconcile their relationship with the nation through rebuilding in the image of the industrial North.[62] Southern universities led the charge between the 1870s and 1920s by hiring Northern-educated faculty and emulating the curricula and activities of Northern colleges.[63] HBCUs did this as well, as their sports were first conducted by "some member of the faculty who had either attended a Northern school or played on such team."[64] Moreover, the *Baltimore Afro-American* noticed in the 1920s that athletic "culture is entering the South by way of the [Northern educated] college football coach."[65] Charles Williams founded the first intercollegiate football and basketball teams at Hampton after matriculating at Harvard in 1909. "The Crafty [John] Barco" did the same at Virginia Union after earning his graduate degree from Newton Theological Seminary of Massachusetts in 1903. John Lyman Whitehead followed suit at Saint Paul's after earning a master's degree in commerce from Yale. The exception in this pioneering bunch was Virginia State's Dr. Thomas Langston Puryear. He started Virginia State's intercollegiate programs after graduating from Howard.[66]

Virginia's HBCU athletic culture helped strengthen the commonwealth's position as the gateway for college football and basketball to enter the New South. UVA and Washington and Lee played the region's first recorded intercollegiate football game in fall 1870 and basketball game in 1892. Other Southern universities followed suit by making both football and basketball official school sports by 1895.[67] The game of football so captivated the interest of the New South elite that it was not uncommon for formal dinners to end in gridiron matches where "both old and young [men] participated."[68] By the turn of the century, the children and patrons of New South academia had become the market by which universities sold college football and basketball to bolster enrollment. These sports were also educational programs that helped professors train the "body and mind" of the New South's emerging leadership class, a group who became increasingly alienated from muscular labor.[69] Furthermore, by participating in the growth of Southern college football and basketball, Virginia HBCUs helped advance the New South cause for national reconciliation after the Civil War.

College football and basketball were not immune to the rise of Jim Crow segregation despite inspiring national reconciliation. Decades of underregulated intercollegiate play throughout the country inspired calls for uniform rules of engagement, namely the creation of athletic conferences between "like-minded" universities.[70] Virginia educators were ahead of the movement to control sports as by 1897, Richmond College (now University of Richmond), Hampden-Sydney College, Virginia Polytechnic Institute, Randolph-Macon College, and the College of William and Mary had formed the Virginia Interscholastic Athletic Association.[71] League creation like this led to more intersectional or national contests, which begot the adoption of a uniform color line in college athletics. By the 1910s, Northern, Midwestern, and West Coast colleges accommodated white Southern colleges by adopting the infamously dubbed "gentlemen's agreement" to bar Black athletes from intercollegiate competition.[72] Necessitating this agreement was the fact that some Black athletes starred in intercollegiate football and basketball at white Northern and Midwestern schools between the 1880s and 1910s.[73] While Virginia HBCUs never played against white colleges, some white schools, such as Roanoke College, played against Indian industrial schools. Carlisle's Captain Richard Henry Pratt once told a group of Choctaw students attending Roanoke College after the game that "if an Indian can kick himself into fellowship with a white man, let him kick!"[74] The color line was firmly set by the next decade, however, and Indians were, like Black athletes, effectively barred from white college football and basketball contests.[75] This reality led to HBCU athletics being a more organized and subversive institution in Southern life.

Virginia HBCUs disrupted Jim Crow segregation by allowing for interracial play. Sports historians overlook that Indian students stationed at Hampton Institute between the 1890s and 1910s played intramural football and basketball with Black students to promote fellowship and Native assimilation.[76] Beginning in 1903, Hampton took the unprecedented step of integrating their intercollegiate football teams, with rosters "consisting of both Negro and Indian boys." This feat did not go unnoticed, as interracial play was previously restricted to campus.[77] The closing doors of white college sports compelled the Carlisle team to travel South and play Virginia HBCUs.[78] Black Virginia high schools even traveled out of state to play Indian boarding schools as well.[79] It appeared that for a time, HBCUs and Black schools in general could have kept integrated college football and basketball play alive in the South. Yet, with intersectional, intercollegiate football and basketball games becoming both popular and lucrative, white and Indian colleges outside the South adhered to the Southern custom of segregation, leaving HBCU football and basketball to grow within the confines of Jim Crow by the 1910s.[80]

As HBCUs were confined to playing in a completely segregated world, the games were imbued with more purpose for Black people. Walter Camp and James Naismith indeed created football and basketball to groom white men in lessons of racial manhood through scientific efficiency and organized competition in elite white male–dominated spaces.[81] Even white Southern communities felt this way about sports such as football, with the *Staunton Vindicator* once telling boys who refused to play the physical game for fear of injury or getting dirty that they "might as well be a girl at once."[82] The growth, consolidation, and Jim Crowing of college football and basketball by later apologists also cemented modern athletics as exercises and displays of white male supremacy.[83] This allowed HBCU football and basketball to become radical exercises of Black New South modernity and autonomy within the intellectual confines set by Booker T. Washington.

Historian Michael Hurd notes that white HBCU administrators in general saw college football and basketball as distractions from the everyday function of industrial and religious education. Thus, they refused to use school resources to fund the games.[84] Black alumni, students, and faculty responded through organizationalism, forming booster, student, and alumni clubs that used gate receipts to fund intercollegiate games.[85] Schools like St. Paul's, where professors and alumni were working-class part-time farmers, used gate receipts to fund financial awards to generate and maintain an on-campus athletic culture.[86] These games, the teams, coaches, and fanatics became a unique reflection of the values taught in Black higher education. Through sports, said the *Southern Workman* in 1903 about Hampton specifically, one saw that HBCUs were not just schools "where knowledge is taught; not a mere church where doctrines are taught; not a mere college where young men are decorated with culture, or turned into a magnificent football elevens, but a great environment of eager young men and women drawn together by one common spirit . . . to redeem their race."[87] By "casting down their buckets" in the segregated world, HBCU sports teams became an all-Black experiment in racial uplift, a reality that did not change until the 1960s.

As HBCU athletics evolved from leisure-time intramural activities to a pillar of racial uplift by the 1910s, Black educators conformed the games to the contemporary standards of Black respectability. Several scandals dating back to the 1890s compelled white colleges to form official alliances (conferences) to regulate their beloved games.[88] Black schools were no different. As Hampton's Charles Williams remembered, "we have similar and sometimes the same problems, only on a smaller scale" as compared to white colleges.[89] The *Southern Workman* best articulated Black concerns in 1903: "While athletics have doubtless done much to improve the morals of our college men, it is nevertheless true that the brutal displays that have been made in connection with some of our football games have been productive of serious harm."[90] Black HBCU presidents called for the implementation of newer rules of engagement as early as 1905 because many football and basketball games resulted in serious injuries on and off the field of play.[91]

Beyond injury, HBCUs dealt with unruly behaviors that distance college athletics from the realm of Black respectability.[92] Hampton's Charles Williams recalled the Bronze Age of HBCU sport in 1932 without fondness, noting that gambling and rowdiness were commonplace; referees were often unknowledgeable about the rules and partial to their betting favorites; fans often rushed the field in the middle of play; losing teams quit during games; "some men," said Williams, "were known to have played football [in college] for twelve years"; and "studies were often considered secondary if a student was a good athlete."[93] Moreover, "it was not an uncommon thing for members of the faculty to play on the school team."[94] By the 1910s, Black HBCU administrators had made it clear that college football and basketball, as Charles Williams once stated plainly, "would have to be controlled or eliminated."[95]

CIAA creation was grounded in the prevailing Black middle-class adherence to respectability politics. Black officials from the five charter CIAA schools met in March 1912 to create the first ever rules of engagement for HBCU sports. They ensured that athletic competition on and off the field reflected Victorian notions of civility, honor, and masculine restraint. CIAA bylaws required members to ensure that "improper and unsportsmanlike conduct of any sort," such as gambling, drinking, brawling, "offering of inducements to players," and ignoring academic standards in athletics, were removed from Black college contests.[96] This emphasis on behavior was part and parcel of the respectability culture pervasive in Black life. Black leaders such as Booker T. Washington along with W. E. B. Du Bois, William Monroe Trotter, T. Thomas Fortune, Clinton Charles Spaulding, and others promoted the idea that Black citizens should bid for racial equality through embracing the social norms and morals accepted by middle- and upper-class white society. Often ignored by historians is that at the forefront of this cultural movement was creating physically strong, refined Black men through "clean" collegiate athletic competition.[97] "May the CIAA ever realize that we are helping to train the factors of a civilization, the leaders of a race," said Howard's Dr. Frank Coleman, as he, like many who founded the organization, believed that "a determination to win by following the ethical course will advance our [Black] civilization." For Coleman and others, there were "no more wholesome influence under which a student may come during his years in college than a code of fair competition, the regulations of which are rigidly enforced."[98]

The CIAA's emphasis on Black respectability through athletic competition had implications beyond the field of play. Educators expected the CIAA to ensure sports built what they deemed to be proper Black men: physically stout, cognitively competent, and morally upright. "We believe that. . . . a healthy body [cannot] exist with a corrupt mind as its leader," said Virginia Seminary athletic coach J. H. Lawrence in 1924.[99] Union's John Barco went further, opining, "one of the chief aims of the Association has been to. . . . train men in terms of courage, independent thinking, cooperation, initiative, habits of bodily activity, and above all, honesty in dealings between man and man."[100] While the promotion of competition was encouraged, Black educators placed a premium on the belief that Black athletes, ultimately, played with one another in advancing the race through the world of sport. "If we are going to play . . . football or basket ball," said Booker T. Washington, "let us have teamwork" among Black men.[101] Hampton's Charles Williams agreed with the former, saying, "honesty in the administration of athletics" translated to better community relations between Black men in everyday endeavors.[102] The CIAA's rules, and the upholding of them, made its member colleges the first HBCUs admitted to the all-white National Collegiate Athletic Association (NCAA) in 1921.

The CIAA's racial uplift mission compelled them to help create a national Black college sports culture. Between 1912 and 1926, the CIAA sent men, materials, and money to help every subsequent HBCU league form.[103] This insistence on helping other leagues form came from the constant criticism by Black college administrators that the CIAA was an elitist organization that prevented deserving Black schools from becoming members. This was partly true.[104] The CIAA claimed to admit only "colleges, universities, and institutions of [higher] learning." Until the 1930s, most HBCUs across the country, while named "colleges" or "universities," were vocational and high schools without professors who possessed graduate degrees.[105] Thus, the CIAA helped HBCUs in the Deep South, Upper South, and Southwest form their own athletic leagues in the CIAA image.[106] The CIAA consummated this national network by regularly scheduling inter-conference football and basketball games with nonleague members at great expense. "We as a group are economically poor, our equipment is not so fine, our coaching staffs not so extensive, nor our gate receipts so great as those of many [white] institutions," said CIAA official Dr. Frank Coleman. "The essential benefits which are derived from our games," Coleman concluded, were the creation of a national network where the Black athletic "spirit is the same."[107]

While the CIAA had touched four separate states along the eastern seaboard (Pennsylvania, Washington, DC, Virginia, and North Carolina) by the 1920s, it was for all intents and purposes a Virginia league. The arrangement was originally the idea of Hampton's Charles Williams, the father of the CIAA, and the first league meetings took place at Hampton Institute. The CIAA's first additions to the league after the five charter members were all Virginia HBCUs—Virginia State in 1920, Virginia Theological Seminary in 1921, and Saint Paul's in 1923. Norfolk State joined the CIAA in 1962. Virginia HBCU leaders also occupied the highest ranks of the league throughout the Jim Crow era. Williams served in nearly every leadership position, ranging from president to executive secretary throughout his tenure.[108] "No man in the CIAA," said CIAA President and Virginia State professor W. A. Rogers in 1924, "knows more of the organization than does Mr. Chas. H. Williams."[109] Other Virginia CIAA leadership included Hampton coach Gideon Edward "Gid" Smith, Saint Paul's registrar John Lyman Whitehead, Virginia State athletic directors W. A. Rogers, Dean Thomas L. Puryear, and Harry "Big Jeff" Jefferson, and Virginia Union dean John W. Barco and athletic directors Samuel Barksdale, Harold Martin, and Henry Boyd Hucles. In aggregate, these men served in every elected and appointed office from the league's inception until 1970. Most of the league meetings took place at Union or Hampton—the home press for the annual bulletins. Hampton (9), Virginia State (7), and Union (3) accounted for one-third of CIAA football titles between 1912 and 1970.[110] The previous three, along with Saint Paul's, Virginia Seminary, and later Norfolk State, earned almost half of the basketball titles in the same time period.[111] Run by longtime CIAA board member Plummer Bernard Young Sr. the *Norfolk Journal and Guide* newspaper functioned as the de facto media wing of the league throughout the twentieth century.[112] The CIAA's place as the first and most prominent HBCU sports league during Jim Crow was centered by its leadership belonging to Black Virginia.

FAST ENGAGING THE ATTENTION OF MEMBERS OF THE RACE

The football and basketball games that began as leisured pastimes on HBCU campuses quickly spread to Black communities throughout America. "Football," in particular, "is good in its place" at the center of Black life, the *Southern Workman* said as early as 1895.[113] This reality compelled Virginia sportswriter and cultural observer Aery W. Anthony to tell Black schools to shape these games in their image to assure that they edified the culture of the race. "Our schools and colleges," said Anthony in 1916, should "encourage the great mass of the youth to participate in such games and pastimes as will develop the manly virtues of courage, endurance, unselfishness, heroism, patience, and nobility of the soul."[114] Anthony's wish had come true by the 1920s, as the *Norfolk Journal and Guide*, in lauding college football in particular, noted that the "recent development of football in the colleges, universities, public schools, and athletic clubs has made it a national sport where it was strictly a college game."[115] By the 1920s, the bygone world of sport was all encompassing, with structured leagues at the college, high school, and grassroots levels.

This distillation of athletics from colleges to the broader communities is best seen in Virginia. Most of Black Virginia's urban working class would never set foot at Union, Hampton, Virginia State, Virginia Seminary, Saint Paul's, and later Norfolk State. Yet, CIAA athletes and coaches promoted "physical education and athletics among the. . . . public schools, and the Negro public generally" before and after graduation, Hampton's Charles Williams recounted in the 1920s.[116] To do this, HBCUs regularly played games against amateur football and basketball clubs throughout the commonwealth between the 1890s and mid-1920s.[117] The intercourse between HBCUs and amateur clubs bred issues, however. One would be the disparity in competition, as powerhouses like Hampton sometimes crushed amateur opponents, such as their 87–0 football victory against Roanoke Athletic Club in the winter of 1916. That same Hampton team beat rival Union two weeks later by a much closer score of 15–6.[118] This was not a one-off instance, as Hampton's 1918 football squad thrashed the amateur Newport News Vandals team 64–0.[119]

Other issues were eligibility related. Between 1923 and 1925, football star Robert Dean Miller transferred between Union, Dunbar High School in Washington, DC, and Howard University while gaining hardly any credits toward high school or college graduation.[120] Eligibility issues and the talent disparity compelled the CIAA to prohibit every member but Saint Paul's—then a two-year junior college—from competing against high schoolers and amateur clubs beginning in the 1928–1929 academic year.[121] This decision helped create an imperative to further the educational control of Black amateur sports through the creation of a Black high school sports league.[122]

Legendary Black referee Benjamin Washington long held that Virginia's first Black nonscholastic football game happened in Hampton's Fort Monroe in 1863 between West Point cadets and runaway slaves.[123] The white-owned *Norfolk Landmark* would disagree, noting in a sarcastic tone that "the darkies," as the paper called Black people, first cowered at the sight of a football in 1876 like the cave men who first witnessed fire, mistaking the rounded pigskin ball for a bomb.[124] However, documentary evidence suggests that nonscholastic Black amateur sports began as an agenda orchestrated by CIAA leadership in the 1910s and 1920s. Led by Saint Paul's athletic coach H. A. Taylor, CIAA coaches regularly encouraged their former football and basketball stars to spread the games beyond their campuses "by organizing and encouraging local teams and leagues" in their hometowns before and after graduation.[125] Howard alumnus James Minnis "Piggie" Harrison lauded former players in 1923 for doing what he had done in his hometown of Norfolk, and that was "returning among his old associates of boyhood" and starting amateur athletic clubs.[126] Fellow Norfolk natives Harvey Webb and Dr. William Bailey of Howard, "Red" Gill Thompson of West Virginia Collegiate Institute, George R. Jackson of Union, and Willey A. Johnson of Shaw founded the Monarch Football Club, Cumberland Footballers, Norfolk Athletic Club, Virginia Rose Stars, Attucks Athletic Club, and Columbia Athletic Club.[127] They, along with alumni from Hampton and Saint Paul's, helped form the Peninsula Basketball Association—a league of amateur nonscholastic basketball teams throughout Virginia's eastern seaboard. This collection of Tidewater area teams played games at local YMCAs and armories throughout Black Virginia communities.[128]

The Black Virginia sports phenomenon happened well beyond the Tidewater. Black middle-class men in Richmond (Adelphia Athletic Club), Charlottesville (Charlottesville Athletic Club), Lexington (Lexington Athletic Club), Roanoke (Autocrat Football Team), Petersburg (Hawks), Bedford, Hampton, Suffolk (Sunbeams) and Portsmouth (Alpha Athletic Club) also formed football and basketball teams that played one another.[129] Urban white Virginians had amateur teams also (basketball was mostly played in Richmond, Roanoke, Northern Virginia, and the Tidewater), however racial segregation ensured that Black amateur football and basketball teams only played HBCUs, Black high schools, and each other.[130] Some Black amateur teams, such as the Leans Athletic Club of Roanoke, played all-Black clubs as far away as Texas.[131] The development of these segregated games was a part of a national urban movement, as middle-class men Black in DC, Baltimore, Philadelphia, New York City, Newark, and St. Louis formed several amateur teams that regularly engaged in interstate play at YMCAs, churches, Black high schools, HBCUs, and public parks.[132]

Black women also created amateur athletic clubs. Female educators were adamant that young girls needed as much athletic attention as the men. Thus, they pooled their monies to rent and construct gyms to host several sporting clubs for Black female youth.[133] Many Black women engaged with Young

Women's Christian Associations (YWCAs) to create amateur women's basketball clubs given that high schools often snubbed female play beyond the intermural realm.[134] This was certainly the case in Virginia, with the Phyllis Wheatley Branch (Black) of the YWCA in the Tidewater organized several intramural athletic clubs in basketball and gymnastics.[135] It would not be until the 1920s, however, that Black Virginia high schools, led by schools in Danville (Danville High School), Roanoke (Harrison High School), Surry County (Dr. John J. Smallwood School), Hampton (Union High School) began playing interscholastic girls sports, with basketball being extremely popular.[136]

The rise of Black amateur sports outside of HBCU campuses resulted largely from urban migration during the New South period. After the Civil War, many Black Virginians left the rural countryside for cities such as Norfolk, Richmond, Petersburg, Lynchburg, Roanoke, and Danville to work in industries such as tobacco, meat packing, flour, textile, shipbuilding, and manufacturing.[137] Of the 690,000 Black Virginians in 1920, 209,000 lived in urban areas. Black urban life would only increase throughout the century, as most Black urban migrants were boys and men between fourteen and forty-five years of age.[138] While Black women moved to urban areas with their sons and husbands, urban migration, in Virginia, had become a masculine endeavor for stable work. "Before 1920 the Negro was primarily a rural Southern person," said Fred M. Alexander. After 1920, Alexander found, "he," as Alexander was clear to masculinize his analysis of Black migration, "has become increasingly urbanized."[139]

Advancements in Black education helped convert the urbanized nonscholastic athletic club culture into a bumper crop of high school football and basketball teams. Between 1870 and 1930, more Black people migrated out of the commonwealth than migrated from the Virginia countryside to its urban centers. Thus, Virginia's Black population remained stagnant at around 600,000 between 1870 (40 percent of the overall population at that time) and 1930 (27 percent of the overall population) while the white population increased from 1 million to 2 million during the same time period.[140] The demographic shift's impact on athletics was seen directly with Norfolk's Lyon Social Club, as the local media reported in 1923 that their football players were vastly relocating to Northern cities.[141] They were not alone.[142]

Just as amateur athletic clubs "petered out" of existence in Black communities, Black educators pushed the state legislature for more public schooling (more schoolhouses and longer terms) for Black youth.[143] With the help of Northern white philanthropists, some sympathetic white Virginia liberals, and Black grassroots organizations, the number of public secondary schools (mostly high schools) jumped from less than five (with none accredited) in 1900 to more than fifty by 1930, with thirty-four being fully accredited. Black school enrollment increased across the commonwealth from 111,677 to 158,531, with high school enrollment going from 910 to 7,676 and vocational school attendance increasing from 1,389 to 14,266 during the same period.[144] As Black educators corralled more Black youth into schools for longer school years, high school sports began to emerge throughout the commonwealth.

Black Virginia's shift toward high school football and basketball conference formation came not from local elites but from their neighbors north of the Potomac. Washington, DC's M Street educator Edwin Bancroft Henderson founded the Public School Athletic League (PSAL) in December 1910. Initially composed of eight Black DC-area schools, the PSAL organized competitions in basketball, football, baseball, and track and field that had long taken place since the turn of the century against schools from Baltimore.[145] Henderson also organized the Interscholastic Athletic Association of Middle Atlantic States. This organization promoted Black high school athletic competition through state league formation.[146] They found success in West Virginia (West Virginia Colored High School Athletic Union), Texas (Prairie View Interscholastic League), as well as Missouri and Kansas (Missouri Valley Interscholastic Athletic Association). Black Virginians, however, struggled mightily to create their own high school league for reasons that are lost to the documentary record.[147] Instead of organized league play, Black Virginia high school sports took place "under the careful supervision" of a few teacher-coaches who appeared to struggle in creating football and basketball schedules.[148] Thus, Henderson—a Virginia native—and other Black DC school officials aided their Southern neighbors by forming the Interstate High School Athletic Association (ISHAA) in the winter of 1924.

The ISHAA was like the CIAA in that it formalized athletic ties that already existed. The ISHAA began with Black principals at DC's Armstrong Technical School, Baltimore's Frederick Douglass School, Newport News's Huntington High School, and Norfolk's Booker T. Washington High School coming together to regulate football competition, an expensive sport that only the largest Black schools could afford to play.[149] Since the late 1910s, Black Virginia schools such as Norfolk's Booker T. Washington (formerly John T. West), Newport News's Huntington, Lynchburg's Dunbar, Christiansburg Institute, and Portsmouth's I. C. Norcom began interscholastic football and basketball competition against one another and Black DC-area schools. It would not be until the 1930s, when the DC suburbs expanded into Virginia via the New Deal, that there were Black high schools in Northern Virginia and that those schools would engage in basketball and football play. Interstate rivalries developed by Central and Eastern Black Virginia schools extended as far north as Baltimore and as far south as Charleston, South Carolina.[150] These games were as much a function of desire as they were a need, as white schools in each state utterly refused to breach the color line for athletic competition.[151]

Black Virginia high school football and basketball was created by segregation like HBCU sports before them. High school sports began intramurally on the nation's few elite white (often Northeastern) preparatory school campuses in the 1860s. Southern white high schools—both public and private—used football and basketball to recruit prospective students as early as 1877.[152] While it was widely believed that the "spirit of rivalry"[153] compelled Alexandria's Episcopal High to play Virginia's first ever high school football game against Johns Hopkins College (now University) in 1888, Episcopal regularly played gridiron contests against the Deaf-Mute College of Washington and Kendall Green College in 1884.[154] Other white Virginia high schools started football and basketball programs between 1880 and 1910.[155] The games were so popular that graduation awards and credentials for college admission included excellent play in athletics.[156] In fact, football and basketball became selling points for private academies in Virginia (Norfolk Academy, St. Christopher's in Richmond, etc.,) and the South who wished for prospective students to see them as peers to noted Northeastern preparatory academies such as Groton Hill, Philips Exeter, and Andover.[157] Their opponents were either one another, white amateur clubs, out-of-state white high schools in DC, West Virginia, Virginia, Maryland, and DC colleges.[158]

Numerous abuses with recruiting and low academic standards compelled white high school officials across the country to begin paying faculty coaches, forming state-level athletic conferences and national athletic associations by the 1920s.[159] Under the direction of UVA's General Studies Department, eighty white Virginia high schools created the Virginia High School Literary and Athletic League—now Virginia High School League (VHSL)—in 1913.[160] The VHSL along with other white state leagues formed an umbrella organization called the National Federation of High Schools in 1920. The umbrella league helped white high school football and basketball mimic their collegiate counterpart by orchestrating intersectional games and "national titles," with the first national championship games being played in Waco, Texas, in 1927.[161] The VHSL's mission statement to "promote wholesome athletics among the pupils of Virginia" did not include Black pupils.[162] With the exception of some Midwestern states such as Illinois, Minnesota, Iowa, and Indiana, white high school leagues barred competition across the color line.

With the VHSL closed to Black students, the ISHAA quickly became a Black Virginia league like the CIAA. This was in part due to Baltimore member schools being "the slough of [ISHAA] football," lagging far behind in terms of talent and training.[163] The Black DC schools, such as Armstrong and M Street, were solid, but Virginia had the most teams in the league (ten), making up half of the league's membership by the late-1920s. This helped Virginia host the league's most dominant football team, that being the "Fighting" or "Scrapping" Bookers of Booker T. Washington High School in Norfolk.[164] Coached by former CIAA football and Lincoln University great Owen A. Wilson, the Fighting Booker "Machine," while having no football facilities, won every ISHAA football title during the league's nine-year existence, beating opponents by a combined 300 points, on average, every season.[165] The Bookers were a sensation in Black elite circles, as W. E. B. Du Bois's *Crisis Magazine* editorialized on the "unbroken record of winning games" by what was often deemed "The South's Finest High School Football Team."[166]

Booker T.'s football dominance created the imperative for Black Virginians to form their own high school athletic leagues. While Booker T. made Virginia the toast of Black high school sports, the ISHAA remained a league run and operated by elite DC men only.[167] This must have caused a rift between them and Black Virginia educators, as by 1927, ten Black Virginia high school principals met at Hampton Institute to form the Virginia Interscholastic Athletic Association (VIAA), with its first official sport being basketball. Football would not become a league sport until 1932 because of prearranged game contracts in the ISHAA.[168] Undoubtedly inspired by the VIAA, smaller Black Southside schools such as Charlotte County Training School, Halifax County Training School, Lunenburg County Training School, Mecklenburg Training School, and South Boston's Booker T. Washington formed the basketball-focused Southern Interscholastic Athletic Association (SIAA) in 1934.[169] That same year, Black schools in the Piedmont, Southwest, and Shenandoah Valley formed the Western division of the Virginia State High School Athletic Conference (W-VSHAC).[170] Black DC schools were not slighted by Virginia's athletic conference development, as they closed ranks and formed a metro-area conference called the South Atlantic High School Association in 1933.[171]

The CIAA maintained a tight-knit Black athletic culture by bridging the gap between themselves and the burgeoning Black Virginia high school leagues. Like the relationship between the Southwest Athletic Conference (college) and Prairie View Interscholastic League (high school) in Texas, CIAA teams had their pick of top VIAA prospects. Virginia State and Hampton were also home to VIAA, SIAA, and W-VSHAC tournament games.[172] In some cases, as with Virginia Union, CIAA schools played basketball games at VIAA and W-VSHAC schools because they lacked indoor facilities.[173]

Beyond recruiting and facility usage, CIAA football and basketball coaches tightened the Black amateur sports community with football and basketball coaching schools and clinics annually hosted at Hampton. Black high school coaches from Virginia and states as far away as Georgia and Alabama regularly attended.[174] Also attending these meetings were Black referees, who, since the formation of the CIAA, VIAA, SIAA, and W-VHSAC, were the only officials regulating Black football and basketball games. In fact, the CIAA set the precedent that all-Black sports leagues (high school and college) should contract only Black referees. This became standard practice throughout the nation by 1930.[175] Called a "labor for a common good" of Black athletics by Virginia State's football coach Harry Jefferson,[176] organized meetings between CIAA leadership and Black high school coaches ensured that athletics were a collective endeavor designed to create a fraternity of leaders dedicated to uplifting the race through organizationalism in athletic competition.[177]

As Virginia entered the New South era, Black residents created and sustained a vibrant, binary amateur athletic culture of college and high school sports. Games that were originally played as recreation quickly became symbols of Black progress after slavery. Football and basketball contests became places where Black leaders and everyday persons communed with a shared purpose to find a respectable reprieve from the indignities of Jim Crow segregation. With Black amateur athletics firmly entrenched and regulated by educational institutions, the games later produced a new vision of Black progress, one where its players and coaches became peak symbols of masculinity and civility. This "New Negro" development would not have happened without Black citizens resisting racial norms, adopting organized contests, and using them to generate a shared, institutionally based autonomous culture during the darkest days of Jim Crow segregation.

2

THE LEADERSHIP, 1910–1929

A FALL 1922 youth football game between heated crosstown rivals Norfolk Athletic Club and Columbia Athletic Club drew the ire of a sportswriter at the *Norfolk Journal and Guide*. The game of football, itself, was not the problem for the *Journal and Guide*. Rather, he took issue with the way the game was played by the adolescent athletes. In a news article titled "Keep the Sport Clean and Manly," the writer reported that continuous "roughnecking" before, during, and after each football play was a "disgrace to the game" and to amateur sports' purpose and meaning for the Black race.

After the game, the writer interviewed Norfolk football great, Portsmouth I. C. Norcom's head coach, YMCA director, and fellow spectator George Ward.[1] The two must have talked ad nauseum about the terrible display of sportsmanship they witnessed. What made it into the *Journal and Guide*, however, was Ward's insistence that he coached Black youth to see football as a training ground for proper Black manhood. "Smart" players understood that victory in football required turning masculine aggression into assertion. Assertiveness required self-sacrifice for the collective benefit, as Black men generally understood that unchanneled aggression was hazardous to the player, the team, the sport, and the race. "Brains will master brawn" inside and outside the gridiron, and "in union there is strength," Ward insisted. Ward shared with the writer the understanding among Black leadership about the efficacy of amateur athletics in the New Negro age of the 1920s. It was not enough that Black boys played amateur sports. They had to play it the right way.

Saturday afternoon football games were not just leisure getaways from the daily grind of industrial and agricultural labor. Rather, they were communal projects designed to uplift the race through making competitive Black men. There to witness this was the Black community, who helped shape the development of Black masculinity through their consumption of sports. "The [Black] public is to witness clean sport," the sportswriter insisted in his critique of the 1922 youth football matchup.[2] When the *Journal and Guide* printed this, the newspaper articulated the widely held belief that the place amateur of sports in Black life relied on its shaping of proper Black manhood in an age when the phrase was oxymoronic to white America and nearly elusive for the segregated race.

Black athletes were Virginia's New Negro during the World War I era.[3] Black Virginia's adoption of the athlete as its version of "the New Negro" was a rhetorical discourse printed in local media outlets. The *Norfolk Journal and Guide*, *Richmond Planet*, and CIAA Bulletins used speeches, articles, and epic tales about football and basketball to define racial progress as a quest for a specific type of manhood—one I deem *Black athletic manhood*. Black athletic manhood was a marginalized masculinity that Black men could attain through the "proper" exercise of sport. It was also an ideological commitment to use athletics to build Black boys and men who would overcome the emasculation of segregation and lead families, communities, and the institutions needed to sustain Black life. The above outlets married Black masculinity to sports because athletic success was an objective metric by which any Black man could achieve manhood. The physical and mental toll of athletics, as well as the exercise of prized masculine virtues such as honor, self-sacrifice, and assertiveness, the above outlets argued, was a venture of manhood that prepared Black men to be race leaders.

I bridge a scholarly gap left by historians who have documented the rise of sports and Black militant journalism in the World War I era. Historians see the 1920s as the Age of Spectacle, when Americans consumed more sports than ever through print media.[4] Yet, Black newspapers, said one scholar, "did not devote significant attention to" athletics until the late 1920s.[5] While not explaining why, this same historian finds that the *Journal and Guide* pushed for more consistent Black newspaper coverage of amateur athletics. I explain the *Journal and Guide*'s pioneering Black sports coverage through the sentiments of founder Plummer Young.[6] He along with the *Richmond Planet* and CIAA Bulletins had a religious dedication to sport that the Black press establishment largely lacked. However, as amateur sports became America's greatest spectacle, Young successfully pushed the Black press to see organized games as proving grounds for Black equality.

Furthermore, the history of Black male athletes belongs in New Negro historiography. The New Negro movement is generally understood as the time when Black Americans redefined "Blackness" between World War I and the Great Depression by leaving the South in the Great Migration.[7] Millions of Black Southerners left rural farms for Northern cities and formed newer patchwork communities where art forms such as jazz, poetry, and literature proved that Black people, despite slave ancestry, had intelligent mediums of expression.[8] To scholars, the New Negro is an intellectual, musician, poet, war veteran, communist, Garveyite, militant journalist, and Civil Rights activist. The New Negro movement was made of several types of New Negroes. Linking them together was a desire to uplift the Black race from the limitations placed on them by the second Ku Klux Klan, lynching, segregation, disenfranchisement, underemployment, and the Confederate monuments that symbolized it all.[9] Yet, the most forgotten New Negroes were Black athletes. This omission remains no longer. When a Black athlete laced up his cleats and sneakers for competition, he, as W. E. B. Du Bois once noted in 1917, "brought the black man to the fore" of American modernity through properly pursuing competitive glory.[10]

Virginia was one place where Black athletes were rhetorically constructed into New Negroes. The Commonwealth lacked a nationally recognized Black arts community, music scene, political class, and intelligentsia that often defines the New Negro movement of the North and Midwest. Virginia fits in the Southern New Negro paradigm, where racial advancements were seen in stable elite-run urban communities anchored by churches, HBCUs, and various uplift organizations.[11] Here, football and basketball players and coaches became thought leaders and cultural standard-bearers for racial progress. Moreover, athletic manhood provided Black men with a classless masculine attainment not seen through typical bourgeois New Negro avenues of business, the arts, and academia. This cultural development proves that the New Negro era was, like the Black press's role in shaping it, a diverse quest for Black manhood often beginning and ending on the baseline and line of scrimmage.[12]

To remember Black athletes as New Negroes requires the analysis of the outlets that created them: the *Journal and Guide*, *Richmond Planet*, and CIAA Bulletins. For it was these three outlets that conveyed a hypermasculine message and image of racial advancement during a critical time in American sports history. In the early twentieth century, male sports were tapestries of ideas, mechanisms to hash out ideological differences, and platforms for social commentary. They rested alongside novels, movies, and stage plays in relying on real people entering artificial environments to act out ideological commitments and convey messages about everyday life. For Black Americans in the World War I era, racial segregation was everyday life. No Black person, from California to Maine, Washington to Florida, could escape its sinister grasp regardless of how educated or wealthy they were. Being Black in Jim Crow America was an exercise of individual and collective thriving under constant struggle. Nothing articulated that lesson better than amateur football and basketball.

THE VALUE OF THE PRESS

The *Planet* and *Guide* were unlikely allies in shaping Black uplift through the prism of athletics. Both outlets were the most widely circulated Black newspapers in Virginia and some of the most read in the South during the World War I era. Yet, they could not have been any more different. Founded in the shadow of the Old South by John Mitchell Jr., the *Planet* was an activist engine against segregation and disenfranchisement. The *Journal and Guide* was a New South creation. Founder Plummer Young Sr. used the newspaper to preach racial uplift through community solidarity and not political protest.[13] Mitchell was an elder Reconstruction-era liberal, and Young was a youthful New South conservative. Both men felt that the other preached a dangerous message that would get Black people killed—as was Young's criticism of Mitchell—or keep them permanently under the thumb of white racists—as was Mitchell's gripe with Young.[14] Nevertheless, the *Planet* and *Guide* were, like their founders, eerily two sides of the same coin. The papers took different approaches to the same issues confronting Black America in the age of Jim Crow.

Contemporary Black male leaders often preached that Black manhood came from intellect and thrift. Young and Mitchell, however, felt that masculinity required the development of mind and body—the cultivation of virtue and morals through physical and mental perseverance. It was because of athletics, and not intellect and thrift alone, said Young, that "we have met a number of the collegians who excelled in sports who have gone out in the world and made brilliant successes." The existence of prominent former college athletes-turned-Black male leaders such as educator Matthew W. Bullock, professional footballer Frederick "Fritz" Pollard, actor and Civil Rights activists Paul Robeson, as well as Virginia State alumnus and Assistant US Attorney General William Henry Lewis, for example, compelled Young to opine that "you can't have strong mental manhood unless you have a strong physical manhood." Thus, Mitchell and Young embraced football and basketball games, as they turned "robust young manhood" into "masterpieces of physical manhood" for the Black race.[15]

Young's and Mitchell's shapings of Black manhood by sports was, ironically, more in tune with how white people viewed masculinity. By the 1920s, white academics, social critics, athletic apologists, and even newspaper outlets had long preached that football and basketball were enterprises of white masculine supremacy.[16] As University of Georgia Chancellor D. C. Barrow told a group of agreeing Hampton students in 1907, "a fellow who can stand his ground in football can stand a good many things. He has sand and he has character."[17] Plummer Young acknowledged this, claiming that "the white race understands subconsciously that it must keep alive the physical forces" to maintain their control over society.[18] The Black bourgeoisie did not embrace this concept. Rather, they believed manhood came from achievements in business, education, and civic service.[19]

The *Planet* and *Journal and Guide* defined Black athletic manhood outside of the New Negro Black press paradigm. Born in 1827 with the *Freedmen's Journal* in New York City, the Black press was a loose network of independently run, Black-owned newspapers that protested against inequality.[20] This agenda left little room for sport despite Black communities across the country embracing football and basketball.[21] There is reason to believe that Black newspaper editors—often being college-educated, upper-crust Black men—saw sporting events as platforms for the worst elements of Black life. This explains, for example, the *Chicago Defender*'s scathing 1910 article titled "The Football Craze."

The most popular Black newspaper in America demonized football specifically, and athletics more broadly, as an "epidemic" that should be phased out of Black life.[22] The *Chicago Defender* even took the time to check the popularity of football among Black women, namely through criticizing their doting over athletes and fancy gameday attire as unbecoming of modest future wives and mothers.[23] A year later, the *Chicago Defender* extended their anti-sports platform beyond female spectating and into the realm of female competition, citing doctors such as Paul Pattison of Spokane, Washington, who argued that a sport like basketball was too rough for women to engage in.[24] The *Baltimore Afro-American*—a known advocate of Black athletics—even expressed dismay at Black football fanaticism with a doomsday article titled "Fiddling While Rome Burns." In it, they bemoaned that on the same day that congressional Democrats killed the Dyer Anti-Lynching Bill, fifteen thousand Black people attended the Howard versus Lincoln football game.[25] The *Pittsburgh Courier* also platformed concerns about the popularity of college football games, as some Black people felt that the race substituted education for popular spectacle.[26] This take was not hyperbole without merit, as a HBCU football coach admitted in 1924 that for many Black elites, "mental picture[s] of. . . . freely flowing spirits, betting of money, insulting remarks, and crooked officials make up the mental picture" of Black sports.[27] The New Negro ethos required Black cultural products to reflect bourgeois respectability. Many in the Black press believed sports to be antithetical to that mission.

Plummer Young and John Mitchell entered the vanguard and shaped Black athletic manhood by propagating the men who embodied it. Among its gripes with football, the *Defender*'s chief criticism in 1910 was that the game created a "false heroism" where Black fanatics hailed players and coaches as race leaders because of their gridiron conquests.[28] What the *Defender* saw as false heroism, John Mitchell's *Planet* and Plummer Young's *Journal and Guide* viewed as examples of Black excellence. An example of this was the *Planet*'s and *Journal and Guide*'s articulation of athletic manhood through Charles Holston Williams and Gideon Edward Smith.[29] Born in Jessamine, Kentucky, in 1886 and graduating from Hampton in 1909, Williams started intercollegiate football and basketball at Hampton as the school's first athletic director in 1910.[30] Gideon Smith was a Salem, Virginia, native and Hampton graduate who returned to coach at his alma mater in 1921 under Williams's direction.[31] Together, Williams and Smith turned Hampton into the model for Black athletic greatness, making the "Seasiders" one of the most feared HBCU opponents for much of the World War I era.

The *Planet*'s and *Journal and Guide*'s analysis of Hampton differed in style and substance. John Mitchell gave Charles Williams and Gideon Smith the editorial freedom to portray Hampton athletics as the symbol of competitive virtue that Black people ought to emulate in everyday life.[32] Hampton often beat football and basketball opponents so badly that opposing teams forfeited games rather than taking an embarrassing loss.[33] Their dominance, as presented in the two newspapers, represented Black achievement and the need for the race to overcome seemingly insurmountable obstacles. Thus, Gideon Smith once took to the *Planet* and denounced quitting as antithetical to what Hampton athletics meant to Black people. "Nothing is ever gained by forfeiting," Smith once said with disgust about Hampton's conference opponents. However, "we," Smith said about Black people as a whole, "do stand a chance to win if the game is played out." John Mitchell saw fit to publish Smith's scathing indictment of quitting to help shape Black athletic manhood as the competitive spirit Black people needed in the age of Jim Crow.[34]

To the *Planet*, Black athletic manhood was not just about physical dominance and perseverance but Black athletes' demeanors when they participated in sports. Charles Williams's summaries of Hampton games in the *Planet* always included reports about sportsmanship and fair play. Williams once lauded a 1917 football game between rivals Hampton and Virginia State for being "the cleanest ever witnessed on the local gridiron."[35] After a Hampton victory over Shaw University in basketball in 1918, Williams also claimed that "the crowd . . . showed real appreciation for the fine playing and good sportsmanship," as "the game was clean and hard fought."[36] Black fanaticism was so great that at most football and basketball games, hundreds of potential attendants were turned away at the gate.[37] That fanaticism, Williams preached in the *Planet*, hinged upon Black athletes representing the race as good sportsmen who fought hard to win through "clean" competition, something that was to be replicated in everyday life.

CHARLES H. WILLIAMS
Hampton Institute

Figure 1. Charles Holston Williams, athletic director of Hampton Institute, courtesy of Virginia Union University Archives and Special Collections

The *Planet* saw Black athletic manhood as a community venture, where Black fanatics enhanced the competitive spirit displayed on the court and gridiron.[38] During a heated football contest between Howard University and Hampton in 1920, Williams recalled that "the Howard team [was] backed by a large student body who exhibited the most perfect cheering." Because of that, "the Hampton players appeared to be suffering from stage fright, from which they never wholly recovered."[39] Black fanatics expected Black athletes to overcome the fear of failure and execute under the supervision of the Black community. Yet, the *Planet* tasked them with maintaining the delicate balance between competitiveness and unruly behavior. After a December 1920 football game between Hampton and Union—the most heated rivalry in the CIAA at the time—Williams criticized both fan bases for rushing the field after a controversial call. The brawl compelled Williams to forfeit on behalf of Hampton. "The unfortunate ending," Williams later wrote, ruined what was billed as the "most thrilling game of the year." He called on Black fans to be the moral backbone that upheld the competitive and collegial attitude the race was to display on and off the field of play.[40]

The *Journal and Guide* focused less on Hampton's exploits between the lines and more on the leadership who built Hampton into a machine that produced Black athletic manhood. Plummer Young documented with keen detail that Hampton's athletic prestige came from Charles Williams and Gideon Smith building a comprehensive physical education program where students underwent regular athletic training as a graduation requirement.[41] Black athletic manhood demanded racial uplift, and thus Hampton allowed underfunded Black high schools in Virginia's "rural and urban districts" to train under Williams and Smith. Hampton alumni were also encouraged to create physical education programs in Black high schools after graduation.[42] Hampton became the example that athletics improved academics, as school officials secured donations to grow the college on the back of its stellar physical education program and intercollegiate football and basketball clubs. "The spirit of Hampton," said the *Journal and Guide*, was one where physical education built the race through enhancing the bodies of men.[43] In looking at the organized nature of Hampton athletics and the "skilled tutelage of coaches Charles H. Williams, [and] Gideon E. Smith," Plummer Young surmised in 1924 that "the entire athletic program of Hampton is bright."[44] Furthermore, Williams and Smith proved that despite the *Chicago Defender*'s criticism, there was no falsity behind the heroism of Black athletic figures.

Gideon E. "Gid" Smith

Figure 2. Gideon Edward "Gid" Smith, football and basketball coach at Hampton Institute, courtesy of Virginia Union University Archives and Special Collections

THE HAMPTON FOOTBALL SQUAD FOR 1925 (CHAMPIONS)

Figure 3. The CIAA football champion Hampton Seasiders, courtesy of Virginia Union University Archives and Special Collections

HAMPTON BASKETBALL TEAM, INTERCOLLEGIATE CHAMPIONS, 1924

Figure 4. The CIAA basketball champion Hampton Seasiders, courtesy of Virginia Union University Archives and Special Collections

Through covering the exploits of Williams and Smith, the *Planet* and *Journal and Guide* helped counter the white media bias that blocked Black sportsmen from the realm of heroism. "The 1920s," said a prominent sports historian, "were the age of the sports hero."[45] White newspaper outlets across the country controlled the image of football and basketball by making heroes out of white athletes and coaches.[46] Through covering Charles Williams and Gideon Smith at Hampton, the *Planet* and *Journal and Guide* established that Black men could be sports heroes, too, and athletic manhood was not just a venture in white supremacy.

The *Planet* and *Journal and Guide* did not limit Black athletic manhood to the success of Hampton. Rather, they also saw it in other Virginia HBCU athletic programs. The *Planet* often celebrated the underwhelming Saint Paul's football and basketball teams for having had "men [who] fought tenaciously for victory" even though wins were often difficult for them to obtain.[47] It was a widely talked about rumor that the CIAA was so reluctant to admit the junior college as a member in 1923 that they had to, and eventually did, defeat Virginia Union in a football game as a part of a bet among CIAA leadership.[48] Virginia State football and basketball players also earned praise for their "solid muscle" developed by dedicated physical education instructors who possessed doctoral degrees.[49] The future ministers of Virginia Seminary were always in "first class shape," making them tough outs for any opponent who faced the "Dragons" of Lynchburg.[50] The *Planet*'s most vivid argument that Black athletic manhood existed outside of the realm of physical dominance was seen in the painstaking coverage of Virginia Union's first football victory over Hampton, in 1917. The *Planet* portrayed the "Hampton Machine" as Goliath and Union as the David using superior strategy to smite them by a score of 3–0.[51] The *Planet* made sure to make Union the example of Black perseverance. After "playing the best game of her career" in defeating Hampton, the *Planet* covered the "heroic" Union defeat of Howard, Saint Paul's, and Virginia State en route to becoming CIAA football champions.[52]

The *Journal and Guide* believed that HBCU espousal of Black athletic manhood made them invaluable to the Black community. To Virginia State professor and CIAA president W. A. Rogers, student athletes were the "heirs and joint heirs of all the past" who, through the play of sport, upheld the customs, morals, values, and traditions the schools were founded upon.[53] Young held similar feelings, as he celebrated Black colleges for "giving robust young [Black] manhood the chance to display its skill and strength," something white colleges would not.[54] In his bi-weekly "Sportboard Reflections," Young urged the Black public to support HBCU football and basketball games because they were "builders of ideals" and "makers of men" through the physical education of intercollegiate sport. It was in these places where "our good coaching are educating boys" and "developing [them into] men for tomorrow." The making of Black boys into men, Young argued, relied on the strong marriage between athletics and academics. "The educational system which places no stress upon physical development has very little appeal to the public," Young once told his journalist colleagues.[55] The "two are interdependent" in the development of Black men.[56] Moreover, HBCUs used sports to turn Black male bodies into "better bodies" and foggy minds into "clearer minds" for the advancement of the race. Because of that, the *Journal and Guide* concluded, HBCUs were "worth working for, trying for, [and] rooting for." They were "worth our best support, not just for one game but for every game."[57]

THE ST. PAUL FOOTBALL TEAM OF 1925

Figure 5. St. Paul's Tigers football team, courtesy of Virginia Union University Archives and Special Collections

THE ST. PAUL BASKETBALL TEAM OF 1925-26

Figure 6. St. Paul's Tigers basketball team, courtesy of Virginia Union University Archives and Special Collections

THE 1925-26 BASKETBALL TEAM OF VA. SEMINARY

Figure 7. Virginia Seminary Dragons basketball team, courtesy of Virginia Union University Archives and Special Collections

THE VA. SEMINARY FOOTBALL TEAM OF 1925

Figure 8. Virginia Seminary Dragons football team, courtesy of Virginia Union University Archives and Special Collections

THE UNION FOOTBALL SQUAD OF 1925

Figure 9. Virginia Union "Red and Steel" football team, courtesy of Virginia Union University Archives and Special Collections

VA. STATE FOOTBALL TEAM 1927

Figure 10. Virginia State Trojan football team, courtesy of Virginia Union University Archives and Special Collections

Young took his advocacy for Black athletic manhood a step further than John Mitchell's *Planet* by recruiting a cadre of writers who espoused the efficacy of Black sports. The most important of them was James "Piggie" Harrison. The fellow Norfolk native embodied Black athletic manhood, Young believed, because he was one of the men who "have made a better position for themselves and their race by stimulating athletics among the young people while neglecting nothing of their business."[58]

Harrison was born the eldest of five children in 1873 to working-class freeman Samuel Harrison and his wife, domestic servant Louis Harrison, who had been born free.[59] The well known football star graduated from Howard University in 1908 with his law degree and became one of the thirty-seven Black men practicing law in the commonwealth.[60] Harrison's respected standing in Norfolk's Black community could not be denied. The stocky, six-foot-tall, three-sport athlete (football, basketball, and baseball) played professional baseball and ran youth athletic clubs (Columbia Athletic Club and Norfolk Athletic Club) before becoming a lawyer.[61] When Harrison divorced wealthy mixed-race socialite Louis Mercedes Wright in 1916, the record never made the local press at a time when nearly all divorces were recorded for public consumption. Symbolizing his success and standing was that fact and his lovely 2,500-square-foot home along Norfolk's middle-class Washington Avenue.[62]

Harrison used memory and epic storytelling to further the *Journal and Guide*'s sports agenda. In February 1923, Harrison began crafting a series first titled Unwritten History of Local Athletes and later called Unpublished History of Football and Baseball.[63] Harrison later claimed that his decision to write such "history" came from "local fandom," which "is showing much interest" in sports as it "received more support [nationwide] than at any time in their history."[64] The histories of Plummer Young and the *Journal and Guide* have not analyzed the unpublished history series because they are quite easy to ignore.[65] The history reads as random stories shaped by moral lessons with Harrison at the center of everything. Even Harrison admitted that "many incidents come as I write, which I had entirely forgotten, until I began this article." Therefore, Harrison's tales were hard to follow because "memory, like quicksand" is a "treacherous" game that often defeats storytellers.[66] The historian's craft allows one to connect these disparate stories and extract from them the messages that Harrison intended to convey. Harrison used sports stories to promote the virtues of Black athletic manhood as he understood and experienced it, given that he felt his stories would be pertinent for "the present generation" of Black people.[67]

Harrison's stories often stressed that Black athletic manhood was a classless binding agent that connected and uplifted Black men. This began at home, as Harrison recalled that gritty sandlot football games helped him and his hardened, formerly enslaved father form a bond after grueling days working along the Norfolk docks.[68] Harrison also recalled that amateur football matches became proving grounds for masculinity where middle-class Black bankers, teachers, and lawyers competed against working-class servers, longshoremen, and drivers.[69] Harrison's relaxed storytelling method fit with the moral of his narrative that sports were a classless medium of Black masculinity that blue- and white-collar men could participate in. One did not have to suit up for a HBCU to undergo the process of Black athletic manhood. Rather, they could take to an open field or an empty lot to enact the physical and mental process of masculinity. Black athletic manhood was, as Harrison called for, "the brotherhood of [the Black] man."[70]

Harrison also used his unpublished history to argue that athletics helped Black men confront the racial violence inherent in Jim Crow America. "Fights would invariably follow our games," Harrison once told his readers. Yet, his men entered the gridiron abyss in search of victory anyway.[71] Harrison once recounted a tale where his Columbia Athletic Club, "with only four players," defeated their cross-river rival Hampton Tigers. Because his team "played the Tigers off their feet," the Tigers resorted to "fierce and bloody" tactics, as he and his teammates "caught it on the nose" several times while making winning plays.[72] During another football game against a team manned by longshoremen, "in an instant," Harrison remembered, "every man" on his team were "a target for blows." As a result, "several sported black eyes, but we won [the game]," Harrison said with pride.[73] It was not uncommon for one of his football players to enter "the field limping with a cane."[74] These stories told readers that the game of football, for example, required Black men to combat aggression with assertiveness, establish order amid chaos, and snatch victory from the jaws of certain defeat. If a Black man entered the game of life as he entered a game of football, he had better prepare for the certainty of white violence in the form of lynching, debt peonage, and police brutality. "Men who are humiliated, beaten and discriminated against because of a color," said Harrison, needed athletics to teach him how to survive.[75] Because athletics "strips the brute from" Black men, said Harrison, "I know no greater asset to good citizenship and health than the free, fair indulgence in athletics."[76] "If daily licking and perseverance counted" for anything, Harrison opined, it made for a race of strong men.[77]

Harrison provided readers with real-life examples of Black men who used athletics to propel them to commercial success. He proudly recalled that of the Black men who engaged in sports early in life, "a majority" entered "professions and larger outlooks" when their playing days ended.[78] Local footballers such as Joe Paige became a pharmacist; Peck Mills and Phil Scott were doctors; Ed Crocker was the only Black clerk for the US Customs House in Norfolk; Plug Carter was a renowned professional musician; and Wiley Crocker was a prominent Tidewater banker. These men did not become commercially successful solely because of their intellect, according to Harrison. Rather, "despite racial discrimination," said Harrison,[79] they and many others used the lessons of sports to navigate the brutal terrain of Jim Crow and find professional success. These men, Harrison claimed, "made good in [their] after life" because of sports.[80]

Featured tales from Piggie Harrison and numerous articles detailing HBCU athletics helped the *Journal and Guide* push amateur athletics into the Black press mainstream. In 1924, Young proclaimed that "all the readers of THE *JOURNAL AND GUIDE* are interested in the physical development and preparedness of the race" through sports.[81] A few years later, he went further to chastise other Black newspapers who refused to follow his lead: "I wonder why it is that every game indulged in by white schools from every hog path have the summary of their contents appear in the white papers. . . . but if a lynching of a Negro occurred, the [Black] papers everywhere would report it."[82]

Young felt that the Black press cared more about dictating to Black people what should be important than explaining to them the nuances of their cultural developments. This sentiment placed him in line with prominent Black sociologist E. Franklin Frazier. The longtime critic of Black middle-class people denounced the Black press as a realm of make-believe, where elites told the working class what to care about.[83] Instead, Young and Frazier believed that Black newspapers should be mirrors of Black life and quilts of living culture. The Black press enjoyed a relative monopoly over Black public discourse because white newspapers often portrayed Black people as unintelligent and criminally inclined. This endowed them with the responsibility to reflect, not dictate, what Black people cared about. Young's message resonated by the late 1920s. In response to yet another *Chicago Defender* hit piece against football in November 1925, the *Pittsburgh Courier* claimed that college football displayed the spirit of uplift in Black life, as seen by Black people pulling their financial resources together to host and travel to games across the South. For it was because of football that "we are investing in our own social development, and are quite satisfied with ourselves and our own standards."[84] Most Black newspapers—*Atlanta Daily World*, *Philadelphia Tribune*, *Chicago Defender*, *Pittsburgh Courier*, *Cleveland Call and Post*, and *New York Amsterdam News*—gave ample space and analysis to Black athletics throughout the country by the late 1920s, even when it ran against their bottom line.[85]

Black Virginia's New Negro development helped improve the relationship between Black media and the sports world, a fact that few can deny. Virginia State athletic director Thomas Puryear once said that Black "appreciation of athletic competitions is very largely traceable to the influence of the press," which began with the likes of Plummer Young and John Mitchell. Henceforth, Puryear urged that "the press and the CIAA must work together for the realization of a common purpose, the highest development and expression of manhood." He did not mince words in saying that above all, "this is their combined task."[86]

ATHLETIC-MINDED RACE

CIAA athletic directors and coaches must have been proud to attend the league's twenty-fifth annual meeting in 1937. As the special guest and keynote speaker, Virginia State football captain Richard N. Dixon gave a presentation to around one hundred sportsmen about the lessons he learned as a collegiate athlete. "It will be impossible for me to translate into action some of the great lessons of life that have come to me through active participation in athletics under the guidance of some of the greatest men that the game has ever known," Dixon humbly began. He continued by praising his coach Harry "Big Jeff" Jefferson for teaching what ended up being the most important lesson he learned while gracing the gridiron at Virginia State: that football was a parable for Black life under Jim Crow, where the game made Black athletes into race leaders.

HBCU football taught Dixon that race leadership was a venture in personal achievement that aligned with community representation. Off the field, Black people tasked their leaders with being competent and accomplished. Through HBCU football, "the athlete learns a lesson of life—one is always responsible for one's own act," as "a player cannot" suit up and "play football unless he keeps out of trouble and stands well in his classes." Dixon let it be known that this reality ensured that "every athlete knows what the student body thinks of him," as was the case with Black leaders in Black communities. Dixon also compared the football team to the Black community by saying that "no athletic team ever reached great success without a high degree of self-sacrifice and self-control." Football taught Black athletes that failing to uphold the race's standards of respectability while being hailed in a position of leadership was seen as not giving "one's all for the good of the team," and that behavior was "punished speedily and definitely by student and public sentiment." Furthermore, football, as well as life outside of it, "will determine which is the better man" for the Black race.[87] CIAA leaders applauded Dixon for articulating the lessons of Black athletic manhood in the manner they crafted it a decade before. At the CIAA annual meeting just a year prior, Saint Paul's football coach Theodore H. Smith exclaimed that "the stage in athletics is [finally] set for making ethical character" among Black men.[88] This stage was "set" in the 1920s, when Black athletic leadership, like Plummer Young in the *Journal and Guide* and John Mitchell in the *Planet*, developed the ethos for athletics uplifting the race through cultivating Black athletic manhood.

Dixon's speech alone was published in the CIAA annual bulletin, a publication that began in 1923. While CIAA annual meetings were invitation-only, their annual bulletins—compiled by Saint Paul's Registrar John Whitehead and published by Hampton Institute—were widely circulated at HBCU athletic events, churches, high schools, and other community circles throughout Black America. In these curated pages, the Black sports public witnessed CIAA leadership preaching the efficacy of athletics as a net benefit for the race. "Why use sports to build a race," Saint Paul's athletic director rhetorically asked in 1934?[89] Because, according to Gideon Smith a decade before, collegiate basketball and football were "the greatest character builders that we have in our schools."[90] Furthermore, Black athletic apologists spent the 1920s cementing the idea that nothing else developed "human character more universally" than the lessons of sport.[91]

CIAA bulletins reveal the process by which Black athletic leaders joined their friends in the media and contributed to the New Negro mentality of the World War I era.[92] Through speeches and articles, Black sportsmen sought to create an "athletic-minded" race: "a nation physically and organically sound as well as mentally alert," a Black basketball coach explicitly expressed in 1933.[93] By athletic race, they did not mean that Black people should prioritize the recreation of sport above all else. In fact, Virginia State football coach Big Jeff insisted that "we should forget about championships, trophies, etc. These do not count; these are not ideals around which we should build our program. Our first aim should be to develop health and morals in the men who come to us in our schools."[94] Through developing athletes into male leaders, CIAA leadership would, as Virginia Seminary athletic director J. H. Lawrence once claimed, give Black men the "spark of self-confidence which will carry one on even when failure seems unavoidable"; the mentality of "I CAN, I MUST, and I WILL SUCCEED" in spite of discrimination, a former CIAA quarterback once said of the coaching he received in the 1920s.[95]

At some of the earliest CIAA annual meetings, league leadership established that Black athletic manhood began and ended with proper coaching. Saint Paul's football coach Theodore Smith told a group of rookie coaches in 1936 that "the immediate responsibility for the building of the good American man through athletics lies with the teacher of athletics—you, the coach!"[96] While white colleges employed athletic coaches as early as the 1890s, HBCUs, particularly those in the CIAA, did not professionalize the coaching ranks until the 1910s, under the advice of Virginia Union's John Barco.[97] Black coaches were to garner their authority from their own achievements as great athletes.[98] However, Hampton's Gideon Smith told league officials in 1923 that in selecting a full-time coach, HBCUs should ensure that he "is a man with right ideals about athletic sports." The "right ideals" centered on reinforcing traditional notions of obedience to elder male leadership, or "obedience without argument," as was often said by Gideon Smith.[99] This obedience was not blind acquiescence but reflected the belief that proper Black men accepted wisdom passed down from previous generations. This was a life lesson, as Black men largely learned to navigate white supremacy with the guidance of more experienced and knowledgeable elders whose very existence proved that they knew how to endure discrimination.

Unquestioned loyalty and obedience endowed Black coaches with the responsibility to make Black athletes into leaders through developing both body and mind. This was seen as the "most important factor to social growth" for athletes and the race.[100] Big Jeff stressed to younger coaches the efficacy of physical training, as it built strong men whose bodies represented the perseverance the race needed under segregation.[101] Yet, as Arthur P. Chippey of North Carolina's St. Augustine College believed and often advocated, "the human body is a machine through which the mind works."[102] Black coaches were to implement "religious" commitments to strengthening the body through dieting and refraining from vice, and mental development through high academic standards.[103] These commitments required ethical fortitude. "While we admit that the victory is wholesome, the finer points of character, such as manliness, tenacity, self-control, and honesty should have first consideration" to Black coaches, said Gideon Smith.[104]

Unquestioned obedience and loyalty also placed tremendous responsibility on Black coaches to steer their athletes in the right direction.[105] "As the coach is, so will the proteges be," a Black HBCU professor once claimed in 1925.[106] Because players often take on the mentality of the coach,[107] Black coaches worked tirelessly and remained transparent about the method of their madness, knowing that, as was said by Gideon Smith, "the real work of a coach is in helping the school turn out honest and industrious men" for the Black community.[108] Proof of a Black coach's commitment to this ethos often stared them in the face. In a 1927 speech, Gideon Smith described a scenario where he once shook hands with a former player "who is one of the leading physicians in the city [of Hampton]." That same instance involved him meeting another former player who was a known "gambler and bum of the town," a fact the Black community criticized him over.[109] Black coaches' results were under constant, righteous criticism by the Black community. "People know of the coach and his work when they cannot even call the names of some of the leading professors in the same school," Gideon Smith assured readers.[110] He was never shy about stating a fact that a Black professor said first in 1925, "successful coaches exert greater and more lasting influence upon virile youth than do the average professors of the classroom." To those who disagreed, the same professor once challenged readers to "show me a professor. . . . who gets best results, and you will find a man in sympathy with athletic activities."[111]

Coaches were not alone in developing Black athletic manhood. Rather, athletes themselves bore responsibility for being capable of learning the lessons of sport. Gideon Smith said as much in 1923, as "the old athletes that you have known. . . . [are] playing the game of life just as they played the athletic games while in school."[112] To do this, Black athletes were to be mental and physical specimens ready to confront racial discrimination. This assured that the most physically gifted person was not always the best Black athlete. In a 1925 speech, Saint Paul's athletic director Winston Douglass opined that "the true athlete must be a thinker. A sine endurable physique must share its honor with a good brain." The mixture of a sound body and mind helped an athlete "curb his anger to check his fear and to banish any semblance of hatred for his rivals."[113] Hampton's Gideon Smith agreed in calling athletics a means to "build up strong characters that will stand the acid test" and "undergo hardships. . . . without ceasing to be a gentleman."[114] Douglass's and Smith's emphasis on Black athletes being cerebral hinged upon the reality that they were to display to the Black public how to deal with racism, as reliance on physical faculties to resist unfair treatment alone would undoubtedly result in incarceration or lynching. "Athletes are students in school endeavoring to prepare themselves mentally as well as physically to play in the game of life," said CIAA official Edward P. Hunt in 1926.[115] The emphasis on using sports to build men was never lost on this generation of Black sportsmen, as Virginia State coach Thomas Puryear admitted that "as the athlete, go the man in the afterlife."[116] This sentiment created a consensus that "the [Black] athlete is a select person" with a divine mission for racial uplift through his performance on and off the field of play.[117] In more practical terms, "the habit of hanging on to a ball" on the court or field, said Hampton's Gideon Smith in 1924, was to "be transferred to hanging on to a job in the outside world."[118]

If coaches and athletes failed to cultivate Black athletic manhood, the football and basketball games aided in that endeavor. "If you want to know the underlying character of a man, his fight, aggressiveness, determination, resourcefulness, and discipline," Saint Paul's football coach Theodore H. Smith once remarked, "have him play a game of football."[119] CIAA annual meetings were filled with discussions about how football and basketball games were to implement the mental and physical lessons of Black masculinity.[120] The issue of shaping the games into a mechanism for Black athletic manhood relied not on the rules of sport but rather on the Black community—those who witnessed the games take place. "Simply playing the game will not develop character," believed Gideon Smith.[121] Rather, in the words of Virginia Seminary's J. H. Lawrence, "spectators must be taken into consideration" as active agents in shaping Black athletic manhood.[122] To Smith and Lawrence, Black sports fans were to honor the sacrifice their athletes displayed on the field by ensuring that the games were wholesome environments for Black excellence to thrive. This meant ridding the stands of gambling, drinking, and brawling. The emphasis on fans ousting unruliness was a direct parable to Black men being responsible for controlling the Black community image and function by ousting wrongdoers. If Black people would not do it at a sporting event, they certainly would not do it in everyday life.[123]

The Black community was also to ensure that their athletes upheld the code of Black athletic manhood off the field of play. By the 1920s, athletes were larger-than-life figures in Black America. This was certainly true in Virginia, where they were among "the biggest persons in [their] community." Moreover, an athlete "commands the good wishes and respect of the grown-ups, and receives the applause of the kids who regard him as an idol." Youth sports leader and former Virginia Union basketball and football player A. B. Ballard once told CIAA officials at an annual meeting that "you would be surprised to know just how many boys can tell you who was on the All-CIAA football team last year." He claimed that his experience as a youth sports coach showed him that Black "boys are hero worshippers" of CIAA athletes: "The reason that they have the inside track in this situation is very obvious. They have a natural appeal for any red blooded, spirited boy who perhaps because of misguided energy has strayed from the beaten path." Thus, "if the social aim of education is to prepare people to be better citizens," said Ballard, "then the athlete has a distinct function and is of tremendous importance in this preparation." Athletes, "trained in body, mind, and spirit," according to Ballard, must "work with youth" as they "can do more than all the law enforcement agencies, all of the social workers, all of the psychologists and all of the psychiatrists in the world."

This respect came with responsibility, as Black athletes, both current and former, were expected to mentor younger Black boys, keeping themselves and their mentees out of "the pool room and the dance hall" and in schools and churches and on the gridiron and basketball court.[124] Aiding in this endeavor was the rapid growth of athlete-run amateur sports clubs throughout Virginia that were "open[ed] to boys between the ages of 12 and 17 years of age."[125] One of the most public-facing was the Negro Boys' Club of Norfolk, a group of "spirited men who [were] interested in the Negro boy [of today] as the Negro Man of tomorrow."[126] Through football and basketball, they wanted to "create, maintain, and extend throughout the school and community high standards of Christian character," such as "clean living, clean speech," and "clean sportsmanship."[127] Black athletes were to pay it forward and help the Black community become what their colleges, coaches, and fanatics had become for them: "Makers of Men" who "see something more" in sports than "the winning of a game."[128]

The New Negro age of the 1920s brought about a dynamism where Black intellects used magazines and newspapers to articulate how the descendants of slavery could become "New Negroes." *Crisis Magazine* and the *Chicago Defender* compelled Black people to become metropolitan connoisseurs of the literary arts. Race radicals found meaning in the words of Marcus Garvey and his *Negro World* newspaper. Virginia-based publications such as the *Journal and Guide*, *Planet*, and CIAA Bulletins appealed to the rank and file of Black America, those who contributed to the race by earning an honest living, staying out of trouble, and enjoying the few luxuries that life had to offer. It was to these people that the *Journal and Guide*, *Planet*, and CIAA Bulletins expressed an accessible, egalitarian vision of New Negro life, one where athletics developed Black men for the challenges of masculinity under segregation. The bygone world of sport assured Black people that they did not have to be well read, join a radical movement, or even openly fight for Civil Rights to be a New Negro. Rather, they could support the proper play of basketball and football as an athlete, coach, administrator, or fanatic.

3

THE GAME, 1930–1944

DUNBAR HIGH SCHOOL'S 1932 state basketball championship must have been bittersweet, if not unfulfilling. The highly respected Lynchburg squad ran through a tough circuit to defeat cross-state rival and Newport News powerhouse Huntington High School by a score of 24–22 in front of three thousand roaring spectators on Virginia State College's campus. While the players, coaches, parents, and fanatics endured three straight title game losses en route to celebrating their second state basketball championship, they did so under unconventional circumstances.[1] On October 29, 1929, the United States entered the Great Depression. Just a few years later, most Black Virginia high schools suspended their sports programs because of a lack of funding and facilities.[2] Chances were that by 1932, Dunbar did not compete against the best Black teams but merely those who were fortunate enough to compete at all. The most hue and cry raised came from the storied Booker T. Washington High School of Norfolk. The principal, teachers, and parents at Virginia's largest Black high school tapped nearly every local Black institution for money to buy jerseys, rent gym space, and secure travel arrangements, only for the team to not be able to compete at the state level in 1931 and 1932. While admiring "local [Black] institutions" for "a fine spirit in trying to scrape up a basketball team," the Fighting Bookers could not compete "because it has to foot its own bills," a task they simply could not do in the early 1930s.[3]

Economic issues did not just impact Black high school sports. Hampton's Charles Williams loathed that by the 1930s, "athletics . . . has been retarded" at nearly every HBCU in Virginia "because of the lack of necessary money, equipment, and facilities for its proper conduct." These issues existed before the 1930s, as the little funding HBCU administrations provided football and basketball in the 1920s never reached the level of peer white colleges. The economic downturn of the 1930s exacerbated the perpetual "difficulty of securing sufficient funds to maintain athletics," and it had "meant a struggle on the part of every [Black collegiate] institution" across the country.[4] Virginia

Seminary and Saint Paul's endured the Depression by suspending their athletic programs entirely.[5] Fellow CIAA members responded to economic realities by reducing their spending on the annual bulletin, as the once full-length magazine with color images and great detailed descriptions became a simple pamphlet without pictures and few words.[6]

The Great Depression posed significant challenges for Black amateur athletics in Jim Crow Virginia. The football and basketball games that began as New South racial uplift ventures and later evolved into popular spectacles of Black athletic manhood now reflected the economic insecurity inherent in Black life. After Reconstruction, white Southern elites seized control of state power and cut many Black institutions (mainly education) off from public funding. Black Virginians followed their Southern brethren by forming their own institutions, and some of the most autonomous and well-funded were football and basketball clubs. By the 1930s, however, the Great Depression had gripped Black educational institutions, making Black sports more susceptible to closure. The economic times challenged Black Virginians to radically rethink their decades-old Bookerite mentality that communal solidarity could weather the storm of Jim Crow segregation. By the 1930s, *The Game* of amateur sports was no longer just about exercising racial uplift and athletic manhood. Rather, amateur football and basketball became tools to fundamentally improve Black life through vying for their fair share of public investment that had been long denied to them.

The Great Depression ironically made amateur athletics a vehicle for public sector investment in Black life. Virginia's Black leaders used amateur athletics to advocate for more public investment in Black communities, overhauling a more solidified cultural dynamism in which Black people did not expect local, state, or federal agencies to help fund their own institutions. This advocacy did not make Black institutions solely reliant on the state. Rather, it aided Black institutional solidarity, as the better funded HBCUs strengthened their athletic bonds with Black high schools during the nation's darkest economic hour. This story is important because after the World War II era (1939–1948), Black amateur athletics entered what is seen as its "golden age"—where HBCU coaches and players became national icons, when Black high schools had enough financial and institutional backing to compete at a national level, and when the two levels of play eventually became integrated.[7] Important and often overlooked is that the golden age of Black amateur sport came from a mentality shift among Black people decades prior, one where they demanded their fair share of state-level funding for public institutions under their administrative control.

This chapter contributes a Black perspective to the white-focused scholarship about American sports during the Great Depression. Historians find that amateur sports survived the market crash because football and basketball apologists articulated their games as pillars of American values in the geopolitical conflict between capitalism and communism. By selling amateur football and basketball as workshops for American democracy, universities maintained their games long enough for them to receive New Deal funding in the late 1930s and support from the federal war department in the 1940s.[8] Missing in this consensus is how Black amateur sports survived the Great Depression. In Virginia, one sees that Black amateur sports survived through distinction and continuity, as Black Virginians mixed community solidarity with activist calls for more educational funding.

This chapter also informs scholarship about Black responses to the Great Depression. Scholars make clear that Black Americans became more politically active because the Depression exacerbated existing public-sector disinvestment from Black life.[9] While substantial literature has focused on Black flirtations with communism, socialism, and other radical movements in the 1930s, Black activists mostly focused their energies on the Civil Rights Movement—a long durée of activism for the equalization and integration of schools and public services—along with growing the Black vote, which ultimately shifted the race away from the Party of Lincoln toward the Democratic Party.[10] This dynamic was particularly true in Virginia. Yet, scholars of Black life during the Great Depression ignore the role of athletics in furthering the "traditional" Civil Rights efforts of the 1930s. Through examining Black Virginia during the Depression, one sees that amateur sports helped platform more vivid calls for racial equality in public education. Amateur football and basketball had become hallmarks of academic excellence, as nearly every accredited Black high school and college in Virginia had thriving athletic programs. White elites used athletics as a metric to judge Black schools' worthiness for accreditation, thus allowing Black leaders to vie for equal access to public funding. This alone reflects the importance of amateur sport to Black Civil Rights efforts during the Great Depression.

This chapter also complicates the historiographic consensus that Black Virginians abandoned their adherence to the "Virginia Way" by World War II and charted a more independent path toward racial equality. J. Douglas Smith and Clayton McClure Brooks find that between the 1880s and 1920s, Virginia maintained "peaceful" race relations because elite Black and white leaders worked to "perfect" segregation through interracial cooperation. This cooperation buttressed Black adherence to Bookeritism and elite white beliefs in the Cavalier ethos—white supremacy required the white ruling class to manage Black progress. While this plan did not pacify Black desires for full equality as white people had hoped, it prevented the widespread violence

Southern Jim Crow regimes were known for.[11] Peter Wallerstein, Brian Daugherity, Julian Maxwell Hayter, and Margaret Edds, along with others, argue that by the 1940s, years of genteel paternalism had allowed for the growth of the NAACP, a group that used the federal courts to undo segregation in ways white elites would not by the 1960s.[12] Virginia scholars portray Jim Crow as a dichotomy in which Black people aided white paternalism and segregation until they did not. Black Virginia's relationship with segregation is more complicated than the picture painted by the beforementioned scholarship.

In focusing on athletics, I find that Black people, while having a different agenda in mind by the mid-twentieth century, continued to use segregation and elite white paternalism to their advantage instead of wholesale fighting in the courts to end it. Edwin Bancroft Henderson correctly assessed by 1934 that "our athletic systems were truly counterparts of our national, political and social systems."[13] In ignoring the world of sport in their analyses, Virginia scholars miss a critical way Black Virginians broke the social contract between Black and white elites by the Great Depression, yet in doing so still maintained a segregated world where they controlled a key cultural theater for Black uplift. By examining educational activism through the world of sport, one sees that Black people sought to make elite white Virginians live up to their genteel paternalism by shifting public funds to Black education by way of athletics—an undeniable demarcation of Black progress that was seemingly harmless to white supremacy while at the same time critical for Black progress. Thus, amateur athletics proved to be both malleable and strong enough to improve Black life beyond its founders' original vision, as the games loosened a calcified system of racial oppression that had existed since the downfall of Reconstruction.

"SEEKING EVERY OPPORTUNITY TO ADVANCE"

Even before the Great Depression, the *Norfolk Journal and Guide* engaged in a single-handed, decades-long media campaign for the commonwealth to fund Black amateur athletics. "It just burns me up when I think about some [white] high schools playing basketball in their gym" while Black school gyms do not have "space large enough to cuss a cat in," Norfolk sportswriter Scoop Johnson once said in disgust.[14] Throughout the heyday of the 1920s, Virginia's most populated Black schools such as Booker T. Washington of Norfolk and Armstrong of Richmond routinely canceled basketball and football games because they lacked space to practice and host games.[15] Booker T. Washington, in particular, "is reputed to be a half million dollar school, modern in all phases and second to none in the entire South," said the *Journal and Guide* in 1925. Yet, the newspaper continued: "after all was said and done, it was found that the school was not modern in all phases so far as [athletic] equipment." This issue went largely unaddressed in the 1920s, as Black Virginians took it upon themselves to ensure the solvency of their games. The fruit of their labor was the growing popularity of Black basketball and football, which in turn precipitated calls for better facilities. "One of the most potent factors in training an individual for efficient service, school, college, and universities," the *Journal and Guide* said, "is physical education and physical education cannot hope to be detained in any appreciable degree without adequate facilities."[16]

The *Journal and Guide* did not have to wait much longer. The nation's economic circumstances exacerbated racial inequality to the point at which Black citizens could no longer accept it. On October 29, 1929, the American economy crashed after an entire decade of overproduction and under regulation. The 1920s party of excess was over for America in a way that it had never begun for Black America. President Franklin Delano Roosevelt sought to fix that upon his election in 1932. His New Deal administration mobilized federal resources to fix the nation's economy through increased public investment in every aspect of American life. Black Americans more broadly saw that as an imperative to push for Civil Rights through receiving their share of New Deal spoils. The Great Depression and New Deal compelled Black Virginians to combine their Bookerite tradition of community solidarity with a newer emphasis on acquiring their fair share of state resources, which had long been denied to them by white elites. State Superintendent for Negro Education Fred Alexander (who had more interaction with Black people than most white people then did), once surmised about Black Virginia life in the 1930s: "The Negro aspires to improve the general cultural level of his group." This aspiration led them to see that the "barriers to this goal are low income and inadequate education."[17]

As was the case throughout the South, the material poverty that defined Black Virginia life in the 1930s manifested most in public education. By the outset of the Great Depression, Black citizens were nearly 25 percent of Virginia's population. More than 50 percent of those Black Virginians were impoverished in terms of occupations, taxable wages, and housing situation.[18] Most Black men and women made well below $600 a year (around $10,000 in 2022) working in either agricultural (sharecropping) or under-skilled factory laborers in the tobacco, food products, textiles, wood, paper, chemical, leather, stone, and metal industries. While most Black Virginians qualified for state welfare benefits, less than 20 percent ever applied for it, as they relied on civic institutions to have their needs met. Nearly 66 percent of Black Virginians lived as renters on white-owned farmland or tenants in apartments, boardinghouses, or single-family units in urban areas. And regardless of whether Black Virginians lived in an urban or rural area, their housing was often located in run-down, segregated, and underdeveloped parts of cities and counties. "Many Negro families live within their incomes, and few have incomes beyond their immediate needs," Alexander said by the 1930s.[19] It was from these urban and rural communities, these impoverished backgrounds, that Black children entered schoolhouses, where they found little reprieve from the poverty that defined everyday life.

Poverty set tangible limits on Black education in Virginia. By the mid-1930s, school enrollment of both Black and white children had been cut in half due to the economy. Around 74 percent of Black kids were enrolled in school and 58 percent attended regularly. Still, 25 percent of Black Virginia children were never enrolled in school and a major reason why was the lack of investment and facilities.[20] Of the nearly 1,800 Black Virginia schools (1,700 being in rural areas), 89 percent were one-room schoolhouses run by one teacher who could sometimes supervise up to sixty students at once. Close to 95 percent of Black schools had no athletic facilities whatsoever.[21] This was the case because Virginia was one of the worst states in terms of funding public education at all levels. The majority of Black Virginia schools were almost fully funded by Northern philanthropic organizations founded by heiress Anna T. Jeanes of Philadelphia. By the late 1930s, Jeanes had given nearly $10 million to the commonwealth for Black education. Still, most Black schools worked with a budget of $0.14 a day (nearly $2.50 in 2022), and most Virginia localities (64 of 89 at the time) profited from this arrangement, as they spent less on Black education than they received from the legislature and Northern philanthropies.[22]

These funding issues, along with the limited opportunities afforded to Black white-collar workers, contributed to the 40 percent Black dropout rate. For the Black children who stayed in school, prospects were not much better than dropping out.[23] "No negro has ever been brought in my courtroom that has passed the sixth grade," a white judge once wrote in an editorial to a Newport News newspaper.[24] Only 20 percent of Black Virginians who ever attended school left functionally literate, with the other 80 percent being "slightly above a fourth grade education."[25] To help solve Virginia's education crisis at the outset of the Great Depression, Virginia governor John Garland Pollard proposed that the commonwealth increase education funding. His proposal, later adopted, included the state funding white higher education to the tune of $3.2 million a year while funding Black higher education with $173,000. There was no mention of increasing funds for primary and secondary Black schools.[26] With Pollard's plan, it became clear that, as was once lamented by the *Journal and Guide*, "the state of Virginia" planned on "doing nothing for the education of its colored citizens."[27]

Led by high school and college educators, the Virginia Teachers Association (VTA) entered the vanguard to increase state funding for Black education. Founded in 1887, the VTA was an umbrella organization of Black teachers and professors who funneled the energies and financial resources of Black civic associations and Northern philanthropies toward improving Black schools through teacher training and facility upgrades.[28] It was because of the VTA that the Virginia Legislature had created and enforced by the turn of the century a compulsory school enrollment policy, which helped lower the Black full illiteracy rate from nearly 50 percent in 1900 to around 20 percent by 1930.[29] However, the Great Depression created a radical change in VTA activity, in that they recruited nearly four thousand members who sought the equalization of public funding between white and Black schools.[30] Much of this was done at the behest of Huntington High School principal L. F. Palmer.[31] VTA activism in the 1930s revealed a most dangerous reality for white leaders, and that was the "Negro is aware of his condition, is realistic about it. . . . [and] is seeking every opportunity to advance."[32] Their idea of advancement was, as Fred Alexander knew, a "rapidly increasing belief that adequate and complete educational facilities should be provided for Negroes."[33]

The VTA first appealed to local white leadership to uphold their elite paternal obligation. As early as 1932, Black VTA members, parents, and ministers met with white school city councilmen, superintendents, and school boards and requested that they fund the construction of new school buildings. White leaders either ignored these requests or made excuses for why they would not invest more money into Black education. White rejection helped amplify more radical Black voices in the education debate. CIAA founding father and Virginia Union Vice President John Barco said as early as 1930 that "Negroes must not depend upon outside [Northern] aid to solve their educational problems."[34] Rather, they should fight for their fair share of public funding that had long been denied to them by white leaders.

At the forefront of the emerging education fight was Black leaders using amateur basketball and football to vie for school improvements. They did this because athletics had been a proven pathway for Black educational advancement. By winter 1932, Virginia's accredited Black schools, which were also the most funded among the underfunded Black schools, all had thriving athletic programs. "It is not without reason that the Huntington High School of Newport News, Va., is considered one of the ranking Negro high schools in the State of Virginia," said the *Journal and Guide* in 1932. Thanks in part to VTA leader L. F. Palmer, Newport News went from not having a Black high school in 1919 to having the commonwealth's only accredited—by the Southern Association of Secondary Schools and Colleges—Black high school. Palmer's secret was his investment in football and basketball, which had "a large following" by Black and white locals alike.[35]

Huntington's accreditation inspired VTA members to get other Black high schools accredited.[36] By the mid-1930s, Virginia boasted ten accredited Black high schools, with fifty-five Black schools accredited overall.[37] Strong athletic programs reflected a school's ability to maintain student attendance, faculty quality, and financial investment from local governments and philanthropic organizations.[38] This was also true for Virginia HBCUs. A CIAA athletic football coach told his peers that "intercollegiate athletics, the surge and despair of every college president of twenty-five years ago . . . is now one of the basic requirements of the Southern Association of Colleges and Secondary Schools for its 'A' rating." To even be considered for accreditation, he continued, "a school must belong to an organized association of intercollegiate athletics."[39] The connection between Black educational improvement and athletics could not be any clearer by the early 1930s. Thus, Black educational activists embraced amateur football and basketball as a tool to argue for more consistent public investment.

With athletics being closely tied to Black progress, Black communities called for more state investment into Black education through the vehicle of sports and recreation. The most notable call came from Black Norfolk residents, who requested that city government provide them with more recreation space in the form of public parks (with football fields and basketball courts) throughout the city and new school facilities.[40] In channeling the prevailing spirit of interracial harmony that Virginia was known for, Black Norfolk argued that public funding for Black athletic space was a "gift of intrinsic value. . . . that will bring tremendous returns in good will and . . . happier citizenship" between the two races.[41] Yet, white responses to what Black citizens saw as their constitutional rights under the *Plessy* decision (1896)—separate but equal—were filled with both rebuke and grandstanding, ultimately leading nowhere.[42]

This new strategy of athletic activism coincided with a general outgrowth of Civil Rights activism in the early 1930s. Historians have focused mostly on this decade because of Black-run state teacher groups campaigning for the equalization of white and Black school funding in the form of teacher compensation.[43] Ignored by scholars is that Black communities throughout Virginia tapped into their paternalist culture of white benevolence and community resilience in trying to improve conditions within the confines of segregation. Black athletic leadership worked together to consolidate amateur athletics further by sponsoring interscholastic play in only five sports (football, basketball, baseball, track, and tennis), with the revenue coming mostly from football and basketball.[44] When that and requesting white help bore little fruit, they later used those community channels to appeal to the federal government through the New Deal. This action did not surprise every white Virginia leader, as Fred Alexander wrote in a report that white leaders needed to work with Black communities in "order to forestall mandatory legal action."[45]

By the summer of 1934, Black Virginians turned to the federal government's New Deal Program to coax white leaders into investing public money in Black life. They did this, however, by channeling their Bookerite culture of interracial cooperation, as they implored the help of a Black conduit who found favor with the Roosevelt administration. In 1934, President Roosevelt appointed a seventy-two-year-old Black lawyer named Thomas Calhoun Walker to serve as the advisor and consultant on Negro Affairs for the Virginia Emergency Relief Administration. Roosevelt may have chosen him because of his gravitas within Black Virginia, his reputation for helping Black people break through local racist barriers to secure resources for their communities, and his background being eerily similar with Virginia native Booker T. Washington. Nicknamed Virginia's Black governor, Thomas Calhoun Walker was born a slave in 1862 just outside of the City of Winchester. While having a father who heavily discouraged him from pursuing anything outside of agricultural labor, Walker left home to enroll at Hampton Institute under an agreement to work his way through school. Walker passed the vaunted Virginia bar, becoming one of only a handful of Black attorneys in the early twentieth century. After becoming a prominent member of Virginia's tight-knit Black legal community and a pillar in working-class civic community networks, President Roosevelt appointed Walker to become a central conduit between the New Deal administration in DC and Virginia localities.[46]

With the help of Thomas Walker, Black Virginians, both poor and middle class, circumvented local white racism to gain access to New Deal programs.[47] Walker helped Black communities throughout Virginia create recreation and athletic projects and apply for New Deal funds through the Works Progress Administration, Public Works Administration, and Civil Works Administration. These projects ranged from building several high school gymnasiums to the construction of public parks with athletic fields under the advisement of Black "community recreational directors."[48] These plans also touted that the work programs would bring thousands of jobs for local construction workers and they would encourage more enrollment and school attendance from Black youth.[49] "An educational campaign is being planned by the committee to acquaint the public with the value and locations of proposed sports facilities in the hope that when they are ready, they will be utilized," said Plummer Young about the litany of proposals from Black Virginia communities.[50]

Yet, local white officials consistently either rejected the plans outright or refused to accept the approved New Deal plans while providing little or no reasoning.[51] Ideologically, white Virginia leaders were like their Southern counterparts in refusing to support the plans because they were afraid of the federal government disrupting local Jim Crow customs using work programs. Practically, white leaders did not have to take the projects on because Virginia's relatively diversified economy (manufacturing, commerce, and agricultural) helped it evade the full brunt of federal intervention, as historian Ronald Heinemann long argued.[52] This was key, as despite the implicit racism found in the Agricultural Adjustment Act, Social Security Act, and Federal Housing Act, for instance, New Deal programs fundamentally improved the Black condition in the South by making Black Southerners less economically reliant on local white elites.[53]

By the summer of 1936, however, white Virginia leaders such as US senator Harry Byrd compelled local white officials to stop grandstanding and approve New Deal recreation and school projects in every corner of the commonwealth. This should not have been shocking given that Byrd reigned as Virginia's most progressive Jim Crow–era governor between 1926 and 1930. While there is little documentary evidence to support this, one could safely suggest that Black leaders used paternalist channels to push white Virginia elites to stop local officials from blocking New Deal projects. Byrd was a known supporter of interracial cooperation groups and a close affiliate to Black leaders like Plummer Young. He also used surplus funding to upgrade Black colleges, worked as an anti-lynching advocate, and supported bringing electricity to rural Virginia, where the majority of Black Virginians lived. In fact, Plummer Young openly campaigned for Byrd's 1934 senatorial campaign in his *Journal and Guide*.[54] Byrd's support for New Deal programs was as politically convenient as it was benevolent, as by the mid-1930s, Black Virginians reentered the political realm and used their votes and voices as leverage in their favor.

Byrd's support for New Deal programs came after more than a decade of Black political mobilization reached a zenith. This political mobilization began in the early 1920s, when white-collar, politically involved middle-class Black Virginians threatened to leave the Republican Party over their refusal to nominate and support Black candidates for office.[55] During the 1932 presidential election, Black leaders registered the most voters since Reconstruction to help elect Franklin Roosevelt to the Oval Office.[56] The mobilization of Black voters and shift toward the Democratic Party made Black Virginians a valuable constituency that state and local white Democrats could not ignore.

This political reality revealed itself when Black Virginians became major players in a national debate over the federal funding of Southern education. Between 1936 and 1937, the US Congress debated whether to pass the controversial Harrison-Black-Fletcher Bill. Sponsored by the all-white National Education Association (NEA), as well as Southern Senators Hugo Black of Alabama and Byron "Pat" Harrison of Mississippi, the bill would establish more permanent federal funding for public education to help relieve struggling state governments.[57] Southern white Democrats, many of whom were affiliated with the NEA, simply requested that Black leaders speak out in support of the bill given that previous federal education legislation (Morrill Act of 1862 and 1890) help grow Black colleges. However, Black organizations such as the NAACP, Washington Bar Association, National Council of Negro Women, along with Virginia's VTA refused to support its passage without specific protections for Black education. With the help of Thomas Walker, Booker T. Washington High School principal Winston Douglass, and Virginia State president John Gandy, the VTA told Congress that the proposed bill should include provisions to prevent Southern states from segregating education and recreation funds. Black and white high schools were to have the same athletic facilities if they were federally funded. If the bill passed as Black Virginia leaders envisioned it, it would undermine segregated educational spending. White Southern legislators desperately wanted federal aid for education, but they refused to add the provisions. Black opposition was one of the major reasons why the bill stalled and was eventually nixed by 1940.[58]

Black stalling of the Harrison-Black-Fletcher Bill bore the intended results. By fall 1936, Thomas Walker, Plummer Young, and Winston Douglass of Norfolk, Hampton's Sylvius A. Moore, Helen Sharpe, Audrey Jackson, and Susie Diggs were some of the creators, shapers, and advisors who organized the construction of newer gymnasiums, football fields, and public parks from Winchester to the Eastern Shore.[59] The WPA in particular funded programs to train Black teachers, professors, and athletic coaches to be better physical educators, which helped Black leaders better dictate where and how athletic facilities were built and run.[60] Virginia localities not only met their financial obligations to receive the federal projects, but the state legislature also matched this New Deal zeal by spending nearly $28.8 million on public education in aggregate by 1937—the most the state had ever spent on public education up until that point.[61] The sudden white reversal on public spending for Black people was not motivated solely by the traditional benevolence Virginia patriarchs believed themselves to possess. Rather, Black Virginians ignored "the age old plan of petitioning" and used their athletic culture as a basis to fight for state spending on Black education.[62]

"A NEW DEAL FOR ATHLETICS"

The Game, as I call it, did not just involve Black communities leveraging their political power and amateur athletic culture to gain their fair share of public resources. It also entailed the CIAA implementing their own plan to ensure the survival and prosperity of amateur basketball and football through their "New Deal for Athletics."

"What are the implications of a new deal for athletics," Edwin Henderson asked the CIAA at the 1934 annual meeting.[63] This new deal was a renewed commitment by HBCUs to reconstitute the ties between themselves and Black high schools that were loosened when HBCUs decided to only play other colleges by the mid-1920s. While HBCUs did not go back to scheduling football and basketball games against high schools as they did in the past, they committed to helping high schools better conduct league operations under their close advisement and direction. "Despite the fact that unprecedented depression made it very difficult for private [collegiate] institutions to balance their budgets we managed to make financial ends," touted the CIAA mainstay Arthur Paul Davis. Thus, CIAA leadership felt obligated to strengthen Black athletic culture and nurture their farm system during the Depression and New Deal age by helping Black high schools reorganize their leagues and play games before state funds came in.[64] It was not enough that HBCUs weather the economic downfall on their own. Rather, "as educators and social engineers," Henderson implored the CIAA, "we should take the lead in preparing youth to live in a changing civilization" through strengthening the athletic connection between HBCUs and Black high schools.[65]

This New Deal in athletics began not with the CIAA itself but with the efforts of Black educators at Virginia State at the outset of the Great Depression. In March 1930, the Virginia Legislature restored Virginia State to its status as a certified four-year state college.[66] This was no small task, as with the help of President John Gandy, history professors Luther Porter Jackson, James Hugo Johnston Jr., and others, Virginia State was home to several statewide educational (primarily the VTA) and civic organizations that helped them supplant Hampton Institute as the cultural and educational center for Black Virginia life.[67] The newly restored college wasted no time using athletics to fight for their share of New Deal funding like Black communities did throughout the commonwealth. In 1934, John Gandy led a university-wide request for PWA funds to upgrade their athletic facilities.[68] This request was not out of the ordinary, as white colleges such as Harrisonburg State Teachers College (now James Madison University), Fredericksburg State Teachers College (now University of Mary Washington), and Radford State Teachers College (now Radford University) took advantage of a recently passed state law allowing educational institutions to issue bonds to secure New Deal projects.[69] With support from Virginia governor George C. Perry and State Board of Education president E. Lee Trinkle,[70] Virginia State acted like its newfound white peers in issuing bonds to secure PWA funding for "improvements to and enlargement of [a] gymnasium" by 1935.[71]

Virginia State's efforts could not come soon enough for Black high schools. By the fall of 1933, urban and rural Black schools shuttered their football and basketball programs to better use their paltry funds for teacher salaries and school supplies.[72] Financial issues had worsened by the following year, forcing many schools to drop out of the Virginia Interscholastic Athletic Association (VIAA), eventually leading to the reformation of the league into smaller entities. The schools who could afford to play football formed the Virginia State High School Athletic Conference (VSHAC).[73] The other league, filled with schools who could not afford to play football, was the Virginia State High School Basketball League (VSHBL). Leadership of the new football conference divided the remaining members into two separate classifications—high schools and training schools. This helped ease the burden of travel and maintain a level playing field between institutions with varying degrees of financial investment.[74] This venture failed, and more Black schools suspended athletics by spring 1934. The VSHAC dissolved a year later and a few of its members created a new statewide league named the Virginia State Interscholastic Athletic Association (VSIAA) in March 1934.[75] Although Black high school leagues adjusted to the economic despair that befell them, finding places to play remained difficult.

Virginia State embraced its full collegiate status by engaging in the New Deal for Athletics, namely helping Black high schools continue their football and basketball programs. Throughout the 1930s, Virginia State helped the VSHBL and VSIAA organize and host basketball and football games and end-of-season tournaments. This help involved Virginia State physical education professors such as J. A. Moore organizing games, rankings, and statewide contests for end-of-season titles and awards.[76] To do this, they took inspiration from their unlikely league member and Black Belt neighbor, Saint Paul's College. Under the direction of longtime CIAA secretary and Saint Paul's registrar John Lyman Whitehead, the Southern Interscholastic Athletic Association (SIAA) thrived during the 1930s with the two-year junior college hosting nearly all the high school basketball games at the two-thousand-seat Kirby Auditorium.[77] This Black Belt dynamism went beyond state lines, as fellow CIAA founding member Shaw University, and later North Carolina A&T, followed Saint Paul's in embracing the athletic New Deal and organized basketball and football contests during the Great Depression, later being home to the North Carolina State Interscholastic Tournament.[78]

The normality and continuation of national competition compelled Virginia State to better organize Black high school sports for the foreseeable future.[79] While Virginia's Black high school leagues broke down during the

Great Depression, other states kept theirs mostly intact through the National Interscholastic Basketball Tournament (NIBT). Created by Hampton's Charles Williams in 1929, the NIBT was a national tournament where the best Black high schools across the country represented their respective states in pursuit of a national hoops title. Although it was founded in Virginia and the award sponsor was the *Journal and Guide*, the NIBT moved sites throughout the 1930s due to Virginia's difficulty maintaining Black high school sports.[80] Yet, Virginia State, with the support of Black Virginia high school coaches, had aligned with Shaw and North Carolina A&T by 1941 to host the NIBT at Fayetteville State Teachers College.[81] This accomplishment did not hide the fact that Virginia teams had a hard time getting into the tournament due to the inability to pay dues and the lack of a sorting mechanism to determine who should represent the commonwealth, a lingering question that state-level athletic organizations were inherently designed to answer.

After years of playing defense against societal issues and the predations of white elites, Virginia State went on the offensive in 1942. "It is high time the prep coaches and the athletic officials resume their talks and plans within the Virginia High School Football Conference organization," said the *Journal and Guide* two years later.[82] Moreover, the expositor of Black athletic life declared, "The Virginia high School football conference should be resumed at once!"[83] Virginia's amateur athletic leadership heeded this demand. By 1944, Virginia State's J. A. Moore had organized around thirteen Black high schools to create what had never existed before: one comprehensive Black high school league, anchored by football and basketball, named the Virginia Interscholastic Association (VIA). By 1950, the SIAA had joined with the VIA to make one statewide Black high school league.[84] The VIA was the crowning achievement of the CIAA's New Deal for Athletics, as league officers included the likes of Virginia Union basketball coach Henry Boyd Hucles and physical educators such as H. M. Nelson of Hampton, Oscar Moore of Saint Paul's, and other CIAA football and basketball coaches.[85] All operations were housed at Virginia State, as they would be until integration in 1970.[86]

Black Virginians repurposed their amateur athletics during the darkest days of the Great Depression. Whereas high school and college football games were instruments of institution building at the turn of the century and expositors of Black athletic manhood in the 1920s, they became platforms to vie for their fair share of public education funding in the 1930s. Black leaders later used new state and federal funds to restore and better organize high school games under the direction of HBCUs. Moreover, through amateur athletics, Black Virginians learn to navigate the troubled waters of Jim Crow segregation through combining their Bookerite culture of self-reliance with activist calls for the fair share of state resources. With their schools receiving more public funding and amateur games being more organized, Black Virginia's athletic scene was operating on a more national stage by the late 1930s and 1940s. This stage empowered the CIAA to reform college football and basketball play, as well as become a foundation to continue sports amid the temporary shutdown of the World War II years.

4

THE CONTROVERSIES, 1932–1951

American amateur sports have never been without existential controversy. Schools have always paid players, inflated grades, extended eligibility beyond four years, and shaved points. The rampant malfeasance compelled some to call for the suspension and abolition of these games considering World War II. Yet, the NCAA shifted from an advisory body into a regulatory agency, making college sports more legitimate in the eyes of the American public. Corruption and reform also strengthened HBCU football and basketball in the mid-century, yet contemporary sports media and historians have not told this story until now. Between the Great Depression and World War II, the CIAA solidified HBCU sports by regulating corruption and commercialization in Hampton football and Virginia Union basketball. By upholding the integrity undergirding Black college sports, the CIAA secured the moral authority to ensure that HBCU and high school sports continued in opposition to some calling for the games to stop during World War II mobilization.

Historians of collegiate sport broadly argue that reform and the patriotic overtures of World War II made college football and basketball more popular between the 1930s and 1950s than they had ever been in the "golden age" of the 1920s.[1] This led to several reforms in player eligibility, recruiting, and player compensation (scholarships) that ensured the games better reflected the values America fought for in Europe. Sports scholars ignore that the same issues happened in the Black sports world. In doing so, they portray HBCU football and basketball as noncontroversial, sanitized institutions that did not go through the same struggles of legitimacy inherent in amateur athletics.[2] The proceeding pages show how the spirit of reform empowered HBCUs to take more top-down control of Black sports amid national crises. Through detailing and contextualizing scandals with Hampton football and Virginia Union basketball, the CIAA helped continue football and basketball play in high school and college during World War II. Reform reinforced Black respectability, or the CIAA's credo of "honesty in the administration of athletics." By doing this, CIAA leadership entrenched football and basketball at all levels, becoming, in the words of Hampton's Charles Williams, the leading "educational force in the development of the youth of the race" by the mid-twentieth century.[3]

"FOOTBALL IN NEGRO COLLEGES"

The CIAA probably wished they'd never created an eligibility committee. Between December 1932 and December 1933, rival football coaches such as Hampton's Gideon Smith and Virginia State's Harry Jefferson demanded that the committee, consisting of Clarence W. Davis from Howard University, Samuel A. Barksdale of Virginia Union University, and N. C. Webster of North Carolina A&T College, investigate coaches for breaking eligibility rules for transfer football players. The eligibility committee hearings reflected the centralization of league power to end football corruption. The previous decade saw few CIAA member institutions—if any—sanctioned for playing ineligible football players. This does not mean that ineligible players were absent from CIAA gridiron competition. In fact, it was quite the opposite. Between 1930 and 1932, however, the CIAA suspended Lincoln University entirely, as well as several players from Virginia Seminary and College, Virginia Union, and Virginia State College. The major shift toward eligibility enforcement came in 1932, when the CIAA launched a public investigation that ended the football dominance of Hampton, one of America's most successful Black college football programs to date.[4]

The issue at hand was the eligibility of transfer football players. By the late 1920s, the CIAA established that athletes who transferred from accredited non-CIAA schools to a CIAA member, or players who transferred from one CIAA school to another, had to sit out at least a year of athletic competition. All student athletes had four total years of eligibility, with a recommendation to sit out their freshman year. This was the stance taken by all NCAA schools, both white and Black, and it would not be abolished until World War II.[5] HBCUs took this issue seriously because college athletics was a pillar of Black athletic manhood (see chapter 2). To violate the rules of engagement was to undermine the image of Black male honor that the games fostered among the race's leadership class. Proper Black male athletes, coaches, and administrators were to be, above all, rule followers who never sacrificed integrity for victory. Moreover, real victory came to the race by upholding the rules even when no one was enforcing them. Black college football coaches regularly flouted this honor code, leading to them being subjected to the national attention on cleaning up college football in general. This movement encroached upon the HBCU football world by the most unlikely person: Black scholar activist and avid football fanatic William Edward Burghardt Du Bois.[6]

College football historians frame academics as anti-football activists, such as Harvard president Charles Eliot (1869–1909), Northwestern University president Henry Rogers (1890–1900), and University of Chicago president Robert Maynard Hutchins (1929–1945).[7] Yet, Du Bois was hardly the enemy of college football. In fact, he embraced it because it developed Black human capital through an activity widely admired by the white middle class. Moreover, the Marxist Du Bois believed HBCU football distilled Victorian morals and ethics from the Black bourgeoisie—who he deemed to be the "talented tenth" of the race—to the Black proletariat.[8] Du Bois celebrated Black sports in the NAACP-funded publication the *Crisis Magazine*—an outlet dubbed "Du Bois's domain," which was founded in 1910 with him as the editor. Less than a year after beginning publication, Du Bois began his football advocacy by dedicating the July 1911 edition to "The Colored Athlete," and, more specifically, to Black football.[9]

The *Crisis* used HBCU football as social commentary to discuss larger issues in Black life. In a section called "The Horizon," Du Bois highlighted the students he termed "Our Graduates" who played "Along the Color Line" in "Leading [white] Institutions."[10] He even helped propel Black footballers such as Dartmouth's Matthew Washington Bullock, Brown's Frederick "Fritz" Pollard, and Rutgers's Paul Robeson into future race leadership by writing several follow-up stories about their off-the-field achievements.[11] The *Crisis* also took interest in Black football players who challenged the gentlemen's agreement, as their experiences on the field mirrored the racism inflicted upon Black people off of it.[12] Much of Du Bois's focus, however, was on HBCU football. Kentucky Normal and Industrial Institute (now Kentucky State University) football coach Paul William Lawrence Jones wrote articles and compiled pictures of HBCU football for the *Crisis*.[13] The articles and images canonized Black athletic achievement in the industrial age. Thus, the *Crisis*'s later criticism was not an attempt to abolish Black college football. It ensured that the game strengthened Black American culture and life.

In the fall of 1930, Du Bois used the *Crisis* to reform Black college football through an in-depth study of player eligibility. This investigation resulted from *Chicago Defender* sportswriter and CIAA official Frank A. Young's refusal to select an HBCU All-American football team in December 1929. "There will be no All-American team this year nor in the years to come," he said publicly after fielding several requests for one by HBCU football coaches. As the chief arbiter of Black college football's all-star selections, Young editorialized his disgust with schools that ignored eligibility rules. Specifically, he claimed that Black colleges played ineligible players, ranging from blue-chip high schoolers to unknown ringers. "Professionalism is rife," said Young: "win, win, win, at any cost" was the attitude adopted by football programs and enthusiasts alike.[14] The missing All-American team is documented by Black football historian Michael Hurd, yet neither he nor other historians explain Young's protest.[15] What Hurd ignored was a call for reform that the *Crisis* would later answer. Hampton football coach Gideon Smith once claimed that "the press is a great power in helping to make athletics better and cleaner in our institutions."[16] With the help of his protege George Walter Streator, Du Bois made good on Smith's assessment.

Streator and Du Bois made the national call for college football reform heard in the HBCU world. Between 1927 and 1929, the Carnegie Foundation funded a NCAA study of corruption within college football. They found that more than two-thirds of white college football programs engaged in trampism—the practice of allowing players to transfer and play immediately without academic restrictions or considerations. It would not be until the 1950s that the NCAA secured the power to police the practice.[17] The report ignored HBCUs, and because of that, Streator told Du Bois in April 1930, "The Carnegie report scarcely scratched the surface" of college football improprieties. "The more inquiries I make" into HBCU football, Streator continued in the same letter, "the heavier my heart gets."[18] Streator was an alumnus of Fisk University and a professor at Benedict College who knew that, like their white counterparts, many Black colleges sacrificed their academic integrity at the gridiron altar in hopes of growing their purse.[19] "The feeling is current among most of the Negro schools of which I have any knowledge, that a winning team (to use the phraseology of one alumni secretary with whom I discussed the matter) is essential to enrollment," he told Du Bois privately.[20] Streator believed "this argument is stupid and a fallacy," but it was pervasive in Black circles because of how true it was for white colleges.[21]

Trampism ran counter to the stated goals of the CIAA and other HBCU conferences. In 1924, Virginia State dean and CIAA official Thomas Puryear used the annual meeting to alert teams that league leadership was well aware of the "tramp athlete" who extended his eligibility through intentionally flunking courses in the fall, transferring to unaffiliated schools in the spring, and dropping out by summer only to reenroll at his original institution before the next football season began.[22] By 1929, the CIAA had closed loopholes that allowed transfers to play immediately. This ruling compelled Howard University, then the largest beneficiary of immediately eligible football transfers and the league's most influential member, to temporarily leave the CIAA.[23] Maybe this situation compelled CIAA leadership to not broach the tramp issue any further. Yet, Frank Young's criticism in December 1929 ensured that the CIAA could no longer ignore corruption.

Streator's finished reports exposed years of impropriety in Black college football. In the 1932 CIAA Bulletin, Streator argued that HBCU leagues should collude to enforce one another's eligibility rules. By doing so, Streator argued, "Negro colleges could present a united front to demand and receive greater recognition in the world of athletic competition."[24] He came to this conclusion after his first report, titled "Negro Football Standards" (1931). Streator found that HBCUs allowed players to transfer between conferences and play more than four years. While noting that the CIAA "has been fairly successful" in enforcing most of its eligibility rules, he criticized Saint Paul's for allowing a captain to play at the then two-year junior college for more than five seasons.[25] Streator used a stronger tone in addressing the game's improprieties in "Football in Negro Colleges" (1932). In dividing every participating college into three tiers—"good," "medium," and "bad" categories based solely on their rule enforcement—the CIAA garnered a "good" rating. Still, Virginia State, Saint Paul's, and Hampton had several recruiting improprieties.[26]

Streator took a special interest in Hampton Institute, then one of the most storied and prominent programs in Black college football. Under the leadership of alumnus and professional football legend Gideon Edward Smith, the "Seasiders" won nine of the CIAA's seventeen football crowns along with an undisputed Black college national title in 1922.[27] The CIAA was the strongest football league in the HBCU realm, and Hampton was the most feared and respected king of that hill. Streator found that Hampton's football superiority came from the inner workings of athletic director and CIAA founder Charles Holston Williams. Williams and Smith used their school's vocational curriculum to solicit major donations from white and Black organizations. Some of these funds went to developing superior athletic facilities that housed Hampton's comprehensive physical education department, a program that many Black Virginia high schools used (see chapter 2). Williams and Smith saw to it that the most promising high school football prospects transferred to Hampton's "Tech or Academy" high school. The Tech or Academy football team was part high school and part college. Its players gained experience playing smaller nonaccredited HBCUs and top Black Virginia high schools. After graduation, they almost always enrolled at Hampton. The CIAA saw these players, who in some cases had up to four years of college football experience upon matriculating at Hampton, as high schoolers with full college eligibility. Streator saw this practice as underhanded, given that "Hampton is considered the pioneer of football standards," Streator said sarcastically.[28]

The sarcasm led Hampton's Charles Williams and Gideon Smith to publicly rebut Streator. "I have just read an article by Mr. George W. Streator on Football in Negro Colleges," and the accusation, said Williams, "is not in accordance with the facts and does Hampton an injustice."[29] Williams and Smith went to the *Journal and Guide* and demanded Streator recant his assessment of Hampton.[30] "It is hoped that very soon," said Williams, "you will correct the unfounded impression you have caused to be formed concerning Hampton Institute's athletic policy."[31] Williams and Smith insisted that Hampton Academy was not a college junior varsity team masquerading as a high school program.[32] Streator refused until January 1933, when he took to the *Baltimore Afro-American* to recant his accusation against Hampton.[33] Streator was not easily moved by criticism, so it is unclear why he apologized to Williams, Smith, and Hampton. While later research proved his criticisms to be true, his initial findings operated as libel. Nevertheless, Streator would not do the same for other coaches who demanded that of him, such as Wallace O. Hawkins of Knoxville College.[34] While the initial claims against Hampton did not stick, they, and the dozens of other improprieties Streator alleged in his two reports, spurred serious talks about the future of HBCU football.

Streator garnered support for reform throughout the HBCU football world. Presidents Matthew Winfred Dogan of Wiley College in Texas, Robert Paige Sims of Bluefield State Teachers College in West Virginia, and J. Kelly Griffin of Knoxville College in Tennessee all wrote in support of Streator's mission and report.[35] The Black press, in the form of the *Norfolk Journal and Guide* and *Baltimore Afro-American*, also supported Streator's call for reform.[36] "Since the April [1932] *Crisis* was placed in the mail, the furor in athletic circles over the article by George W. Streator on football in Negro colleges has not ceased," said the *Journal and Guide*.[37] Even famed Black academic Horace Mann Bond used the report to call for the complete abolition of football in Black colleges. "If it is argued that [football] is a good advertisement [for HBCUs], I should like to reply that it is the wrong kind of advertisement," Bond said critically.[38] The public attention compelled the CIAA to take the lead, once again, in reaffirming football as a righteous pillar of Black respectability. That would now require investigation and reform.

CIAA secretary treasurer and Saint Paul's registrar John Lyman Whitehead always believed that "the statistics of George Walter Streator published in the *Crisis* for April 1932 are authentic." Thus, Whitehead asked Streator to "send us the full information relative to the athletes who migrated to CIAA institutions."[39] Streator did just that. One of the players who Whitehead and the CIAA investigated was Pine Bluff, Arkansas native and blue-chip Hampton running back Ivory "Ike" W. Richmond.[40] The power runner would go on to become an all-time best tailback in Hampton football history. His quest began after just one game where "the people's choice for all-star honors" gashed North Carolina College for a couple of scores and nearly 100 yards rushing on just a few carries.[41] Streator and later rival Virginia Union alerted CIAA leadership that the talented freshman was in fact a transfer from Arkansas Agricultural, Mechanic, and Normal College—referred to then as Arkansas State (now University of Arkansas at Pine Bluff), where his status as either a high school or college student was up for interpretation. When confronted with what was later deemed the "Richmond Case," Hampton's Charles Williams and Gideon Smith admitted that Richmond was, indeed, a transfer from Arkansas State. Yet, they maintained that he was no tramp athlete because Arkansas State was a de facto high school.[42] John Whitehead and Arkansas State president John Brown Watson all disagreed with this assessment, placing the CIAA's flagship athletic program at the center of the national call to reform Black college football.

John Brown Watson assured the CIAA that Arkansas State was a recently accredited college (as of 1930) who played peer schools in the Southwestern Athletic Conference. "Our students are received with full credit by such colleges as Morehouse, and our graduates are acknowledged by [white] Northern colleges. . . . This fact, too, I made clear to Mr. [Charles] Williams by sending a copy of our catalog," Watson assured Whitehead. Watson confirmed that Ike Richmond was enrolled at Arkansas State's high school wing for three years but that he also spent one final season at the college ranks. While there, he performed as a "poor student" who "passed his work with low grades."[43] CIAA officials initially found Watson's account to be accurate and concluded that while "few know much about Arkansas State College" because of its sheer distance from CIAA schools along the eastern seaboard, it was clear that "Arkansas State College is an A-1 school."[44] This led the CIAA to rule Richmond ineligible from CIAA football until the 1934 season.[45]

But Hampton did have reasons to be vindicated. For one, Arkansas State played fellow Southwestern Athletic Conference teams, yet they could not afford to be a regular member with them or any other HBCU conference. Many of their players lacked proper academic classification, and Arkansas State played their first full season of college football the year Richmond transferred to Hampton and not when he was a student there. Watson admitted this after Charles Williams and Gideon Smith pressed him on the facts.[46] In sum, Williams and Smith had a strong case that Arkansas State was an accredited college in name only.

Gideon Smith verbally sparred with CIAA officials over Hampton's innocence. At a league meeting, he claimed that the best HBCU sports did not take place in the CIAA, but in vocational schools and junior colleges that "are not eligible for membership in this association," like Arkansas State.

Thus, he regularly recruited star football players from those schools and felt "free of breaking any of our rules" in doing so. When told that his interpretation of the rules was underhanded and denigrating to fellow Black schools with aspirations of being respected colleges, Smith claimed "other schools in our Association have used them," namely, players from low rated Black colleges. If "they were and are right for doing so," Smith concluded, Hampton was as well.[47] He must have felt that Hampton was being targeted because they were the best at bending the rules. Thus, Smith reiterated his point by telling league leadership to "look up the matter" and that they would find that his accusations of league-wide cheating were true.[48] However, Smith's mentality brought to light the caste system in Black higher education, one that the CIAA would enter the vanguard to correct in the realm of athletics.

The Richmond Case brought to light the issues inherent in Black education during Jim Crow segregation, a reality that confirmed that neither Hampton nor Arkansas State were definitively right or wrong. While the prime motivator for white colleges bending eligibility rules was winning games, HBCUs did so largely because of the porous state of Black education. After Reconstruction (1867–1877), white Southern state legislatures defunded Black education to the point that many Black schools relied almost exclusively on elite white philanthropy and Black community investment.[49] CIAA leadership knew of the systemic divestment, as in the few Southern states where they operated at the time (Virginia and North Carolina) there were few Black public high schools.[50] This did not limit Black desires for post-elementary education. As detailed by James Anderson and Adam Fairclough, the line between Black high/trade schools and colleges grew extremely thin, as many HBCUs like Hampton and Arkansas State embraced the age of racial uplift by dedicating portions of their campuses to high school–level training.[51]

By 1930, Black education activists, namely HBCU graduates who had trouble gaining admission to respected white postgraduate programs, called for HBCUs to be in line with white colleges by gaining regional accreditation.[52] This would require the closure of high school wings. While George Streator went on the record in the *Chicago Defender* to criticize the accreditation movement, which he believed allowed too many "race colleges" to seek an accreditation they could not manage, his call for football reform was only an extension of that very same movement to gain more respectability for Black institutions and people in the separate and unequal world of Jim Crow America.[53] The call for accreditation and football reform unearthed the Richmond Case, which revealed that these processes were not yet feasible for the gamut of Black education by the 1930s. In fielding teams at colleges that were not yet respected as such, many HBCUs, like Arkansas State, made up for the systemic state-level divestment from working- and under-class Black education.

The actions of Arkansas State president John Brown Watson also deserve attention, too, as it was part and parcel of the troubles inherent in leading a HBCU during Jim Crow. By the time of the Richmond Case, Arkansas State was both what Gideon Smith and John Brown Watson claimed it to be: an accredited Black college that was, however, on par academically with most high schools, and Watson knew that fact very well.[54] The Smith County, Texas, native and Cornell alumnus assumed the presidency of Arkansas State in 1928. This was at the same time when the Arkansas Legislature matched philanthropic funds to help transition Arkansas State from a junior college into a fully accredited four-year institution. Watson responded by immediately pioneering the school's first intercollegiate sports teams that same year.[55] By 1929, his school was, compared to fellow HBCUs, "run down" with less than fifty students and even fewer professors. While he helped grow the institution to nearly one thousand students by the end of his tenure in the 1940s, Arkansas State was, as Gideon Smith claimed them to be in 1932, a glorified high school. Watson could have easily validated Smith's assessment of Arkansas State given the school's relatively unknown status in CIAA country and the newness of its football squad. But to do that would be to ignore the recent financial and sweat equity investments that Black people made to raise the school's profile to the rank of elite HBCUs, some of which were CIAA members. Watson's integrity was not the question, as while serving as a professor at Morehouse College in 1905, he was one of the first Black academics to call for conference formation and uniform rules enforcement.[56] Hence, Watson fits into the mold crafted by historians, as Black HBCU presidents during Jim Crow lived between a rock and a hard place. They were tasked with the impossible goals of building and running accredited colleges to uplift Black students while under the economic and political thumb of white elites who actively sought to limit Black advancement.[57] This pressure compelled these presidents to always put their best foot forward to maintain a high reputation for their schools, which were pillars of respectability for the race.

For these reasons, "there is no specific CIAA reputation which clearly covers this case," league officials admitted after reviewing the evidence.[58] The CIAA had a duty to the Black football world, its members, and the overall goal of helping uplift Black colleges writ large through the proper administration of athletics. Yet, the Richmond Case put these goals into conflict for the first time ever, making it "the most important case properly ever to be considered" by the league.[59]

HAMPTON INSTITUTE 1932 FOOTBALL SQUAD

Figure 11. The controversial Hampton Seasiders 1932 football team, courtesy of Virginia Union University Archives and Special Collections

Rather than challenging Gideon Smith's claim, CIAA leadership, under the direction of John Whitehead, ended the Richmond Case entirely. Hampton received no official punishment, and Ike Richmond was deemed eligible. Henceforth, however, CIAA members were tasked with reporting any eligibility infractions, and the accused programs were to turn over all evidence or face an indefinite ban.[60] The proceeding years were filled with lengthy eligibility meetings and investigations, as football coaches alerted the league to any new transfer or freshman whose playing status was in question. By 1934, these hearings were the longest and most contentious at the annual meetings.[61] The CIAA once wrote with pride in 1939, "One needs only to recall . . . the Richmond case . . . to understand. . . . the unrelenting efforts of the Eligibility Committee to track down offenders and to apply the rule with absolute fearlessness and fairness." They went on to assess that "this procedure has been attended at times with great personal inconvenience and the loss of friendships. The extent of this discomfiture is greater on some occasions than this body knows."[62] One extent that became immediately clear was that the HBCU world was watching, as they followed the CIAA's lead in cracking down on ineligible players.

John Brown Watson was right about one thing, and that was Ike Richmond's lack of academic acumen. The tailback's grades were just as poor at

Hampton as they had been at Arkansas State, forcing him to transfer after his sophomore year to Wilberforce in January 1935. The Midwestern Athletic Association member and elite liberal arts college faced criticism after making him immediately eligible for the 1935–1936 football season. There was no way that Richmond could have gained admission to Wilberforce on his academic merit, and Wilberforce agreed, arguing that Richmond was to be admitted as a freshman because he gained no credits toward graduation at Hampton. In the spirit of George Streator, the *Crisis*, and HBCU football's new commitment to uniformly upholding leagues' rules, the Midwestern Athletic Association banned Wilberforce for the 1935–1936 season.[63] While Streator once deemed reform efforts as "bunk" because of the CIAA's treatment of Hampton, HBCUs later implemented his plans after the Richmond Case.[64]

One uncomfortable fact of the CIAA's crackdown on eligibility was the end of Hampton's football dominance. The Seasiders did not win another CIAA title under Gideon Smith's tenure, which ended in 1945. They did not become a dominant football program again until the early 1990s, under the direction of coach Joe Taylor.[65] During this time, other programs usurped Gideon Smith's Hampton, such as Florida A&M under Jake Gaither and Eddie Robinson's Grambling State. By regulating Hampton's dynasty out of existence, the CIAA reassured clean and fair play as the foundation of Black college football, bringing about the glory days as detailed by historians Michael Hurd and Derrick White. HBCU sports legitimacy did not end on the gridiron. Rather, it continued with the CIAA sacrificing America's most dominant college basketball team nestled in the former capital of the Confederacy.

VIRGINIA UNION DREAM TEAM

Friday, March 7, 1941, was perhaps the most important and unremembered day in American sports history. That day, the best professional and college basketball teams in the world took center stage at Richmond's Blues Armory and played with a few thousand in attendance. The visiting Harlem Globetrotters brought with them a mighty record of 1,868 wins and 138 losses, earning a few world basketball championships (Black only tournament) along the way. They would later break the color barrier and handily defeat the legendary George Mikan and the all-white Minneapolis Lakers in 1948 and 1949.[66] The hometown Virginia Union University "Dream Team" entered the match with three consecutive CIAA titles, defeating two nationally ranked white college teams—one being the all-white national champion—all while compiling an 83–7 record. Nevertheless, the Globetrotters won the "Classic of the Century" 40–38 after eight lead changes in the final minutes.[67]

The Classic of the Century was the zenith of Black athletic excellence during Jim Crow, as the two best all-Black teams clashed against one another after dominating both the Black and white basketball worlds. The Globetrotter footprint on American sports history and culture during Jim Crow is well documented. The Union Dream Team's legacy, however, remains largely forgotten by historians and the contemporary sports public.[68] This ball club earned a nickname that was later appropriated by the 1992 US Olympic Basketball Team, headlined by the best professional Black and white basketball players in the world. The 1992 US Olympic Basketball team aided in the collective forgetting of the real Dream Team, their original purpose, and what their moniker represented.[69] The Union Dream Team embodied Black athletic ideals of integration under Jim Crow segregation, where the best Black athletes wanted to defeat the best white athletes in fair competition. Moreover, the Union Dream Team proved that Black athletes, and Black people more broadly, could achieve the *dream* of undeniable greatness despite racial discrimination.

The Dream Team also personified the reasons the CIAA rid HBCU sports of blatant corruption. Union coaches and school officials allowed ineligible players to compete in exhibition games, one of which (the Globetrotter game) was for profit. The NCAA never investigated any HBCU program during Jim Crow because interracial games were exhibitions; and HBCUs were not admitted to postseason tournaments. Yet, CIAA leadership refused to allow the NCAA's neglectful bigotry to stop them from ensuring the integrity of Black college athletics. In the winter of 1941, the CIAA sanctioned the Union Dream Team out of existence with a six-month "death penalty," forcing them to relinquish their league titles and accumulated wins and records.[70] This sanction prevented future generations from even knowing the Union Dream Team existed. Thus, they are never considered a part of the pantheon of "Black Fives" (in reference to the starting five of a basketball team)—New York Rens, Philadelphia Quick Steppers, Harlem Globetrotters, Tennessee A&I, and so on—who are credited for popularizing Black basketball during the days of segregation.[71] This sanction represented the integrity and honor of Black amateur sports under segregation. When no one was looking, and even fewer people cared, Black men placed honest competition above the glory and acclaim of winning games.

Union's path to basketball greatness did not come easy. At the behest of then athletic director Harold "Doc" Martin, Union pushed to make basketball an official CIAA sport as early as 1924.[72] The CIAA agreed three years later, imploring all member programs to "give basketball the high place that it deserves in our athletic program."[73] However, the financial burden of building gymnasiums ensured that the CIAA encouraged, but did not require, members to play basketball until the 1940s. That was great for Union, as they were, until the late 1930s, widely considered a "football school." A Union student complained in the 1920s that in spite of Martin's push, "very little interest was taken in basketball" on campus.[74] This changed in 1926, with the hiring of Union football legend Henry Boyd Hucles Jr., as athletic director and head basketball coach.[75] It was Hucles who ensured "that for the first time in the history of the school," lauded a Black Richmond minister in 1935, "the basketball team has . . . an adequate court" to play games.[76] Hucles began his tenure by compelling Union leadership to build an outdoor dirt court for practices and contract their home games at the off-campus Richmond Community Gymnasium and Richmond Mosque. Union was the last CIAA basketball program to build an on-campus gymnasium—Barco-Stevens Hall, completed in 1946.[77] Union was well behind other CIAA members in basketball development, as the poorest CIAA institutions—Saint Paul's and Virginia State—competed in their own basketball gyms by 1928.[78] Hucles's efforts reflected that in his earliest years, Union did not have the makings of a marquee or competitive basketball program.

Despite early struggles, Union led the CIAA's mission to help integrate college sports through interracial, intersectional basketball play. Between the 1890s and late 1920s, HBCUs focused mostly on football, ensuring that their basketball product was grossly inferior to that of white colleges around the nation.[79] By the late 1930s, however, "basketball in the CIAA" and HBCU world had "reached a new high," Virginia State coach Harry Jefferson told his peers with glee.[80] The stellar quints at Morgan State, Virginia State, Hampton, and North Carolina College compelled CIAA leadership to "consider the Negro athlete as a goodwill ambassador" to the mission of interracial play.[81]

Charles Williams and other CIAA leaders reached out to Northern white schools to begin a set of "diplomacy games" in 1937. Some Northern white basketball-focused universities agreed to play these games in New York City beginning in the 1937–1938 season. These games stimulated needed tourism for white Northern basketball boosters. HBCU officials used the games to showcase Black excellence through competition.[82] "I believe that one of the great objectives of the future for institutions in the CIAA," said Hampton's Charles Williams at the 1937 CIAA annual conference, "is to establish athletic relations with some of the leading American [white] colleges and universities."[83] Union was one of the first HBCUs to take part in this endeavor designed to add "respect to Negro institutions" through interracial competition.[84]

Segregation shaped Black athletic understandings of integrated play. Black leaders did not invite white schools to join their conference, nor did they advocate for white players and coaches to join HBCUs. Rather, they sought manly competition between white and Black schools. Northern white colleges agreed to these games with little white backlash because the gentlemen's agreement (see chapter 1) was mostly enforced in football—the peak exercise of white masculine supremacy. Basketball, a finesse game played mostly by ethnic minorities in non-Southern inner cities, helped ease the gentlemen's agreement because it was seen as less manly. Thus, interracial competition and Black victory was not considered a major threat to white physical prowess.[85] This reality helped CIAA leadership use interracial games as proving grounds for racial equality. Black sports media outlets accepted this reality, yet some still held contempt for the CIAA's scheme. The *Pittsburgh Courier*, in reporting on the diplomacy games a year later, opined that "in the athletic realm, race, creed, or color should be inconsequential."[86] The *New York Amsterdam* newspaper, however, venerated CIAA leadership for using whatever opportunity they could to disprove, as they stated, "one of the biggest arguments" that these games should not take place because "Negro teams are not in the same class as the white outfits which they would play."[87]

Union was not the ideal basketball program to prove Black equality. Hucles fell in love with basketball at New York University under the tutelage of coach Howard Cann Sr.[88] It was this love that helped him "develop a team of almost entirely new material," as he "worked with a limited budget and a scarcity of prospective players" at Union throughout the late 1920s and early 1930s.[89] Union basketball suffered because they had one of the smallest student bodies and highest scholarship requirements of most HBCUs throughout the nation.[90] This ensured that they had gone from bad to mediocre by the 1937–1938 season. The 9–5 Union aggregation finished fifth in the CIAA that season, earning them a last-minute call to play the Long Island University (LIU) Blackbirds in the diplomacy games.[91] Although the *New York Amsterdam* noted that Black Americans would "like to see the Panthers win this one," Union, like their CIAA counterparts, lost against LIU on March 24 and 29, 1938, at Harlem's Renaissance Casino and Orange Armory.[92] "They [Union] play a great brand of ball and will improve," LIU coach Clair Bee assured after participating in the clean sweep of CIAA teams.[93] When asked if LIU would reschedule Union next year, Bee said, "There is no reason why we shouldn't."[94] The backhanded compliment reflected Bee's arrogance and, more importantly, that white Northern colleges played CIAA schools because they felt that white athletic supremacy would never be threatened.[95]

Union's participation in the CIAA's experiment stretched beyond the "campaign to promote games between Negro and white schools."[96] While other CIAA squads went home after their losses, Union stayed and took more losses against New York City–based amateur teams; the most embarrassing defeat came against a group of Harlem high schoolers.[97] However,

Coach Henry Hucles used the New York trip to add Black Northerners to his underperforming roster. In doing so, Hucles engaged in temporarily reversing the Great Migration of Black Northerners back to their ancestral homeland to represent the race on the hardwood. Black ballers who could not gain admission to white colleges found a home at Union. The most important was Pittsburgh star Wylie Alexander "Soupy" Campbell—regarded as "one of the greatest basketball players to ever leave the state of Pennsylvania."[98] Campbell's commitment aided in New York City stars Melvin "Mel" Glover, Gilbert "Pickles" Frazier, and three others committing to Union as well.[99] The skills of the "New York school boy[s]" along with Campbell compelled the *Pittsburgh Courier* to later warn the HBCU basketball world that "most of all [Union's] boys from New York or thereabouts," they said, are "shooters, runners, floor men, defense and, above all, they work. Boy, how they hustle!"[100]

Union was primed for their rematch with LIU the following season. They dominated the CIAA regular season, finishing with a 12–1 record.[101] Union scored 1,081 points while surrendering 789 points all season in front of record crowds (nearly 4,000 on average) wherever they played.[102] Northern white boosters slated Union to rematch LIU at Harlem's newly constructed State Palace after winning their final conference game against rival North Carolina College.[103] The LIU game location was significant for Union as "two former Harlem scholastic stars" Melvin Glover and Gilbert Frazier were eager to help their team avenge the previous year's blowout losses in front of their friends and family.[104] Union shocked the basketball world when they defeated LIU 35–26 on March 24, 1939, a week after LIU won the National Invitational Tournament's (NIT) national title.[105] Union's dominance was felt by LIU, as they led the entire game.[106]

Hucles's coaching and the influx of talent aided Union's rise during the 1938–1939 season. "Coach Hucles has a smile on his face. . . . [That's] unusual of coach," a school program once joked about Hucles.[107] Hucles was hard on the few men who decided to play for him, as he knew that racism in everyday life would be even harder. A Union athletic handbook noted that "his former players prefer to think of him as a builder of men."[108] Upon Hucles's retirement in 1967, one of his former players who later became an attorney recalled: "I obtained a great deal of knowledge and 'know-how' as to ways to cope with many of the problems that have confronted me in subsequent life. Even though I caught hell from him and was cursed-out on many occasions, I realize that these were for the purpose of conditioning me for future life, and such has been quite beneficial."[109] Former Union athlete Lewis White confirmed the previous sentiment, claiming that "freshmen may not understand his [Hucles's] rigidity at first but they soon learn that he is a straightforward, ethical coach. He produces men of character."[110] Hucles was a hard-nosed coach because if he wanted to both win and develop men of substance, he could be nothing else.

The media became like the hardwood: a battleground in the war for Black athletic excellence. To the *Atlanta Daily World*, Union's victory over LIU ensured that they were "one of the greatest college teams in the history of the game."[111] The hometown *Norfolk Journal and Guide* was more boastful in their belief that interracial competition proved Black athletes to be superior to their white opponents, saying that "the Blackbirds were terrible on the white boys, but when they faced the black boys, it was a different tale."[112] This different tale threatened beliefs in white masculine supremacy, thus the Black press criticized their white media counterparts for first burying and later delegitimizing Union's historic victory.[113] "In Newark," said a *Baltimore Afro-American* sportswriter, "I was unable Sunday to convince a group of sports fans that Union had really beat[en] LIU" because the "Metropolitan newspaper which headlined the deeds of Long Island University's undefeated basketball team all winter, failed even to mention defeat of that team."[114] LIU officials later claimed that the game was not "official" and that their bench players and ineligible freshmen played the whole game.[115] The *New York Amsterdam* refuted this claim by printing the box score, which showed that LIU's starters played the whole game, especially after they trailed 22–7 going into halftime.[116] Union's hometown white newspaper, the *Richmond Times-Dispatch*, dismissed Union's victory as well, claiming it to be a "side-playing" scrimmage for "extra money," with the outcome debated by both ball clubs.[117] The Black press was relentless in combatting these untruths, as they spent much of spring 1939 touting that Union defeated "the same boys whose sparkling play netted them a national cage title and an unbeaten regular season," said the *Atlanta Daily World*.[118]

Coach Hucles and other Black leaders used regional pride to coax white Virginians into agreeing with their narrative about Union's victory. "There was no argument of any kind between the two teams" about the outcome, and "the finest possible spirit of sportsmanship existed throughout the evening," Hucles said in an editorial for the *Times-Dispatch*. Local Black theology professor S. Russell Wilson wrote the *Times-Dispatch* as well, arguing that Union's victory was worthy of veneration because the small Southern Baptist school defeated a superior Northern program while not being "blessed with first-class equipment."[119] The *Atlanta Daily World* caught onto Hucles's and Wilson's strategy, claiming that "Union not only brought recognition to Richmond, but the state of Virginia as well."[120] Placing Union's triumph in a larger, long-nineteenth-century tradition of Southern and Virginia pride compelled the reluctant *Times-Dispatch* to accept Union's victory for what Black people believed it to be. "Local sportsmen, regardless of creed, class, or color, have greeted with justifiable pride the somewhat startling feat of the Virginia Union University basketball team," the *Times-Dispatch* later said. They went further in correcting their previous take on the game, stating: "The team which was beaten by the [Union] Panthers was made up of the regular Long Island lineup . . . virtually the same team which had just finished winning the national intercollegiate invitational tournament at Madison Square Garden."[121]

With the local white press conceding to the Black narrative of Union's victory, the Black press issued Union a nickname that symbolized their meaning to Black America.[122] The CIAA crowned Union conference champions in spite of Virginia State and North Carolina College both having claims to the title.[123] The CIAA never justified their selection because Union, as the *Pittsburgh Courier* said for them, "added ever greater glory" to Black basketball "by upsetting the great Long Island University team of New York."[124] Moreover, the *Baltimore Afro-American* found that "down in the Old Dominion they're calling the Panthers the Dream Team."[125] The *Journal and Guide*, who had offices in several cities along the East Coast, also found that Black "sports fans throughout the country" labeled Union the "Dream Team."[126] This was no coincidence. Union created "a different vision" of and for Black athletic excellence.[127] Union overcame their well-known handicaps and "soared to the heights in the CIAA and landed in the blaze of glory," said the *Atlanta Daily World*.[128] Like Black Americans more broadly, systemic barriers should have prevented Union from defeating LIU, let alone competing with other elite HBCU quints. As Black America continued to do during segregation, Union overcame and became "inspiration to those who will follow," the *Chicago Defender* said a year later.[129] The Dream Team reflected the collective Black striving for opportunity and achievement during Jim Crow. This striving, Bluefield State athletic director James H. Rowland Jr. believed, helped to push integration more broadly through "democratic athletics," as Union showed that Black people could go twice as far with half as much.[130] By becoming the Dream Team, moreover, Union basketball symbolized Black America in the sports world.

Union broke more barriers in the 1939–1940 season, proving that some of the best college basketball was played by HBCUs.[131] The Dream Team became CIAA champions with a 14–1 (12–1 in conference) record, with a close loss to North Carolina College. Their "speedy break and lightning passing attack," as described by a CIAA Bulletin, helped them to average 75 points per game.[132] Union was so dominant that the first ever CIAA all-star game in March 1940 featured them versus a team made up of the best players from the rest of the conference.[133] As expected, Union won the game.

Figure 12. Virginia Union "Dream Team" of 1939, CIAA basketball champions, courtesy of Virginia Union University Archives and Special Collections

Union inspired yet another dream, and that was white Southerners breaking the custom and law of segregation. White fans, players, coaches, and referees regularly attended Union games.[134] The increase in white attendance created a shortage of tickets, as hundreds were regularly turned away from the gate before the jump.[135] "You know they must have put on a show when white people begged for a return engagement," said the *Atlanta Daily World*.[136] They further surmised that after the season, "Hucles was satisfied that his team . . . prove[d] to even the most prejudiced and hard to convince that it was not a matter of luck that his crackerjacks won the title again in the CIAA this year and that winning the title two years in succession was no fluke."[137] Breaking down segregation in the South allowed Union to generate a desire for integrated competition at the national level.[138] When asked in 1938 about all-Black teams playing for national championships against all-white teams, LIU's Clair Bee said, "I see no reason why the better colored teams shouldn't be booked at the [Madison Square] Garden," host site for the NIT.[139] History disagreed with him.

Union burst onto the scene when basketball national titles were a relatively new venture that conformed to age-old customs. The Amateur Athletic Union (AAU) hosted the first national basketball tournament in 1897, consisting of college, YMCA, and recreational teams.[140] It was not until the late 1930s that sports boosters created college-only national tournaments such as the NIT in New York, National Association of Intercollegiate Athletics (NAIA) in Kansas City, and NCAA Basketball Tournament in Evanston, Illinois.[141] As end-of-season tournaments made college basketball a national game like football, universities implemented the already established gentlemen's agreement. Many argued that if Black players and schools played for national titles, white Southerners (teams and fans) would not participate. The Dream Team's 1939–1940 season cast doubts upon that. Black basketball became a national spectacle in the mid-twentieth century, and "his ambassador" for integrated competition was, the *Pittsburgh Courier* believed, "Virginia Union University's far famed *Dream Team*."[142] This ambassador opened college hoops to integrated competition. Thus, some felt they could also help Black schools compete for national titles.

Unfortunately, the Dream Team would not become the first HBCU invited to a national basketball tournament. Union representatives and the Black press lobbied New York basketball promoter and sports journalist Ned Irish for a spot in the 1940 NIT.[143] Irish promised to include Union if they received enough support in the form of letters from fans promising to attend.[144] Many letters filled Irish's mailbox, yet the Dream Team never received an invitation for the March 1940 tournament.[145] The Black press later blamed Union's omission on the gentlemen's agreement, a claim LIU's Clair Bee acknowledged and Ned Irish originally denied.[146] Irish later recanted, claiming that white teams, coaches, and fans were, "regardless of ability or prowess are just not interested in having to do with anybody or anything colored."[147] Union's popularity in the white South led some Black newspapers to speculate that Bee, himself, rallied Southern white schools to boycott the Dream Team as revenge for his embarrassing 1939 defeat in Harlem.[148] Whether it was bigotry or vendetta, the truth behind Union's failed effort to break the color barrier on a national stage, as with many historical mysteries, likely lies somewhere in the middle.

The Dream Team's demise, like their rejection from the NIT, evolved from their on-court success. Halfway through the 1940–1941 season, Union defeated opponents by nearly 1,000 points en route to their third straight CIAA title.[149] Northern white basketball booster Frank Forbes solicited Union privately, without CIAA approval, to play against a top-tier white squad in another set of diplomacy games in Harlem and Baltimore in December 1940.[150] The popularity and profitability of these games grew significantly, as now

Figure 13. The 1940 Virginia Union "Dream Team" denied a spot in the NIT, courtesy of Virginia Union University Archives and Special Collections

they took place during the season. Around nine thousand people were expected to watch each game live.[151] The Dream Team accepted in order to earn a payday that would help build an on-campus gymnasium. Union's opponent was LIU rival, fifth-ranked Brooklyn College, "considered one of the leading contenders" for the NIT title.[152] Coach Artie Musicant believed his Brooklyn College Kingsmen had nothing to fear because he had the better team. He ignored the fact that the Dream Team would play with extra motivation due to being unjustly barred from the NIT just months before.[153] Union traveled to New York and trounced the Kingsmen in "the biggest upset of the current basketball season," said the *New York Amsterdam News*, by a score of 54–38.[154]

Union's subsequent loss to the Globetrotters in the Classic of the Century foreshadowed that their downfall would come by Black hands, not white. Shortly after losing the Globetrotter game, CIAA leadership held a special meeting at Virginia State to punish the Dream Team and coach Henry Hucles for numerous rules violations. Specifically, Union played ineligible players in unsanctioned games (Brooklyn College and the Globetrotters) that operated as professional in nature.[155] This meeting was the corollary of the CIAA's decades-long mission to ensure the legitimacy of HBCU sports.[156] Union had no chance of escaping the sanctions, and representing Black America in the basketball world made the situation worse.

UPTOWN ITS

La Mar Cheri

"SHOW PLACE OF THE HILL"

739 St. Nicholas Avenue

CORNER 147th STREET AUDUBON 3-9321

TASTY FOOD — CHOICE WINES AND LIQUORS

GOLDEN GATE OFFICIAL BASKETBALL PROGRAM

SANCTIONED BY METROPOLITAN A. A. U. MONDAY DECEMBER 27th

BROOKLYN COLLEGE

vs

VA. UNION UNIV.

(C. I. A. A. CHAMPS)

Next

Basketball

ATTRACTION

Va. STATE

vs

W. Va. STATE

(MID-WEST CHAMPS)

JAN. 11th 9 P. M.

MID-TOWN ITS

Audubon 2-9327 AUdubon 29348

CELEBRATING 15 YEARS

Of satisfaction in the Heart

Harlem

SMALL'S

PARADISE

7th Ave at 135th Street

COMPLETE NEW REVUE

3 SHOWS NIGHTLY

10:30 — 12:30 — 2:30

Secure Reservations Now For

New Years Eve

CELEBRATION

FREE NOVELTIES

SPECIAL DAWN REVUE

Spend New Year's Eve

DOWNTOWN ITS

WELLWORTH TAVERN QUINN'S

7th Ave. at 126th St. (N. W. Cor.) 8th Ave. at 115th St. (S. W. Cor.)

UNiv. 4-9661 — UNiv. 4-7120 UNiversity 4-8446

Foods, wines and liquors at the most reasonable rates in town.

FITZ & MAX at your SERVICE

Figure 14. Flyer for the Union "Dream Team" versus the number-five-ranked Brooklyn College Kingsmen, courtesy of Virginia Union University Archives and Special Collections

Union's infractions paled in comparison to the issues plaguing college basketball writ large. Intersectional "diplomacy" basketball games earned urban boosters such as Frank Forbes and Ned Irish much criticism. Liberal arts college faculty and other reformers argued that profit-driven games led to corrupt recruiting and the de-emphasis of academics, as had long been the case in college football.[157] The CIAA could have simply ignored Union's infractions given how influential they were to integrating college basketball and the fact that they did not garner nearly the same level of attention as that of white colleges. But CIAA leadership did not care. They took pride in HBCU athletics being the pillar of honest competition, thus they refused to allow even their flagship programs to flagrantly violate the rules of amateurism. Union's issues did not happen in a bubble created by the color line. Rather, they took place in a college sports climate rife with corruption, calls for reform, and Black desires for sports to remain a pillar of Black respectability.

The CIAA voted unanimously to ban Union from all league competition, strip them of their conference titles and voting power, and remove them from all CIAA promotional material for at least a year's time. The punishment lasted only six months, however, as Union's compliance and the graduation of key players convinced the league to allow them back in by fall 1941.[158] Union did not challenge the CIAA's sanction, accepting "in a sportsmanlike manner the reasonable penalty imposed by the association," the CIAA recorded.[159] After being readmitted, it was clear to all that Union's basketball dominance in the HBCU and white basketball world was over.[160]

The remnants of the famed Dream Team finished 13–1 with a CIAA title in 1941–1942.[161] This did not come without controversy, as elite HBCUs (in and out of conference) refused to play Union in basketball until all Dream Team members had graduated.[162] The ones that did, such as Clark University, beat them pretty handily.[163] Yet it was the "Dream Team's nemesis" of North Carolina College, and legendary coach John McLendon, who continued the CIAA's Black basketball dominance.[164] McLendon's Eagles implemented Union's fast-paced, full court play. His team not only dominated the CIAA throughout the 1940s, but they also earned the honor of being the first HBCU to play and defeat a Southern white college (Duke University) in spring 1944.[165] McLendon would later lead his future ball club, Tennessee A&I, to college basketball glory, as his Tigers won three straight NAIA national titles between 1957 and 1959. It is hard to imagine that had Union gone unpunished, Hucles and the Dream Team would have cemented their legacy by accomplishing everything that McLendon did after them.

VIRGINIA UNION UNIVERSITY BASKETBALL TEAM (C. I. A. A. 1942 CHAMPIONS)
LEFT TO RIGHT: Clyde J. Davis, Jr., Washington, Pa.; Richard T. Culberson, Iowa City, Iowa; Melvin L. Glover, New York City, N. Y.; Warren G. Kelley, Buffalo, N. Y.; Wilmotte A. Burton, New York City, N. Y.; Coach Henry B. Hucles, Jr., Richmond, Va.; Kavanzo M. Hyde, Philadelphia, Pa.; Robert Daughtry, Buffalo, N. Y.; Levi G. Bough, New York City, N. Y.; Howard J. Irvin, Buffalo, N. Y.; Garnett E. Blair, Carnegie, Pa.

Figure 15. The 1942 Union “Dream Team,” CIAA champions, courtesy of Virginia Union University Archives and Special Collections

The Dream Team's story is truly a heroic tale. Hucles and his Northern players triumphed over the seemingly insurmountable odds created by segregation. In the process, they symbolized the Black ideal that integrated competition proved Black equality and that Black athletic excellence could lead to racial integration more broadly. Yet, CIAA leadership ensured that the Dream Team was a cornerstone and not a capstone for Black athletic achievement. While Black Americans were "singing paeans of praise for the heralded Virginia Union Dream Team," said the *Atlanta Daily World*, the CIAA sanctioned them to establish Black athletic achievement as a voyage in honest competition.[166] They would not allow Black success to be marred by the corruption that plagued white colleges, and thus the Dream Team remained what they had become: trailblazers for future HBCU programs to learn from.

"CARRY ON! CARRY ON!"

December 7, 1941, changed college sports throughout America. No one discovered a major scandal; rather the Japanese Empire issued a successful attack on the US Naval Base of Pearl Harbor. This attack led to immediate American entry into World War II and the mobilization needed to fight a two-front war in the Atlantic and Pacific Oceans. As with World War I, many white universities debated whether to play college football and basketball given the inevitable manpower and supply shortages. The solution for most programs was to consolidate control into the NCAA and US military by converting athletic programs into battlefield efficacy centers. This put federal money into the hands of universities, via the GI Bill of Rights, to house and educate soldiers who would ensure the continuation of college sports, but for a higher purpose.[167]

HBCUs such as Howard, Hampton, and Tuskegee benefited from this program. Most HBCUs, however, wished to pause all sports as the GI subsidies would not overcome the manpower and supply shortage inherent within warfare. To play or not to play was the question, and "we must determine where we stand," a Black Virginia minister said to the CIAA over the pending issue plaguing HBCU sports. There was no shame in quitting. Storied HBCUs such as Tennessee's Fisk University, Texas's Bishop College, Georgia's Fort Valley State College, and Florida's Talladega College determined that playing anything beyond intramural sports was out of the question.[168] The majority of the HBCU world, however, looked to the CIAA to set the tone, as "the issues are clearly drawn" but not clearly solved.[169]

Black Virginia CIAA officials such as Hampton's Charles Williams, Union's John Barco, and Virginia State's Harry Jefferson wanted to continue intercollegiate sports. However, they faced backlash because to play games while men were dying was deemed unpatriotic, not to mention that football and basketball required much manpower, money, and fuel for travel. Even celebrity Black athletes Joe Louis and Jackie Robinson not only served in the war but also raised money for the war effort.[170] Some anti-sports voices used this point of crisis to generate public debate about ending HBCU sports altogether. Many HBCU professors felt the "luxury of football" and basketball long rotted their institutional commitment to academics, said the *Journal and Guide*. Thus, many worked behind closed doors to make sure "the war crisis will succeed where athletic reformists have failed" in ending the games entirely or, at least, converting them to on-campus intramural ventures. While not openly supporting the abolition of HBCU sports as called for by their faculty, noted CIAA schools such as Howard, Lincoln, and St. Augustine supported the cancellation of all intercollegiate football and basketball for the 1942–1943 season.[171] This move reflected that "toes will be stepped on," said one CIAA coach, if Williams, Barco, Jefferson, and others did not call off the games by the fall of 1942.[172]

Black Virginia educators used their position in CIAA leadership to guarantee that college basketball and football continued during the nation's mobilization phase. While each member institution had equal voting power on league issues, the president and secretary treasurer held significant sway, as all decisions were either approved or denied by them. This system worked well as CIAA president George G. Singleton, Virginia State Professor of Commerce, and secretary treasurer John Lyman Whitehead, Saint Paul's registrar, had not the slightest intention of canceling a single game. Rather, they believed that the league was obligated to maintain its position as the leader in Black college sports. This could not happen, they felt, if the CIAA refused to stay the course and play games because the road had been made uneasy by global warfare. Both men came together and created what was later dubbed the "Carry On" policy. This required the CIAA to subsidize members to play the revenue sports of football and basketball. The league would help schools consolidate schedules, locate games in major cities, and subsidize the mass transportation of teams to host sites. Teams who did not participate would lose their portion of league revenue. Singleton and Whitehead knew that this plan would be met with reprisal; thus they used the May 1942 CIAA annual meeting to ensure that their stance on the issue was unwavering and clearly articulated.

The May 1942 CIAA annual meeting was Singleton's and Whitehead's finest hour. In the highly anticipated "President's Address" drafted by Whitehead, Singleton criticized everyone who rallied opposition to football and basketball. "A program which contributes to the development of . . . character should be enhanced—not curtailed; such a program should be promoted at any cost and not suspended for the duration of any time," Singleton said to the captive audience of CIAA coaches, athletic directors, and school presidents. Singleton compared himself to British Prime Minister Winston Churchill, stating that "he was not elected Prime Minister of Great Britain to preside over the liquidation of the British Empire, and I was not elected President to preside over the liquidation of the CIAA." Therefore, "Carry On, Carry On," as he exclaimed that the final days of his CIAA presidential tenure (1940–1945) would be defined by Black athletic resilience and not forfeiture.[173] Other HBCU leagues such as the neighboring Southern Intercollegiate Athletic Association, Eastern Intercollegiate Athletic Association, and Southwestern Athletic Conference followed suit by announcing their own versions of the Carry On policy between August and September 1942.[174] Agreeing with Singleton and Whitehead was the *Journal and Guide*, as they posited that "strong athletic programs will [not only] be an asset" to a nation dealing with the trauma of war, but it would also be an exercise of the freedoms that the men were fighting to defend in Europe and Asia.[175]

Figure 16. Carry On policy advocate and CIAA president George G. Singleton, courtesy of Virginia Union University Archives and Special Collections

Singleton felt that the CIAA had moral grounding in its decision to "carry on" with football and basketball. Singleton instructed every CIAA member to compile statistics of every current and former player serving in the US military. The CIAA had hundreds of alumni soldiers, and "61% of the CIAA athletes reported serving in the armed forces are leaders, and the fact that they are leaders is no mere coincidence," he later said in support of continuing the games. "Their training on CIAA gridirons . . . and courts had contributed toward their achievements," lauded Singleton. Thus, CIAA play during the war was justified in Singleton's mind. While CIAA Bulletins cost money to purchase, servicemen received free copies with letters thanking them for their service to the nation.[176] There is not much evidence indicating how veterans felt about CIAA games continuing, but one could imagine that they supported it. The policy of using CIAA Bulletins to honor living and deceased soldiers continued until 1945.[177]

Singleton and Whitehead also led the vote to not award any official championships until the conclusion of the war.[178] "The justification for sports now is to win the war" and not conference crowns, said Edwin Henderson, then president of the CIAA's officials' board, in support of the decision.[179] Union's John Barco and Virginia State athletic director Harold "Doc" Martin compelled Whitehead to include sections honoring CIAA veterans who were serving and died in warfare.[180] With this, the ultimate sacrifices of CIAA stars such as Union's Gilbert Frazier, who died while serving in the 51st Defense Battalion of the United State Marine Corps, remained at the center of CIAA football and basketball play.[181] Singleton, Whitehead, and their supporters tied the games to the ongoing war effort, ensuring that CIAA basketball and football was unmistakably seen as an honor of the Black men serving in World War II.

The Carry On policy received significant resistance by a few non-Virginia member institutions. Much of this dissent came from Singleton's and Whitehead's ability to marshal enough votes to ease eligibility rules to continue basketball and football play. The interim eligibility rules allowed players stationed near opponent CIAA schools to transfer and play without sitting out a year. Academic standards for all players were also temporarily suspended.[182] "To throw out all considerations for academic standing for the sake of putting a team on the field during the most serious period of our nation's history," said St. Augustine College President C. D. Halliburton, "would be to confess" that the criticism of anti-sports activists were true that football and basketball were "the most important element of [Black] college life."[183] Halliburton and other CIAA presidents pushed Singleton and Whitehead to reinstate the normal eligibility rules in 1944, making it harder to field athletic teams.[184] Singleton and Whitehead also faced protest from several members

Figure 17. St. Paul's registrar and Carry On policy supporter John Lyman Whitehead Sr., courtesy of Virginia Union University Archives and Special Collections

(10 of 14) who refused to play intercollegiate sports in defiance to the Carry On agenda. This refusal was mostly limited to football, as nearly every CIAA school played basketball between 1942 and 1945. While they all cited "manpower" shortages from dropouts and enlistments, "we begin to suspect that there was something deeper and more fundamental involved," said Carry On supporter, the *Journal and Guide*.[185] This "something deeper" was a combination of faculty dissent and a general disdain for Singleton's and Whitehead's refusal to budge on the issue.

Virginia HBCUs stood behind Singleton's and Whitehead's Carry On policy. Singleton's very own Virginia State, as well as Union and Hampton, led the way by playing several basketball and football games against all-Black Army and Navy units at Fort Lee in Petersburg and Naval stations in Norfolk, the proceeds of which went to support the war effort.[186] Saint Paul's made the ultimate sacrifice by suspending their program entirely until the conclusion of the war.[187] Whitehead supported this plan because Saint Paul's was, at the time, transitioning into a four-year institution, so they used every discretionary dollar they had to build newer academic programs. Thus, Whitehead wanted to ease CIAA eligibility rules to help Saint Paul's athletes fill the ranks at other member schools.[188] What seemed hypocritical on the part of Whitehead and Saint Paul's was actually a noble endeavor to aid the Carry On policy. With every Virginia HBCU on board, dissenting CIAA members such as Howard, Lincoln, North Carolina College, and Shaw ended their football boycott in the fall of 1944. A year after that, by the final year of Singleton's tenure, all CIAA members had resumed normal sporting activity.[189]

Singleton's Carry On policy allowed the CIAA to take more control and authority of Virginia's weakened Black high school sports world. The Virginia Interscholastic Athletic Association (VIAA) ceased all operations between 1942 and 1945.[190] The issue of war covered for the fact that while HBCUs struggled to play their own games, "no leadership" or support was "given [to Black] athletics either by local [all-white] boards of education or by the State Department of Virginia," a Virginia State professor criticized.[191] As the war progressed, school boards allowed Black athletics to die.

While it is difficult to gauge Black sentiment on indefinitely postponing high school sports, a later opinion piece published by someone I suspect to be a Black teacher gives insight into how unpopular it may have been. In 1951, the VIAA—then reorganized as the Virginia Interscholastic Athletic League (VIAL)—published a letter in support of Black high school sports during World War II. The letter begins by challenging anti-sports advocates who see that "[high school] sports is a diversion for . . . personal enjoyment" and a business whose "success is measured by the cash register." Rather, the author saw sports as "bread and butter, milk and medical care to many thousands of people who are very seldom thought of as being involved in sports." They go onto argue that agricultural and industrial firms (those who make balls, jerseys, and other sports equipment) rely on the play of sport to feed their families. To not play the games would be to harm the "millions of unknowns who plant, harvest, breeds animals, manufacture sell and buy" high school sports for a living. "In sports," said the author, "are all members one and another and, in a very real way, our brother's keeper. Yes, sports help to keep the wheels of our economy going and our economy keeps sports going—from the most insignificant field hand to the cloistered financier."[192]

The pro-sports advocates must have made their feelings known to the CIAA. By 1945, Hampton, Virginia State, Union, and Saint Paul's had organized basketball and football regular seasons and tournaments for Black high schools throughout the commonwealth.[193] When asked about HBCU involvement with organizing high school games in lieu of VIAA suspension, Virginia State's Harry Jefferson said that "through the catastrophe of war, we will all learn where the values in athletics are and what standards are really significant."[194] The *Journal and Guide* agreed with Jefferson, opining that "athletics is designed for boys and they came to the rescue of these boys. No gesture more concretely manifests the type of spirit athletics ought to develop."[195]

CIAA leaders put into action what they felt in their spirit: societal uncertainty meant that Black people needed strong leadership, and the training ground for such people came from sports.[196] The decision to help high school football and basketball continue compelled VIAA members to desire more CIAA oversight. When the VIAA resumed operations in 1946 under the new name VIAL, they did so under the leadership of Virginia State physical education director J. A. Moore.[197] Not only did CIAA coaches (Henry Hucles of Union and J. A. Moore of Virginia State) serve as commissioners, and VIAL was set up identically to the CIAA, with eligibility committees and all, but the league briefly printed bulletins that were, in structure and message, mirror images of the CIAA.[198]

By the eve of *Brown v. Board* (1954), CIAA leadership helped grow the league by recruiting half (around sixty in total) of Virginia's Black high schools to join it while reestablishing VIAL's membership to the National Federation of State High School Athletic Association.[199] "What has been accomplished in an organizational way has been the result of the principal having the courage to think that those so delegated could Carry On such a program under the highest possible ideals," said J. A. Moore.[200] The CIAA's leadership was paramount in resolidifying Black high school sports under the leadership of HBCUs. This reality compelled a gracious VIAL principal to predict the league's future direction. "Although strong men played a major part in bringing into being the VIAL, even stronger men would be needed in the future to Carry On the work to its ultimate goal"—that being the understanding that amateur sport was a crucial pillar of Black life under segregation.[201]

The interwar period stressed Black amateur sports to its limits. Scandals and war generated debates about the direction of games that just decades before were on-campus pastimes. Under these circumstances, the CIAA, by then still the nation's leading Black athletic organization, took more control of the direction of Black sports. By punishing their own elite programs, refusing to suspend athletic competition during World War II mobilization, and restarting Black high school sports in spite of global warfare, the CIAA brought Black athletics back in line with the original mission of racial uplift, as set forth by its founders at the turn of the century.

V. I. A. L. IN ACTION

Figure 18. VIAA 1951 state basketball game between Peabody High School of Petersburg (winner) and Lawrence Dunbar High School of Lynchburg, courtesy of Virginia Union University Archives and Special Collections

AWARDING OF THE TROPHIES AT THE STATE TOURNAMENT—1951

Left to right: Mrs. S. F. Griffin, President of V.I.A.L.; Mr. S. Blue, Coach of Peabody; Dickerson, Captain of Peabody, State Champions: Co-Captain Bennett and Co-Captain Thomas of Dunbar, runners-up; Mr. Waters, Coach of Dunbar, Dr. J. A. Moore, Commissioner of Basketball.

Figure 19. Award ceremony for the VIAL state basketball tournament, courtesy of Virginia Union University Archives and Special Collections

V. I. A. L. IN ACTION

Figure 20. Live shot of a VIAL football game, circa 1951, courtesy of Virginia Union University Archives and Special Collections

Their experiences with Hampton, Union, and continuing sports during war did not prepare them for what lay ahead. The watershed of racial integration in colleges and high schools throughout the nation presented another unique challenge to Black football and basketball. On the one end, integration was the logical conclusion of nearly a century of Civil Rights activism by local Black communities and national organizations. On the other end, the parallel sports world created by segregation was on the brink of elimination. The CIAA would not be alone in straddling the fence between Black progress and institutional survival, as Virginia's all-Black high school league faced similar challenges in the years to come. Furthermore, full integration became a contested terrain where Black sports struggled to maintain their existence and relevance in opposition to a societal outcome that undoubtedly advanced the race far beyond where segregated sports could take them.

5

THE INTEGRATION, 1951–1970

The post–World War II era brought about a new reality of integration to Black football and basketball play across the country. Before the war, people viewed integrated games more broadly as white and Black athletes competing against each other in the same arena on equal footing. As the last troops came home from Europe, however, the sports world viewed integrated competition as Black and white people playing not against but with one another. This new understanding was in line with postwar social and moral sentiments that America was to function as an interracial democracy.

By 1970, Black footballers and basketballers were playing at formerly all-white Virginia universities.[1] Most of these Black men were born and raised in Virginia and they played prep ball for high schools that underwent court-ordered desegregation.[2] Those still in denial about the end of segregated sports by 1970 needed to look no further than the recently integrated T. C. Williams High School of Alexandria. Under Black coach Herman Boone, the Titans finished a historic undefeated football season by crushing the Andrew Lewis High School Wolverines of Salem 27–0 in the winter of 1971.[3] Disney later turned the team into legends by recounting their story in the 2000 Denzel Washington film, *Remember the Titans*.

By the 1970s, integrated competition was a logical conclusion of the modern Civil Rights Movement, a result that historians have long documented Black Virginians taking an active part in through a steady stream of legal and street-level activism. This spelled the end of Black-only football and basketball, one of the few crown jewels of segregation. While Black Virginians eagerly experienced the end of segregated schools, employment, housing, and political office, they were not willing to surrender their all-Black games.

Between the 1950s and 1970s, Virginia underwent a unique phenomenon of Black people seeking to prevent integration from ending their segregated games. "The grave problem of integration" compelled the CIAA to fund scholarships for both Black and white athletes and schedule white opponents.[4] The Virginia Interscholastic Association (VIA—previously the Virginia Interscholastic Athletic League) lobbied and received state appropriations to create the first ever comprehensive all-Black high school league. While both the college and high school ranks employed different strategies, they aligned on employing the age-old practice of institutional solidarity. In all, the CIAA and VIA failed to maintain the prestige of HBCU sports and the existence of all-Black high school athletics. In that failure one sees the importance of Jim Crow athletics to Black people, as integration undid generations of work to make the games community mechanisms of uplift.

I complicate the narrative that when integration came, Black athletes embarked upon it as an inherent good, if not a desired result, after decades of societal agitation.[5] Instead of focusing on courageous Black athletes enduring physical and psychological harm to integrate previously all-white colleges and high schools, I focus on the forgotten Black leaders who worked within the dissipating segregated world to reap the potential benefits of integration while mitigating its effects on all-Black sports. Black people valued their segregated games in ways that few people today understand. These games were not just operations of necessity: they were a source of pride. Black people had reason to fight the tide of history to prevent the talent diaspora that later befell Black communities once the doors of white society were fully open.

I disrupt the prevailing narrative of Black-only institutions during the age of integration. Scholarship dealing with Black institutions during the Civil Rights age generally focus on the adverse impact of integration. HBCUs and Black secondary schools lost significant human capital to the "brain drain" of academically prepared students and talented Black faculty from Black schools, as well as the flight of upwardly mobile people from Black communities.[6] The realm most irreparably damaged was high school and college athletics. Between the 1960s and 1980s, most talented Black football and basketball players spurned HBCUs and all-Black high schools were closed down and or integrated with white schools.[7] This chapter reveals the hidden layer of resilience that Black Virginians showed in seeking to ride the wave of integration and stave off certain demise. At the high school level, this fight made Black Virginia unique, as it was perhaps the only Southern state where Black leaders sought to maintain segregated sports. While Black leaders at both the college and high school levels used different methods to achieve the same outcome, their games succumbed to the national move toward integrated education.

"TRAGEDIES OF THE INTEGRATION NONSENSE"

Integrated (Black versus white) sports in Virginia have an interesting origin. There was no court order, national media pressure, or street-level demonstration to allow Black and white boys to play against one another. Rather,

World War II compelled Virginians to defy the decades-old color line in search of a sensible solution to a colorblind problem.

The Commonwealth experienced the war years like every other state. The US military drafted young men; others simply enlisted. Everyday citizens limited their food, water, and oil consumption to aid the troops in Europe.[8] The manpower and supply shortage compelled many Black and white Virginia high schools and colleges to cancel their football and basketball seasons. The coaches, players, and families who continued playing ball, however, quietly set up a series of integrated high school and college football and basketball games as early as February 1943 at Hampton Institute. More interracial football and basketball contests took place on military bases throughout the Tidewater later that year.[9] These games would be canceled as some white Virginians expressed outrage that white schools openly violated the existing Racial Integrity Act of 1924, which barred interracial contact in all dwellings and events.

Under normal circumstances, white Virginians would never have allowed integrated play on the gridiron and hardwood at the college or high school level. Yet, wartime conditions proved how fickle segregation was given the commonwealth's love for athletics. Historians often cite the vaunted "Secret Game" between Duke University and North Carolina Central in 1944 as the first intercollegiate or interscholastic game between Black and white Southerners. However, not-so-secret games took place throughout Virginia a year prior to that at both the high school and college levels.[10] These events, like the Secret Game would a year later, reflected that Virginians and Southerners alike were ready to make integration in sports match what many felt integration should look like in the postwar period.

Virginians confronted racial integration in sports at a time when it was an evolving concept. To the dismay of Black newspapers, Black fanatics were fixtures at many white Southern college football and basketball games. White fanatics and media members were also regular attendees at Black high school and HBCU contests.[11] For those who did not attend the games played by the opposite race, the game highlights were always recorded in various newspapers. Spectating was always an integrated experience, despite racial divides enforced in the gallery. What was not integrated was the gridiron and hardwood themselves, as the coaches, players, and referees were all the same race. That would change as the nation entered the modern Civil Rights Movement of the 1960s. "Athletic integration," said the *Norfolk Journal and Guide* in 1962, was "becoming fact in dear ol' Dixieland."[12]

Underpinning the move toward integrated sport was the fair play movement. Historians Charles Martin and Donald Spivey document how liberal white Northern college students and administrators called for Black and white athletes to share the field of play as teammates by the 1930s.[13] This movement produced some successes, such as Iowa's Ozzie Simmons in 1934; UCLA's Kenneth Washington, Jackie Robinson, and Woodrow Strode in 1938; Kansas State's Harold Washington in 1949; and Syracuse's Jim Brown in 1954. Southern white universities such as UVA (1947), Oklahoma State University (1949), Duke University (1944 and 1950), and University of Oklahoma (1955) allowed Black athletes to play on their campuses if they were members of the opposing teams. The NCAA permitted the integration of postseason football, such as the Cotton Bowl in Dallas, Texas, and the Orange Bowl in Miami, Florida, beginning in 1948. By 1952, the NAIA allowed Black competitors in postseason basketball tournaments as well, opening the door for both HBCUs and integrated squads to compete against all-white squads for national titles. The CIAA participated in this by requesting, and ultimately receiving, admission to NCAA postseason events akin to their existing participation in the NAIA.[14] The gentlemen's agreement was on life support by the late 1950s.[15] While most Southern universities did not recruit Black athletes until the 1960s, they did, in the previous decade, join the national movement in allowing Black and white people to play with one another as teammates.

HBCUs were generally unprepared for the fair play movement's logical conclusion. The Virginia Union "Dream Team" led the CIAA and the Black college world in promoting integrated play through college basketball in the 1930s. CIAA member Lincoln University also enrolled HBCU football's first white player during the same decade.[16] But when the definition of integrated athletics changed from Black and white players competing against each other to Black and white players competing with each other, the CIAA made note of the "growing trend to influence Negro stars to enroll in white colleges." For HBCUs in general, and the CIAA in particular, integration "offers a challenge . . . which must be met with direct action," said CIAA official Charles C. Hawkins in 1947.[17]

Yet, the CIAA did not meet the threat head on. Rather, they signaled to the sports world that they were ready to receive white players and coaches by changing their name from Colored to Central. After getting some flak for implementing the name change, CIAA president Paul J. Moore rhetorically asked league members in 1950: "Do we wish to set aside our league as being different? I think not." He continued by claiming, "I believe we want to integrate ourselves in a sports world where there are no barriers of religion, color, or creed. Yet we apparently continue to set ourselves apart by that name." Moore embraced the new integrationist sentiment in postwar America, and that was removing all identifiable color barriers between the races. "Many of our institutions have interracial faculties and student bodies," Moore argued.

Thus, as Moore's logic went, the league's name should reflect that and the fact that the HBCU world was open for integrated sport. By changing the league's name, Moore believed the CIAA would better align with "the Mid-Western Athletic Association, The Ivy League, The Pacific Coast Conference, [and] The Big Ten"—white-run leagues that the CIAA saw themselves as peers to.[18]

The name change did not deflect the fact that integration would force the CIAA to change its long-standing view on athletic scholarships. With the exception of schools in the Southwestern Athletic Conference, the HBCU world generally shunned athletic scholarships, or what Hampton's Charles Williams once called the "subsidizing of athletes," which he deemed "one of the major athletic problems in this country."[19] HBCUs unofficially embraced the liberal-arts scholarship model, where student athletes were offered on-campus jobs to defray tuition costs.[20] By the postwar era, however, scholarships were the primary means by which most white colleges recruited decent athletes, including Black athletes. It did not help that the burgeoning Southeastern Conference institutionalized scholarships as early as the 1930s. As scholarships funded the Black athletic migration to white colleges after World War II, the CIAA had no choice but to reevaluate their resistance to subsidizing athletes.

Leading the CIAA's Committee to Aid Athletes in 1956 was a league founding father: Saint Paul's College president Charles R. Frazier.[21] Frazier compiled a report showing that when it came to scholarships, the CIAA was essentially two leagues operating as one. Twelve of the twenty members did not offer athletic scholarships, while the other eight did. "The impression [is] that in summary," he concluded, many "feel for the most part that the level of competition should be strengthened, and that liberal grant-in-aid [athletic scholarships] should be provided to meet the challenge of the new day." To Frazier, neglecting athletic scholarships was to ignore that "desegregation is the law of the land." Thus, he concluded: "We need this support . . . to keep pace with . . . [white] institutions" by convincing "the administrators in our institutions that we need increasing support for intercollegiate athletics."[22] Frazier's urgency compelled the league to, by 1961, allow every member to offer the equivalent of forty-four full athletic scholarships across all sports, with the expectation that the majority would be spent on football and basketball.[23] Scholarships were a "major step in the direction of integration in sports and there must be no faltering," the CIAA stated publicly about their league agenda going forward.[24]

The CIAA and HBCU world simply waited too late to institutionalize the use of scholarships. By the early 1960s, league members complained publicly of blue-chip Black basketball and football talent making their way to white colleges.[25] "Let's face it: all the best Negro football players are going to

Indiana, Illinois, and Michigan State. If we are going to get second rate anything, we are getting second rate athletes" Kentucky State President Rufus B. Atwood told the *Chicago Defender* in 1962.[26]

This issue did not go unnoticed by the Black press, as the *Journal and Guide* decried in 1963 that "the quest for the talented ones [Black players], athletically and academically, among them [Black colleges] became tougher for coaches on the colored collegiate front."[27] This migration created an inferiority crisis among Black colleges in general, as Black athletes signaled that HBCUs were lesser schools than their white counterparts. This hurt even worse in Virginia, as local HBCUs had long held a monopoly on Black high school talent. "The threatening loss of competitive competition on the [Black] scholastic sports front," the *Journal and Guide* lamented as early as 1958, a time when many talented Black high school ballers chose the Big Ten over the CIAA, "is one of the current tragedies of the integration nonsense that is harassing the state of Virginia."[28] As for the HBCU sports world in general, former North Carolina College great John McLendon opined that "integration at major colleges has made recruiting at Negro schools more difficult" because the "good negro players can go to almost any school they choose" regardless of Black schools now embracing athletic scholarships. Thus, McLendon offered a new solution. "All it would take would be one good (white) boy," he claimed. If HBCUs could offer an integrated athletic experience akin to white colleges, "I think that would get us started," said McLendon, in the direction of reclaiming their monopoly over Black athletic talent.[29]

The consensus was clear by the mid-1960s that the HBCU world's only salvation in athletics was to open their door and integrate their previously all-Black game. "As integration advances to stardom," said the *Journal and Guide* in 1963, "it's logical to assume that the day isn't too far off when the colored mentors will compete with the major college coaches for the competent white athlete."[30] CIAA members and other HBCUs aggressively recruited white football and basketball players in the 1960s. While stud Black high schoolers did not stop going to white colleges, nearly every CIAA school added white football and basketball players (mostly from the North) between 1966 and 1970.[31] Other HBCU leagues followed suit soon after.[32] School integration helped them in this regard, as HBCU coaches were better received in integrated schools than they ever would have been in all-white schools.[33] By 1970, "white players are no longer novelties on predominantly Negro teams," celebrated the *Journal and Guide*, as HBCUs finally appeared to be in a position to compete with white colleges.[34]

HBCUs went further in making themselves appealing to both white and blue-chip Black players. Between the 1950s and 1970s, every Black college league pushed for and received admission from the NCAA and NAIA to participate in postseason basketball tournaments and football bowl games. This resulted in Tennessee A&I (1957, 1958, 1959) and Grambling (1961) winning NAIA basketball national titles. The only CIAA school to bask in the glory of integrated postseason play was Winston Salem State, as they captured a Division II NCAA basketball title in 1967. Other HBCUs organized televised football bowl games between themselves to increase the national profile of Black colleges.[35] To get Black "blue-chip athletes to reverse the current trend and enroll in predominantly Black colleges and universities," HBCUs also began playing against white colleges in regular season contests. In Virginia, this led to newer rivalries between Black and white colleges that shared the same city, such as Norfolk State University and Old Dominion University (white) in the Tidewater, as well as Virginia Union and Virginia Commonwealth University (white) in Richmond.[36]

Virginia HBCUs even integrated the ranks of athletic leadership. While nearly every CIAA member had some white low-level staff by the 1970s, Virginia Union took the unprecedented step in hiring the league's first white head coach. Nicknamed the "White Shadow," Dave Robbins accepted the job as Union's basketball coach in 1978 after leading Richmond's integrated John Marshall High School to a 136–48 record and earning a state basketball title in 1974.[37] While a highly controversial hire in the Black college world, and even in Black Virginia circles given the school's basketball legacy with Henry Hucles, Robbins achieved an unparalleled level of success at Union, racking up 713 wins (nearly 80 percent of the games he coached), fourteen conference titles, and three Division II NCAA national championships over three decades before retiring in 2008.[38]

Integrated college athletics, however, came with issues that emerged to the level of national news. White colleges experienced an outpouring of Black athletic activism in the 1960s and 1970s, symbolized by the "unforgettable fists" of Tommy Smith and John Carlos in the 1968 Olympic games. This brought student athlete activism to the forefront. The movement consisted of incremental acts of resistance in the 1950s evolving into public demonstrations by the 1960s.[39] Many Black athletes protested racism from fellow white players and coaches, as well as the student body, faculty, administration, and the campus community writ large.[40] Much of the bigotry involved controversy over what the "Syracuse 8" complained was the implicit and explicit rules to "stay away from white women" if they wanted to remain in good standing with the university community.[41]

Other issues involved Black coaches walking on eggshells while disciplining white players.[42] The few Black coaches who had to deal with this issue were ironically among the anointed, as Black coaches found it nearly impossible to get coaching jobs at white colleges, even as football and basketball rosters became majority Black.[43] Other issues gained lesser attention, and that was the unfamiliar faces of white players at Black colleges. In 1968, the *Michigan Chronicle* reported on the harassment that white footballers faced from the Black campus community at Bethune-Cookman University in Daytona Beach, Florida. This was one of the few situations where white athletes learned how it felt when the "shoe is on the other foot," and they were the targets of racial ill will.[44] In sum, integrated college athletics, while being a natural outgrowth of the Civil Rights Movement, led to more problems than many anticipated.

While the CIAA evaded most of the racial drama happening in places like Bethune-Cookman, they experienced a rapid decline that had long hidden under the blanket of segregation. As early as 1959, Winston Salem State recommend that the CIAA acknowledge the eight-hundred-pound gorilla in the room, and that was that "the CIAA should be divided and schools with similar philosophies should be grouped together."[45] Just five years before, Virginia Seminary bowed out of the league after three decades of competition. The year after Winston Salem's recommendation, Lincoln University left as well. "There is . . . a geographical problem," said CIAA's council of presidents in 1962, as the Virginia and smaller Carolina schools were being looked down upon for their paltry investment in athletics as compared to the Northern and prominent Carolina members.[46]

The problem was that the CIAA—led by its Virginia members—spent the last few decades adding small teacher colleges (Fayetteville State, Elizabeth City State, Livingston, Bluefield State, and Saint Augustine College) and athletically minded schools (Delaware State, Morgan State, and Maryland-Eastern Shore) with little regard for a shared athletic vision. The athletically minded members wanted to reprimand smaller members for their inability to invest in athletics, a move the Virginia members refused to do.[47] The reason was simple: Virginia leadership were bound to their decades-long commitment to uplift the race through institutional solidarity. Although they pioneered interracial competition, they refused to completely abandon their racial uplift commitments to keep up with the newer push to remake Black college athletics in the image of white colleges, namely through abandoning smaller schools who could not keep up with the rising cost of interracial play. Almost immediately after the CIAA added the underwhelming Norfolk State in 1962, the Northern schools (Howard, Maryland-Eastern Shore, Morgan State, and Delaware State) and prominent Carolina schools (North Carolina A&T, North Carolina Central, and South Carolina State) expressed their desires to leave the then eighteen-team league.[48]

By 1970, six of the eighteen CIAA teams (Howard, Maryland Eastern Shore,

Morgan State, Delaware State, North Carolina A&T, and North Carolina Central) defected and formed the rival Mid-Eastern Athletic Conference (MEAC). MEAC was dedicated to competing at the highest levels of college sports by investing in facilities, full scholarships, and campus upgrades, something the smaller CIAA schools could not do.[49] The Virginia CIAA members even met in 1972 to ponder if they should leave the smaller North Carolina teaching colleges behind and create the Virginia Collegiate Athletic Association, but that initiative fell through.[50] While the CIAA lost some of its charter members in 1970, all of its Virginia members—with the exception of Virginia Seminary, who dropped athletics entirely—remained in the league until the 1990s, when Hampton and Norfolk State finally left for the MEAC. Integration did a number on HBCU athletics, namely facilitating Black athletic migration to white colleges and the breakup of the CIAA, which created the conditions by which Virginia HBCUs were no longer seen as leaders in Black college athletics.

"VENTURE IN FAITH"

Virginia's Black high school sports were not spared from the pending demise by way of racial integration. More than a decade before the *Brown v. Board of Education* decision (1954), states such as New Jersey, Indiana, Iowa, Illinois, and Minnesota played integrated high school games.[51] In the 1950s, Black high schools in Washington, DC, played white Catholic schools from Delaware to New York in football and basketball.[52] Even the former Confederate South joined the national movement toward integrated competition. Kentucky's Carlisle High School integrated its football team in 1955.[53] The love of good football compelled Texas to integrate high school sports in 1959.[54] Georgia saw integrated high school sports by 1966.[55] Integrated games both North and South did not signify the emergence of racial harmony in athletics, as Black athletes were routinely taunted with racial epithets and sometimes spat upon on the field of play.[56] Rather, integrated high school basketball and football games reflected that segregated schooling was nearing its end.

Yet, no state stood more opposed to integrated high school football and basketball after *Brown* (1954) than the Commonwealth of Virginia. Since the 1960s, historians have analyzed Virginia's Byzantine legal system that maintained segregated schooling after *Brown* (1954), ranging from pupil placement boards, school closures, private school vouchers, and Freedom of Choice Plans.[57] These accomplished works ignore that Virginia's refusal to integrate schooling reached the realm of athletics, where it took a peculiar turn. Southern states maintained segregated schools writ large while integrating high school athletic competition, in that Black and white schools played against one another while a minority of schools were forcibly integrated by the federal courts.[58] Virginia was out-of-touch with the region and nation in this regard. In fact, Black Virginians used the white desire for segregation against them by securing public funding to better consolidate, organize, and run their own high school sports league in the twilight years of segregation.

In April 1954, the all-Black Virginia Teachers Association (VTA) met privately at Virginia Union's Hawthorn Hall and Virginia State's Virginia Hall. The topic of discussion was how they could use the state's commitment to all-white schooling to strengthen all-Black sports should the US Supreme Court outlaw school segregation a month later.[59] They concluded that if white Virginians insisted on evading legal mandates to integrate schools, then they should ask the all-white legislature to fund the formation of an all-Black league that would provide every Black high school and training school—both large and small—with a chance to better compete against one another. This would take place under the direction of Virginia State College's Physical Education Department, like what had already been done in 1903 for white people with the Virginia High School League (VHSL), which was under the direction of UVA's General Education Department. Moreover, the VTA insisted on doing the unthinkable: becoming a finger on the hand of what would later be dubbed "massive resistance."

This "venture in faith," said Southampton County Training School principal Charles Womble, hinged upon white leaders not understanding the contradiction of being so ideologically bound to segregation that they would do what they never did before: pay a premium for segregation by funding Black amateur sports.[60] By framing Black high school sports as the servant of "separate but equal," Black-run high school athletics stood a chance of not only surviving but flowering amid integrated competition across the nation. Months after the May 17, 1954, *Brown* decision, the Virginia Legislature agreed to fund the project along with their other anticipated measures to maintain segregated schooling. With state funding in fall 1954, the struggling Virginia Interscholastic Athletic League (VIAL) became the Virginia Interscholastic Association (VIA)—a statewide coalition filled with Virginia's 116 sport-playing Black high schools and training schools.

It was one thing to convince white racists to support segregated athletics in the age of integration; it was something totally different to convince Black people—many of whom fought for school integration—to do the same. With state funds in their pocket by fall 1954, VIA executive secretaries traveled twelve thousand miles in-state and held community meetings at more than forty-two Black schools to promote the league.[61] Ninety-seven of Virginia's 116 Black secondary institutions became full members.[62] The selling point was that integration would be a long process in Virginia, thus the VIA was the only surefire way to ensure Black children continued playing high school sports. While there is no evidence to support this, one could imagine that VIA members told Black communities that should their boys be integrated into white schools, they faced limited opportunities to play football or basketball due to racist coaches and faculty.

By December 1954, VIA's executive, legislative, and administrative committees had organized the league into three groups (Eastern, Northern, Western), with fifteen districts comprising both vocational and liberal arts schools. Black Virginia athletic leadership's ability to organize the league so quickly considering *Brown* (1954) showed both a renewed commitment to all-Black athletics and a collective Black disbelief that school integration was happening in the commonwealth anytime soon. More than the VIAL before it, the VIA was heavily interwoven with Virginia HBCUs.[63] Unlike the VIAL, HBCU presidents (Dr. Robert Prentiss Daniel of Virginia State), professors (Drs. James A. Moore, William Bennett, Nathaniel Gatlin of Virginia State, and H. M. Nelson and Ben Whaley of Hampton), and athletic coaches (Harry Jefferson of Virginia State, now at Hampton, and Henry Boyd Hucles of Virginia Union) controlled VIA's executive committee.[64] These same people organized district and state tournaments that were later held at Hampton (basketball) and Virginia State (football).[65]

The VIA was also a break from the past in that it allowed for athletics to reflect the growing influence of Black women in public education. Female high school administrators such as Mrs. Dorothy J. Harris, a teacher at Mecklenburg County's West End High School, served on the VIA executive committee upon its inception.[66] Her voice was powerful, as she created the statewide group setup and fought for the inclusion of smaller high schools, such as Alexandria's Parker-Gray, Danville's Langston, Powhatan's St. Emma Catholic School, and others "whose enrollment did not warrant it, but whose scope of activity . . . should be included" in the VIA.[67] Moreover, she ensured that big-time high schools in the Richmond and Tidewater areas did not simply dominate the VIA as they sought to, as the league's survival relied on smaller schools and communities buying into it.[68] Harris's inclusion into high leadership ranks reflected that since the 1930s, women had become prominent members of Virginia's Black educational leadership, ranging from principals, professors, and administrators.[69] Moreover, Harris's place in the VIA reflected that the totality of the Black community was needed to do the impossible: save all-Black high school sports from succumbing to integration.

Black women did not get the red-carpet treatment upon their inclusion into what had long been a men's club. After Harris upheld a controversial call that cost Newport News powerhouse Huntington High School a chance to play in the Group 1 state football tournament in 1955, for example, Huntington principal W. D. Scales objected to her authority on the grounds that she was a woman. "I am of the opinion that the adjudication of a dispute arising out of a football infraction involving coaches and official would require a greater knowledge of the game of football than ladies normally possess," Scales wrote in his scathing rebuttal to her decision.[70] Scales's disrespect of Harris belied a general apathy Black men had for Black women in the competitive sports realm.

In December 1954, VIA officials voted unanimously to "not approve state tournaments for girls' athletic activities."[71] After significant opposition from Harris, other Black female district-level committee members, and girls' basketball coaches such as Mrs. Beatrice McKenzie of Petersburg's Peabody High School, Misses Eva Davis of Richmond's Armstrong High School, and Mattie P. Smith of Charlotte Court House's Central High School, "the committee does not approve state tournaments for girl's athletic activities was deleted from the minutes," the executive committee later ruled.[72] Rather, they allowed the female teachers to form Virginia Interscholastic Association League for Girls (G-VIAL). VIA leadership underwrote all their state tournaments so that Black girls could more equally participate in sport (mainly basketball) alongside the boys.[73] This Black women's activism reflected that they were now equal partners in fulfilling the VIA's mission to "broaden the scope of activities within their individual schools by providing a wider area for student participation," as expressed by the league in December 1954.[74]

Barring Black women's demands for inclusion, VIA hit several unexpected snags with organizing the statewide high school league. Black athletic leadership quickly learned that Black communities throughout the commonwealth demanded respect for their regional rivalries. Many Black schools in Southwestern Virginia, such as Tazewell County High School in 1955, forced the VIA to constantly redraw district lines because they "already have long established relationships with many of the schools" closest to them.[75] VIA also resolved several disputes or "protests" that threatened to undermine the league's solidity. Schools as large as Richmond's Maggie Lena Walker High School and as small as Hopewell's Carter G. Woodson High School debated controversial calls, acts of violence, and rules violations in basketball and football games. Some schools threatened to leave the league entirely and play out-of-state opponents when the executive committee did not rule in their favor.[76] Other issues involved smaller rural schools refusing to adhere to eligibility rules involving age, academic performance, and the payment of fees. VIA leadership nipped these issues in the bud by helping several schools with delinquent fees and suspending every school who, knowingly or unknowingly, violated league rules.[77] The VIA's strong, top-heavy leadership kept the ship afloat during its inaugural years, using the revenue from basketball and football to financially float state tournaments in every nonrevenue sport.

The VIA hit its stride in the final years of the 1950s. While the nation and later scholars recount this time as the nadir of public education, where the Virginia Legislature closed schools in Prince Edward County, Norfolk, Warren County, and Charlottesville to prevent integration, VIA membership remained around one hundreds schools, with nearly 60 percent of members playing football and basketball annually.[78] This had much to do with the VIA providing base-level insurance through Roanoke's Clifton Whitworth Firm for all Black football and basketball players.[79] The VIA certified more than 150 referees across the commonwealth. A few basketball teams, such as Alexandria's Parker-Gray, Newport News's Huntington High, Richmond's Armstrong High, and Williamsburg's Bruton Heights, represented the VIA by competing for national titles in the all-Black High School Basketball Tournament in Nashville, Tennessee. Black football and basketball coaches regularly attended VIA coaching clinics at Virginia State and Hampton, learning the most up-to-date strategies and fundamentals. The VIA also did not lose any money between 1954 and 1959, which assured that the Virginia Legislature would not intervene in league affairs. "Although there can be much improvement," said the executive committee in 1959, "the Virginia Interscholastic Association may well be proud of the progress made during the past four years."[80] An executive committee member continued that "needless to say our new effort" at creating a statewide sports league during the Civil Rights era "was a successful one."[81] There was even talk of the "VIA becoming self-sufficient," operating 100 percent without administrative appropriations from the Virginia Legislature. The realities of the 1960s, however, quieted that talk.[82]

Chinks had appeared in the armor by 1960. It was this year that the VIA was "still experiencing growing pains," such as "redistricting and reclassification" of smaller schools to help them cut down on travel costs. VIA golf star Arthur Ashe also left the commonwealth to continue his high school career at the integrated Sumner High School in St. Louis. "Tennis in the VIA cannot be thought of without mentioning" Ashe, the 1960 annual report stated after his departure. It continued that, "although Arthur Ashe left Virginia, we are proud of his achievements and wish for him the best of luck in all his endeavors."[83] While Ashe left for an integrated school out of state, his abrupt exit from the league signaled the oncoming tsunami of Black schools dropping out due to integration throughout the commonwealth.

In 1961, Black Northern Virginia principals at Culpepper County's George Washington Carver, Leesburg's Frederick Douglass, Alexandria's Hoffman-Boston and Parker-Grey, Manassas's Jennie Dean, Fredericksburg's

Walker Grant, Warrenton's Walter C. Taylor, Spotsylvania's John J. Wright, and Fairfax's Luther Porter Jackson met secretly to form their own league. They claimed that this was done to save money and maintain rivalries. Many felt that this was the first step in them transitioning away from all-Black athletics. It was no secret that white liberals in Northern Virginia were planning to end segregated schools in defiance to the state.[84] Luther Porter Jackson High School principal C. P. Hazzard confirmed the VIA's suspicions of the Northern district's secession, saying in 1963 that "some of the effects of integration are now being felt by some schools in the Northern District . . . which in time will affect the entire State organization."[85] Charles Womble tried desperately to work with Northern Virginia schools to remedy the issue, yet none were willing to listen.[86]

C. P. Hazzard's prediction was correct. Between 1960 and 1967, the VIA went from 116 members to a mere fifty. Executive Secretary Charles Womble regretfully reported in 1968 that "practically all large urban high schools have been lost to the VHSL," "no VIA school exists west of the Blue Ridge Mountains," and "only one school remains in Northern Virginia." The declining participation led to financial ruin, as the league ran a yearly deficit of $3,000 (nearly $30,000 in 2023).[87] It became clear by the end of the decade that, as Womble said, "VIA's problem today is survival." As schools left due to either closures or consolidations with white schools, the remaining schools expedited the VIA's destruction, a fact often ignored by those who remember this short-lived experiment. "Participation in this meeting is needed. We will be disappointed if we do not see you at this meeting," Womble said in a 1966 general memo. Many league meetings were canceled due to lack of attendance.[88] General apathy took over Black amateur sports in Virginia, as remaining VIA schools either stopped playing sports, refused to pay dues, or flagrantly disobeyed league rules without repercussion. It was "conditions within the Association and conditions outside the Association," said Womble in 1968, that pushed Black schools out faster than integration was letting Black kids in.[89]

The VIA lost complete control of the league during its decline. Decreasing participation in basketball and football compelled the VIA to allow schools with delinquent dues to play games, such as the newly reinstated Prince Edward High School and Lawrenceville's J. S. Russell. This policy irritated other VIA members.[90] S. M. Hawkins, athletic director at Franklin County's Lee M. Waid School, told the VIA in a strongly worded letter that game participation and end of season "honors should be financial." He like many other Black athletic leaders felt it unfair to compete and possibly lose space in postseason events to teams who, regardless of reason, evaded their financial responsibilities to the league.[91]

The weakened VIA also said nothing when member schools such as Salem's George Washington Carver High School and Appomattox's Carver-Price High School hosted their own basketball state tournament.[92] Schools such as Charlottesville's Jackson P. Burley refused to send in their eligibility lists, making it harder for VIA officials to ensure that only eligible players participated in games.[93] These issues went unresolved. Womble later lamented the "general reluctance of district councils to adjudicate cases of reported violations of regulations, particularly eligibility and sportsmanship rules."[94] Some coaches and fans verbally assaulted referees without VIA punishment.[95] Member schools had to reconcile their own issues without VIA help, such as postgame brawls and items stolen from locker rooms by the away team.[96] Other schools became so bitterly divided over controversial endings in basketball and football that they refused to play one another again, such as Nansemond's Training School and Cumberland County's Luther Porter Jackson High School, and Lynchburg's Dunbar High School and Gretna's Northside High School.[97]

Whereas the VIA had lost control of the league by the mid-1960s, they ensured the league had a respectful demise. As early as 1966, VIA leadership began negotiating with the all-white VHSL about "an honorable merger."[98] VIA records only call this obvious league death a merger to maintain Black respectability, as admitting the truth "weakens VIA's image" as a legitimate entity run by and for Black people. Addressing the "subject of merger cautiously and tactfully,"[99] VIA officials presented VHSL officials with their terms for a formal merger in summer 1967, which would have combined the two leagues outright, with the leadership ranks being equally shared by both races. VHSL flatly rejected this offer.[100] VIA officials came back in the winter with a nine-point merger proposal that allowed existing Black schools to maintain their VIA districts and rivalries as a part of the merger. Black principals and VIA officials also wanted to have similar voting powers in VHSL as they did in the VIA, and VIA referees would be grandfathered into the VHSL.[101] The most controversial part was that the VHSL would reimburse the VIA for the missing dues of all the teams that left the VIA to join the VHSL because their schools were integrated.[102] The VHSL never responded to the offer. Yet, the VHSL reset the table for discussions by admitting Franklin County's Lee M. Waid High School as the league's first all-Black member in 1967 without a dissenting vote.

The merger discussions were so one-sided because, as the VIA told the *Journal and Guide* in 1967, "We are losing schools because of integration." The losses were so severe that VIA's Group 1 had hardly any teams and Group 3 no longer had divisions.[103] By 1968, all-Black schools in heavily segregated areas such as Petersburg's Peabody, Chesapeake's Crestwood and Carver,

Richmond Armstrong and Kennedy, Machipongo's Northampton, and Accomack's Mary N. Smith left for the VHSL. The VIA also dealt with a student-athlete exodus, as talented Black football and basketball players left all-Black high schools to play for integrated squads. The need for a merger escalated as the Black high school stars, such as Newport News footballer Leroy Keys of George Washington Carver and Hampton's hooper Howard White of Kecoughtan, who left the VIA for the VHSL, also left the state for colleges such as Purdue and the University of Maryland given that white Virginia universities were still largely segregated and HBCUs were not playing prominent universities.[104]

The VIA and VHSL agreed to a "merger" in May 1968. This was not an equitable coming together of former competitors. Rather, the VIA was to be dissolved by summer 1968 and all accredited VIA schools absorbed into the VHSL by April 1969.[105] VIA football continued until 1969 because of lucrative preexisting game contracts. Few people from VIA would be fully incorporated into VHSL executive administration. Franklin County's Hayden High principal Leon Armistead controlled the redistricting format. P. D. Vann of Ridgeview and Campbell County's O. J. Duncan later served on the VHSL executive committee. Norfolk's Walker Junior High principal Clarence Jones was named the VHSL's state program supervisor. Only the most senior VIA referees were allowed to join the VHSL.[106] In 1970, Hampton alumnus Phillip Smith III became the VHSL's first Black head football coach at a previously all-white school, taking the reins at Newport News's Denbigh High School after compiling a 36–10 record at the previously all-Black Westside High School.[107]

The VIA schools, coaches, and players who entered the VHSL dispelled any notion that they could not compete at the highest level in basketball and football. The stigma attached to the VIA was that it was a de facto junior varsity league compared to the VHSL.[108] This myth succumbed to reality when Norfolk's Booker T. Washington, Suffolk's John F. Kennedy, Franklin County High School, and Richmond's Maggie Walker all finished their first VHSL football seasons undefeated, while Lynchburg's Dunbar went on to win the VHSL district basketball title over the traditionally white Northside High School of Roanoke by nearly 20 points in 1970.[109] Other former VIA giants such as Petersburg's Peabody and Newport News's Huntington regularly thumped their crosstown white counterparts in district football and basketball play.[110] By 1971, the VHSL saw its first traditionally all-Black school win a state championship in basketball when Richmond's Maggie Walker defeated Staunton's Robert E. Lee by a score of 80–63 for Virginia's esteemed 3-A (then the highest division in public school) state title.[111] Walker's Black coach Pierce Apollo Callahan Sr. joined T. C. Williams of Alexandria's legendary football coach Herman Boone in being the first Black coaches to win VHSL state titles.[112]

While VIA schools found success on the VHSL hardwood and gridiron, many Black Virginians felt that something was lost with the merger. That something was the sense of racial uplift that high school football and basketball long buttressed under all-Black male leadership.[113] With that sentiment prevalent throughout Black Virginia communities, VIA leadership stood strong in their convictions, knowing that integration was ultimately the better outcome for Black Virginia. "In thinking about the merger," former VIA official Charles Womble said after its completion, "conviction and honesty" compelled him to say that "educationally, the merger paves the way for the removal of crippling restrictions against Negro boys and girls in the high schools of Virginia."[114] He further opined that, "in the wake of integration . . . this decision was overdue, it was just, it was American, and it was necessary for the best interest of boys and girls we serve. The decision, while in general has opened doors for our group which were heretofore closed, has presented us with challenges we have not had before."[115]

VIA leaders understood that for Black progress in America to live, their segregated games had to die. But that death was honorable, one that reflected the morals and values that brought them into existence in the first place. At the final VIA meeting, leaders had a catered dinner at Virginia State's Foster Hall where they all thanked and congratulated one another for their service to the uplift of the race through sports. "A feeling of nostalgia swept over" the VIA to the point that the final legislative act was to appoint someone to archive league records; retrieve copies of insignias, metals, and honors from Jostens; and "make provision for a History of the VIA to be written."[116] The provision was for $1,300, the remaining balance in the VIA account.[117] To my knowledge, this chapter is the only history ever written on the VIA, and I did not receive a dime of this allocated funds. No matter: I fulfilled the task in making sure that the "history of the VIA" was, indeed, written.[118]

Integration dealt the death blow to all-Black football and basketball in Virginia. The most traumatic result was not the end of segregated games. Rather, it was the removal of Virginia as the capital of the HBCU sports world and the interweaving of Black Virginia's athletic culture with the rest of the South and nation. As Black athletes and coaches made their way into formerly all-white schools, and the reverse happened in formerly all-Black schools, issues arose that highlighted the generational separation between the races created by Jim Crow. Some Black coaches quit coaching at integrated schools due to constant scrutiny by white players, families, and school administration.[119] This was the case with Alexandria's T. C. Williams head football coach

Herman Boone despite the Disney retelling of his dream season of 1971. This issue even happened with Black high school and college players, as formerly all-white schools refused to abandon their Southern "traditions" when Black players came in.[120] White coaches also resigned in protest to Black athletes voicing discontent with conditions on campus and in society.[121] The conflict between players and coaches sometimes became violent, as a Black North Carolina high school football star violently attacked his white coach over a dispute in 1970.[122]

The issues inside of college and high school football and basketball mimicked society writ large. Court-ordered integration did not solve racial separation overnight. This reality was best summed up by the Syracuse and Cleveland Browns legend Jim Brown. "Black and white athletes shake hands, slap palms, embrace, slap each other on the backside on the field but after the game is over they go their separate ways," he said in response to questions about segregation in athletics. For Brown, occupying the same spaces did not eradicate the biases, misconceptions, and downright hatred the two sides had for one another. "That's why Black athletes don't socialize with white athletes," Brown concluded.[123] While this issue worked itself out over the coming decades, newer issues with commercialization arose later to ensure that the bygone days of amateur basketball and football, where the games were tools of racial uplift, institutional solidarity, and Black manhood, remained gone forever.

CODA

The Bygone Days Are Gone, 1970–Present

THE BYGONE ERA of Black amateur football and basketball is over, and it is safe to say that it will never return. For the reasons why, inquiring minds should first turn to the current state of HBCUs, which were the longtime standard-bearers of Black amateur sports culture.

Since *Brown v. Board* (1954), only one HBCU (Florida A&M football in 1978) has won a Division I NCAA national championship in basketball or football. Of the 107 surviving HBCUs, only twenty-three compete at the Division I level in basketball and football, with twenty of the twenty-three unable to win football national titles because their conferences cannot afford to compete for them. In fact, few HBCUs make more than their expenses from basketball and football on a yearly basis.[1] Few sports fans can name current HBCU basketball and football players or their coaches.[2] This reality is even truer for Virginia HBCUs, as it has only two Division I Black colleges (Hampton and Norfolk State), neither of which has a national name in the world of sport. This reality is a far cry from that of Black high schools and amateur clubs, which have now become some of the most recognizable institutions in American sports.

Majority Black high schools regularly win state titles in basketball and football. However, their best players are often recruited by predominantly white Division I programs. The most success is seen in Black-run AAU basketball organizations, as they dominate the circuit year in and year out under the control of some of the most iconic sportsmen in the country.[3] This reality signals a fundamental shift in Black amateur athletics, as HBCUs have been usurped in terms of athletic cultural relevance by secondary schools and the nonscholastic grassroots. Yet, commercialism is so married to amateur Black football and basketball that the games no longer center on racial uplift as was the case in the past.

In the age of integration, the commonwealth took a step back from its generational role as an amateur Black sports leader because of the declining athletic prestige of their HBCUs. This allowed secondary schools and grassroots organizations to become cornerstones of Black amateur football and basketball culture. School integration created a nationwide paradox where HBCUs failed to compete with white colleges on a national level. Yet, school integration had an adverse effect at the secondary level, as resegregation ensured that many Black prep football and basketball players remained isolated in majority Black high schools oftentimes located in majority Black communities. It is in these same communities where Black-run AAU programs have risen to national prominence. Still, integration has helped make Black high schools and AAU programs a branch in the hyper-commercialization of sports, ensuring that the bygone spirit of racial uplift is not the foundation of Black amateur football and basketball.

To even my surprise, scholars take an anti-integrationist focus to the current state of Black athletics. They do not advocate for the reinstitutionalization of Jim Crow segregation. Rather, they highlight the exploitative issues plaguing integrated football and basketball to the point where some suggest that Black athletic migration back to HBCUs might be the only means of curbing it. The most pertinent issue they discuss are the mistreatment of Black sportsmen, from systemic racism in the coaching ranks to the limited compensation Black players receive while historically white colleges grow insanely wealthy. In sum, authors such as Billy Hawkins, William Rhoden, Andrew Zimbalist, and others see Black athletics in the integrated world as a colonized institution, where Black amateur athletes are converted to commodities for white profit instead of pillars of Black community uplift as they were before integration. In the process, Black athletic prowess solidifies a broader systemic racial poverty where Black excellence becomes white profit to the point that Black human and financial capital perpetually leaves Black communities.[4]

This coda attempts a more bottom-up analysis to explain the current state of Black amateur athletics. While not debunking the well-informed scholarship, I discuss elements that they ignore, such as the use of bowl game capitalism by HBCUs in their attempts to "keep up with the Joneses" in the integration age, as well as the kernel of Black communal resilience that exists at the high school and grassroots levels. Furthermore, I show that Black institutions took an active part in tethering commercialization to amateur sports at the sacrifice of Black uplift. The result is that the bygone world of sport, where amateur football and basketball were institutional pillars of Black masculine resistance to Jim Crow, is long gone.

"NEED TO GET THEIR ACT TOGETHER"

The post-integration age of HBCU football and basketball is a not-so-simple picture of decline. Yes, a few HBCUs climbed to the mountain top of athletic glory, à la Kentucky State's NAIA basketball threepeat between 1970 and 1972; Coppin State's NAIA national basketball title in 1976; Texas Southern's NAIA national basketball title in 1977; Florida A&M's NCAA I-AA national football title in 1978; and Virginia Union's NCAA Division II national basketball titles in 1980, 1992, and 2005.[5] However, HBCUs generally struggled to win at a high level after integration because they could not afford to compete on the national stage.[6]

This failure to compete was not for a lack of trying, as HBCUs attempted to compete at the highest levels of sport despite the realities that they were no longer the best show in town. This odyssey to reclaim the golden age through direct competition with white colleges removed the bygone spirit of Black amateur football and basketball from HBCUs—the places that gave it birth. This spirit could not exist in the commercialized sports world, a realm where winning and profit are the only things that ultimately matter; a realm that HBCUs were largely spared from under Jim Crow; a realm where white colleges have dominated since the 1890s.

If there is one place of origin for the HBCU athletic decline, one would be hard pressed to ignore the rarely talked about "brain drain."[7] In the 1970s, white colleges included themselves in the Civil Rights struggle by increasing their recruitment of Black students and faculty. The Black middle class also opted to attend and work at traditionally white colleges over HBCUs in search of the best opportunities in the integrated world.[8] The downstream impact was that HBCUs were left with small enrollments filled with academically unprepared students and faculty shortages.[9] This is a trend that has not significantly reversed to the present day.[10] Talented Black athletes were a part of the brain drain, routinely choosing white colleges instead of HBCUs.[11] As Black middle-class students, talented Black faculty, and blue-chip athletes abandoned HBCUs in aggregate, Black colleges suffered financial deficits that made it impossible for them to invest in competition at the highest levels of football and basketball.[12]

The brain drain was but one issue HBCUs in Virginia and the nation had to confront. The other was the NCAA's divisional reorganization. Just as HBCUs were losing enrollment to white institutions, the NCAA, in 1973, used school size and sports investments to divide its members by classifications of Division I–III.[13] The split deepened five years later when Division I football was itself split between Football Subdivision Schools (FBS I-A) and Football Championship Schools (FCS I-AA). This reorganization ensured that similar-sized, like-minded (more so like-budgeted) schools played one another for national accolades. Yet, it created a caste system where smaller schools suffered financially from the lack of national exposure. By 1980, only twelve HBCUs qualified to become FCS members. Two—Tennessee State University and Florida A&M—ascended to the ranks of FBS at one time, but neither are there today. Not one CIAA or Virginia HBCU became a Division 1 school upon the new NCAA format because they could not afford the rising costs (scholarships, travel, on-campus upgrades, etc.) of Division I sports.[14]

The inclusion of HBCUs in the integrated athletic world propelled their financial issues to the forefront. The Black press, by way of syndicated sports columns titled "Black College Tidbits," "Black College Sports," or just "Tidbits," publicized the financial issues various HBCU leagues faced. The biggest issue was that not one of them offered the same amount of full football scholarships as major white colleges. While the financial issues varied from school-to-school, they often escalated to the league ranks as the upstart MEAC (future home to Norfolk State and Hampton[15]) almost closed its doors after just a few years in Division I basketball and FCS football in the 1980s.[16] Other HBCU leagues were not too far behind, as they could barely afford to compete in Division II play.[17] Some HBCUs even dropped nonrevenue sports to keep football and basketball afloat.[18] The money issue is probably best seen in the shuffled conference affiliation, as HBCUs regularly rotated from one Black conference to the next because of peer schools failing to maintain their Division I or Division II status.[19]

HBCUs suffered even more when the NCAA lost its cartel-like control over television rights and profit-sharing. On June 27, 1984, the US Supreme Court ruled in favor of the Universities of Georgia and Oklahoma to prevent the NCAA from controlling individual schools' television rights.[20] This allowed the Big Ten, SEC, ACC, and other predominantly white leagues to become wealthier as they negotiated their own television contracts based on whatever the free market would bear. HBCUs were devastated and further impoverished by the ruling. Instead of relying solely on the NCAA-controlled television deal, which allotted them at least one nationally televised mid- and postseason game, Black college leagues struggled mightily to convince any television company, including the then upstart ESPN, to bid on any of their games in the 1980s.[21] This led to HBCUs giving their television rights up for free to smaller entities such as Black Entertainment Television.[22]

The exposure problem did not end on-screen. Given that Black athletes were integrated into every major sports league by the 1980s, the Black press began giving as much space to football and basketball outside of HBCUs as they did in them. Many Black colleges quit advertising sports all together. "Major universities promote all their sports, whether the record be 0–10 or 10–0. Few Black colleges adhere by that policy," lamented the *New York Amsterdam* in 1980.[23] Others were just neglectful, as the same outlet criticized the once great CIAA by saying its "teams need to get their act together. Many fail to even send their statistics to league headquarters. That's pathetic."[24] This was a far cry from two decades prior, when the CIAA celebrated their cooperation with the media in 1959 as "its most successful year" to date.[25] HBCUs did not have a single national publication or television outlet solely dedicated to their football and basketball in the 1980s, a time when national exposure set the financial foundation that many major college programs enjoy today.[26]

Virginia HBCUs, which were by this time second-tier athletic institutions, took part in bowl classic capitalism to help revive Black college sports. Events such as the Bicentennial Bowl (beginning in 1975), Gold Bowl (beginning in 1976), and others shared space with existing bowl games, such as the Turkey Day Classic, Fish Bowl Classic, Southern Heritage Bowl Classic, Orange Blossom Classic, and Bayou Classic to help drum up interest in the Black college football product.[27] The financial motives were never mistaken, as a 1993 Gold Bowl program told spectators that one of the main reasons for the games were to provide "additional revenue to the athletic budgets of participating institutions," as well as "to provide additional visibility to these predominantly Black institutions."[28] To sell the games, HBCUs often harkened back to the Jim Crow days, when "classics" were end-of-season celebrations and fellowship for alumni, current students, and HBCU leadership.

But even bowl classic capitalism, which pit the best HBCU football schools against one another in majority Black Virginia cities such as Norfolk and Richmond, regularly faced attendance issues. The reasons for this vary, but one that stands out was the competition disparity created by the NCAA's division setup. Division I schools were able to offer more scholarships than Division II and Division III, which has no athletic scholarships. This created a major talent disparity, as Division I schools ended up being drastically better than non–Division I schools by the 1980s. The Division I MEAC, for example, regularly blew out the Division II CIAA in Gold Bowl contests. The first few matchups were so bad, and attendance lagged so much, that by the early 1980s, CIAA and MEAC champions had opted out of the Gold Bowl to play in the Division I FCS and Division II football playoffs. This left the Gold Bowl with the second-place teams from both leagues, which still resulted in a MEAC domination of the CIAA.[29] Eventually, the Gold Bowl consisted of just CIAA teams, while the MEAC entered into bowl game agreements with the Southwestern Athletic Conference (SWAC), the only other Black Division I league.[30]

HBCUs also struggled to compete on a national level because of academic reforms implemented by the NCAA. In the 1980s, nearly 75 percent of Black football and basketball players either flunked out of school or did not graduate once their eligibility ended.[31] This created a new stigma for Black athletes, one where they were seen as "dumb jocks" instead of real college students. This was a reversal of the days of Jim Crow, when HBCU football and basketball players were lauded for their academic prowess.[32]

Figure 21. Ad for the 1979 Gold Bowl, courtesy of Virginia Union University Archives and Special Collections

The NCAA sought to fix this sudden shift in the perception and realities of the new Black athlete. In 1986, NCAA member schools enacted the then controversial Proposition 48 measure, which placed a minimum high school grade point average (2.0 on a 4.0 scale), course credits, and standardize testing score (700 SAT) for athletes before they were to receive scholarships from Division I schools. Division II and III schools were exempt from this ruling. Many in the Black news media complained that "the most critical blow would be delivered to the Black athlete," said the *Pittsburgh Courier*.[33] That was true, as year after year, Black athletes were the most disqualified by Proposition 48.[34]

While some, such as Civil Rights leader Jesse Jackson, claimed that this was done to create roster spots for lesser white athletes, the reality was much more complex.[35] White colleges were okay because they had, for at least a decade, secured the most academically prepared Division I Black athletes. Some white colleges simply admitted academically ill-prepared Black athletes and provided them with remedial courses to meet the NCAA's new requirements. HBCUs, on the other hand, were further priced out of Division I sports as in the round; they could not afford the luxury of admitting a student-athlete on scholarship and allowing him to only take classes until he became eligible.[36] The NCAA later passed Proposition 42 in 1989. This eliminated ineligible high schoolers from even being offered scholarships that were contingent on them becoming academically eligible after a probationary year.[37] This led to a flourishing of the postgraduate high school and junior college ranks, as other predominantly white institutions gained more access to talented Black players they normally would not have. With academically eligible blue chippers flooding white colleges and academically ineligible talents entering postgraduate and junior colleges, making it easier to later sign scholarships to white colleges once they became eligible, HBCUs threatened to leave the NCAA. Yet, the majority stayed and never sought full Division I status.[38] Moreover, these rules helped jumpstart a newer trend, prevalent from the 1990s forward, of talented Black prep athletes migrating away from majority Black high schools (traditional HBCU pipelines) to secure a better chance at Division I eligibility.[39] Given the commonality of this trend, it is a shame that it has not gotten nearly enough scholarly attention.

The decline of HBCU athletics has also impacted the way Black coaches are viewed. While so much popular and academic attention has been paid to Black coaches not getting a fair shake at basketball and football coaching jobs at white colleges where the rosters are overwhelmingly Black, few have taken notice of the historical decline in prestige of HBCU coaches.[40] We are a long way from the days of Gideon Smith, Henry Hucles, Harry Jefferson, Jake Gaither, Eddie Robinson, Mario Casum, Clarence "Big House"

Gaines, John B. McLendon, and others who commanded national acclaim for their coaching genius and recruiting prowess. The overall declining notoriety of HBCU coaches has come from the Black coaching profession not being the same as it was under Jim Crow. In an age where profits and winning take precedent over mentorship and character development, Black HBCU coaches have not had the athletic material to build sustained excellence on the field and court. Those who have, such as Willie Jeffries (South Carolina State University to Wichita State University), Deion Sanders (Jackson State University to the University of Colorado), and Willie Simmons (Florida A&M to Duke), for example, are and will be lured away with more lucrative opportunities at white colleges.

The decline of Jim Crow–era HBCU football and basketball has also shifted the zeitgeist of the Black college athlete. During segregation, Black college athletes were trained to see their physical excellence as a form of resistance to racial discrimination. Now, however, they are conditioned to see themselves as celebrity entertainment. Many focus so much on sports and neglect the other faculties of racial manhood that was once taught by HBCUs under Jim Crow. This has turned the Black college athlete into, as Billy Hawkins long argued, "a colonized body," where many see their worth to society through the prism of being star athletes when few will ever make that leap beyond college.[41] While Black athletes' graduation rates have increased tenfold since the 1980s, they still lag significantly behind those of white athletes.[42] It is tough to quantify, but one would be hard-pressed to argue that Black college football and basketball players see themselves as their predecessors under Jim Crow did: as future leaders who used athletics to train the mind, body, and soul for the daunting task of uplifting their respective Black communities.

From the 1990s to the present, HBCU football and basketball has had the same troubled existence since the immediate decades after integration. The CIAA has experienced flight, reorganization, and decreased national prestige as Hampton and Norfolk State left the now solidly Division II league in the mid-1990s. The Southern Intercollegiate Athletic Conference suffered the same fate when marquee programs such as Florida A&M bolted for greener pastures in the Division I FCS MEAC and then, more recently, the SWAC. Even with the MEAC and SWAC considered, HBCU basketball and football remains unable to consistently compete on a national level. The more recent booster efforts from the Black celebrity caste as well as more national exposure through lucrative ESPN television contracts has not changed this reality.[43]

The present world of integrated college football and basketball has ensured that the bygone days are indeed gone. HBCUs failed and continue to fail at their attempt to win in the for-profit game as their control of talented Black athletes has dwindled. In the process, HBCU athletic prestige has waned; Black college coaches are no longer household names; and Black athletes are not groomed to primarily see their sports as training grounds for future community leadership. Integration has made HBCUs just like other schools, but only in the unsuccessful ways. I do not doubt that, on an interpersonal level, Black college coaches use athletics to teach racial manhood and community uplift. However, coaches and programs are under more pressure to win now than ever. HBCUs now run basketball and football programs for the same reasons white colleges do: to advertise their colleges, make television money, and bolster undergraduate enrollment.

"A DEGREE FOR FREE"

History was made at Hampton University's Armstrong Stadium in December 2018, but not by the hometown Pirates—formerly the Seasiders. Rather, the overwhelmingly Black Highland Springs High School football team, the Springers, coached by Loren Johnson, traveled seventy miles down Interstate 64 to face off against the mostly white Stone Bridge High School of Loudoun County, an affluent DC-area suburb. The Springers dominant display of power and speed, aided by a roster filled with Division I talent, defeated Stone Bridge for their fourth straight Virginia High School League (VHSL) title. This was only the third football "four-peat" in the post-integration era, allowing Henrico County's "Beast of the East" to join the ranks of recent VHSL football legends and nearly all-Black squads of Phoebus High School Phantoms (2008–2011) and the Hampton High School Crabbers (1995–1998). By the winter of 2022, the Springers would win their fifth state title in eight years.[44] Not to be undone, in March 2022 the basketball Springers, coached by Reggie Tennyson, won their third state basketball title in the new millennium, making them one of only three teams in Virginia to accomplish that feat.[45] The Springers are uniquely positioned to help continue some remnants of the bygone era because they maintained their athletic dominance in basketball and football with a majority Black student base, represented by nearly all-Black rosters headed by Black male coaches.

Highland Springs's football and basketball dominance unveils what appears to be an irreversible reality for the nature of Black amateur football and basketball in the commonwealth and nation. Highland Springs is for all intents and purposes a Black school.[46] Yet, the almost all-Black students, teachers, and administrators sit in a Black enclave within majority white Henrico County. Highland Springs is one of several majority Black high schools across the country (Duncanville High School and Yates High School in Texas, Parkview Magnet School in Arkansas, Booker T. Washington High

School and Miami Northwestern in Florida, etc.) who have kept the bygone days of athletic success under Black leadership alive. Unlike HBCUs, these schools have football and basketball games regularly sold to capacity with a sea of Black faces in the crowd, as well as several alumni playing high-level football and basketball at the collegiate and professional ranks. Yet, despite the incessant boosterism by HBCUs during the same period, not one of them in Virginia or anywhere else has sustained the previous levels of success or Black community investment they had before integration.

Whereas HBCUs have had to compete in an integrated athletic world, there is a case to be made that Black secondary schools have, to a large degree, avoided this. The reason for it lies in the rapid resegregation of public schools in Virginia and the nation after the 1970s. Education scholars have meticulously documented that since the litany of federal school desegregation cases and judicial orders of the 1970s, white parents have and are migrating away from school districts filled with Black and brown children. De facto "resegregation" is so prevalent that public schools are less racially integrated now than in the 1970s.[47] This reality is even more pronounced in Virginia, where Black students rarely attend majority white schools.[48]

Left by this resegregation are majority Black high schools, sometimes in a majority white jurisdiction—such as Henrico County's Highland Springs High School—filled with Black faculty, administration, and athletic coaches. These leaders garner tremendous community support in their grooming Black athletic greatness, as majority Black high schools regularly win state-level basketball and football titles across the country. In Virginia, specifically, this resegregation has allowed the bygone era to live on in the spirit of rivalries such as Norfolk's Maury, Granby, and Booker T. Washington, as well as Portsmouth's I. C. Norcom and Churchland, Petersburg and Hopewell in the Petersburg area, Richmond's "Southside Classic" of George Wythe and Huguenot and Thomas Jefferson and John Marshall, Hampton's Phoebus and Hampton High, Newport News's Warwick and Heritage, Lynchburg's E. C. Glass and Heritage, Roanoke's Patrick Henry and William Fleming, and the Blackbelt battle between Greenville and Brunswick. These high schools routinely square off for bragging rights in the majority Black communities they serve, often with the games being sold out. These schools have also produced legendary, long-tenured Black coaches, such as William "Bill" Lawson of Petersburg High School (1966–1999), Walter Brower of Hampton High School (1982–2015), George Lancaster of Huguenot and Highland Springs (1976–2016), and Frank Threatts Jr. of John Marshall (1962–2010). From these rivalries, where Black coaches instruct Black rosters, numerous state champions in basketball and football have arisen to replace the Black athletic supremacy once held by HBCUs.

Yet, it is even deeper in the grassroots basketball world where the bygone spirit has evolved from success at the national and international levels. HBCUs and high schools in Virginia secured control of the Black athletic world from nonscholastic entities by the 1920s. However, this changed when Virginia, the South, and the nation devolved into chocolate cities and vanilla suburbs in the late twentieth century. Whereas high school athletics had restrictive academic and behavior standards for athletes and coaches, grassroots/AAU basketball became a rugged terrain where elements of the bygone era flourished. Most AAU ball clubs lacked the stable facilities and funding of public high schools. Yet, they were filled with strong Black male athletic leadership who ran mission-based organizations anchored by supportive Black communities.

Like the HBCUs and amateur clubs in the early twentieth century, Virginia AAU explosion began like the organization of high school basketball, with ambitious Black men, inspired by those in the North, looking to give meaning to basketball play in the heavily Black Northern Virginia, Tidewater, Richmond, and Southwestern Virginia. As for Northern and Southwestern Virginia, one should look no further than Preston Kim "P. K." Martin's Potomac Valley AAU club and Delmar Irving's Roanoke Jaguars. Martin was a pioneer in using the YMCA's and local sports organizations to get Black boys from the DC area involved with AAU basketball in the 1970s and early 1980s, a time when the league was predominately white and affluent. It was his organization that platformed the likes of Grant Hill, who first hit the national scene in 1989 as a fifteen-year-old phenom. Irving, a longtime member of the Roanoke City Water Department, did the same in the Southwest city of Roanoke, where he used his Roanoke Jaguars to help pipeline talented Black players into private schools to assure their transition to Division I colleges.[49]

The most notable Black-run AAU organization in Virginia is in the Tidewater. Boo Williams AAU club was founded by Hampton native Marcellus Spencer "Boo" Williams Jr. in 1982. Inspired by Philadelphia grassroots basketball guru Sonny Hill, Williams returned home to Hampton and started an AAU basketball team after a short professional basketball career in France and Ireland to sell insurance.[50] By the 1990s, Boo Williams basketball had an executive board and several AAU teams that competed around the nation and overseas. Boo's success is mostly seen in the construction of his multimillion-dollar facility (the Boo Williams Sportsplex—constructed in 2008), Nike endorsement, and rise of prominent alumni and NBA Hall of Famers such as Alonzo Mourning and Allen Iverson.[51]

Martin's, Irving's, and Boo's successes inspired two rival organizations from Richmond. Frank Threatts and VCU basketball alumnus Kendrick

Warren founded Richmond Metro Gold, and William A. "Tony" Squire created the Squires Running Geeches—now known as just the Squires—by 1988.[52] These organizations, while spread thin throughout the commonwealth, aligned on using basketball to give Black boys access to the best free college education their on-court talents would allow them. More than that, they gave Black men, some of whom were uncredentialed, the opportunity to become legitimate athletic leadership at a time when most high-level Black athletes were coached almost exclusively by white men. Tony Squire often recalled the days when high school coaches (Black and white) hated men like himself, P. K. Martin, Delmar Irving, Frank Threatts, and Boo Williams, as they were seen as predatory interlopers who gave college coaches more direct access to talented Black basketball players.[53] Yet, these men reopened the door of coaching to many Black men who, like Squire, did not have a college degree, akin to the amateur basketball days of old. It was in AAU where Black boys could see men with similar backgrounds lead them in an official manner befitting the respect that athletic coaches generally garnered in Black communities.[54]

Given its impact on American sports, there has been an embarrassingly little amount written about the AAU basketball world.[55] Black communities embraced AAU upon its founding in 1888.[56] In the late twentieth century, however, AAU basketball, like other grassroots basketball movements, such as the And-1 Mixtape Tour, became very popular in impoverished Black urban communities because the NCAA and NBA had become too sanitized in their nationalization and commercialization for profit. This influx of corporate money and national notoriety made the post-integration's biggest Black stars (such as Earvin "Magic" Johnson Jr., Michael Jordan, and Shaquille O'Neal) not only Black icons but American icons. Moreover, Black athletes became a national symbol of the "multicultural" or "colorblind" age, as they were culturally disconnected from Black urban dwellers who gravitated more to the game of basketball than any other. College and professional basketball players would not directly appeal to Black urbanity again until the rise of Allen Iverson in the late 1990s. Thus, it was not uncommon for Black communities who could not afford to attend major Division I basketball or professional games to pack out local playgrounds and high school gymnasiums to watch the less structured, faster paced, and flashy grassroots basketball, as it became what rap and hip-hop was becoming at the same time—an authentic medium of Black cultural expression.[57]

P. K. Martin, Delmar Irving, Boo Williams, Tony Squire, Frank Threatts, and Kendrick Warren unknowingly channeled the spirit of the charter generation of Virginia HBCU coaches by using the media to preach the efficacy of Black-run amateur athletics as a tool for uplift. Boo Williams in particular had a penchant for attracting major Division I talent to his travel teams, and that was not by mistake. It was the design of his academic mission that was in line with early sports boosters, such as Norfolk editor Plummer Young. "I'd be happy if our educational programs got all the publicity" instead of basketball, Williams told the *Journal and Guide* in 1991, as he provided college preparedness courses for all his players.[58] The Squires and Metro offered similar services, as they regularly gained space in local papers to advertise how they kept "idle youth" with athletic talents off of the streets and in the classroom through basketball.[59] "A degree for free is our motto," and it remains Tony Squire's ultimate goal for his players.[60] This insistence on using the press to preach the efficacy of basketball for Black male development was similar to that of Hampton coach Gideon Smith, Charles Williams, and "Piggie" Harrison of the 1920s. The Virginia media is to be given credit too, in that they regularly printed the accomplishments of local teams and players, as well as the free academic and athletic services the organizations provided in urban and remote rural areas where Division I talent was few and far between.[61]

Virginia's AAU circuit, run by Black urban men and filled with Black urban youth, made Black athletic expression a standard-bearer for hardwood excellence in the South and nation. By the 1990s, Boo, Metro, and the Squires were household names in national basketball circles. Virginia's big three sent several players to elite basketball colleges while winning several AAU national titles. They also represented America in world competition, as they regularly switched their organizational logos for USA emblems while competing in Europe and Latin America.[62] Their basketball excellence made some wonder if "Virginia is for lovers?" questioned the *Richmond Times-Dispatch* in 1992. "A more apt slogan," they opined, "might be: Virginia is for college basketball recruiters."[63] Boo, Metro, and the Squires compelled major shoe companies such as Nike, Adidas, and Reebok to sponsor AAU tournaments throughout Virginia, some of which hosted household names such as Jason Kidd, Chris Webber, Kevin Garnett, Ray Allen, Kenny Anderson, and many others.[64] These tournaments helped make Virginia an AAU basketball Mecca where the "who's who of coaches" often traveled in search of the nation's best basketball talent.[65] Tony Squire once remarked that it was not uncommon that he'd receive calls from notable basketball coaches such as Jerry Tarkanian of UNLV, Rick Barnes of Providence College, Billy Tubbs of Oklahoma, and Tubby Smith of the University of Kentucky. "I get calls every day from somebody," Tony Squire once lamented about the stress of facilitating his mission of a degree for free.[66]

The prominence of AAU basketball, however, has come with realities and controversies that assure the bygone days are all but gone. Richmond Metro founder Frank Threatts once admitted that AAU basketball, at the level he coached, "is a corporate venture."[67] As AAU teams locate and consolidate the best amateur basketball talent in the country, unscrupulous coaches often traded player commitments for financial compensation. This is not new. What is new is the corporate side of amateur athletics sinking deep into the realm of grassroots basketball. The issue garnered national attention with the April 2000 FBI arrest of Kansas City AAU baron Myron Piggie.[68] After another high profile arrest involving Florida AAU coach Jonathan Augustine, the NCAA stepped in and restricted contact between colleges and players at early ages, where some AAU coaches became the financial brokers.[69] While this helped push the majority of recruiting to the high school ranks,[70] distrust of AAU remains high given the recent FBI case against Maryland's Curtis Malone and Missouri's Christian Dawkins.[71] Virginia's AAU clubs were caught up in some scandal. Tony Squire faced suspension from AAU in the early 1990s for allegedly hosting unregistered tournaments.[72] Even the beloved Boo Williams faced accusations—albeit unsubstantiated—of selling players Alonzo Mourning and Allen Iverson to Georgetown, Joe Smith to the University of Maryland, and Ronald Curry to the University of North Carolina at Chapel Hill.[73] While Squire long ago insisted that "this [AAU basketball] is definitely not a way to make money," recent scandals prove that for some unscrupulous coaches, AAU basketball is quite lucrative.[74]

AAU's impact in the basketball world has even extended into the realm of football, a development that Virginia's Black communities have been a part of. Around 2008, at the height of its power in basketball, the AAU national organization branched into tackle football, a realm previously dominated by Pop Warner Little Scholars. This Philadelphia-based football nonprofit was founded in 1929 by lawyer Joseph J. Tomlin. It operated as a mostly northeastern youth organization until the mid-twentieth century, when it sprouted into several states with thousands of teams, hundreds of subsidiary leagues, and a national championship game first played in 1947. By the early 2000s, Pop Warner football was youth football in America. That was until AAU partnered with existing youth football leagues across the country who sought other alternatives. Mainly, Pop Warner divides teams by age grouping and player size, whereas AAU leagues divide teams strictly by age. Today, Virginia's AAU football scene is most prominent in its metropolitan regions of Northern Virginia, Roanoke-Lynchburg region, Richmond metro-area, and the Tidewater. Teams organize like AAU basketball, where Black community leaders use youth sports to provide Black boys the lessons of manhood that cannot be learned in a classroom. They also value winning. Teams such as the Virginia Vipers of Richmond, Virginia Wolverines of Roanoke, and Central Virginia Wolfpack of Lynchburg have won AAU national titles since 2018. While these organizations are relatively new, it is safe to say that they will become what youth basketball is in Black communities in Virginia and the nation.[75]

Because of integration and commercialization, gone are the days of amateur football and basketball as exercises of racial uplift. With integration and commercialization, Virginia's Black colleges became like HBCUs in general in losing their central importance as athletic institutions. Virginia also became the site for another national development. Majority-Black high schools and grassroots clubs became the relics of the bygone era where Black institutions maintained both their community relevance and athletic dominance under the leadership of Black men. It is here where Black high school coaches and AAU barons have the same staying power and national recognition of HBCU coaches in years past. Moreover, there is some hope given that secondary school coaches and grassroots leaders help Black boys compete in a world of their own while HBCUs must compete against white colleges for talent and relevancy. Therefore, if the bygone era is to return, AAU basketball and football, as well as high school sports, must take the lead.

Notes

Introduction

1. VIA Heritage Association, "Inaugural Meeting for Virginia Interscholastic Association Story Website," *VIA Story*, September 30, 2017; VIA Heritage Association, "Awards Banquet and Planning Meeting," *VIA Story*, July 1, 2018; and VIA Heritage Association (VIHA) Hall of Fame 2018 Press Release, January 28, 2018.

2. "50 Years Later, Black High School Athletic League's Legacy Endures," *Daily Press*, February 18, 2018, 1–7.

3. "About the Black College Football Hall of Fame," Black College Football Hall of Fame Webpage, undated; and "History of the Prairie View Interscholastic League," Prairie View Interscholastic League Coaches Association Webpage, undated.

4. T. H. Breen, "Horses and Gentlemen: The Cultural Significance of Gambling Among the Gentry of Virginia," *William and Mary Quarterly* 34, no. 2 (April 1977): 239–57; and Aram Goudsouzian, "House of Cards: Leisure, Freedom, Authority, Revolution, and the Diary of Landon Carter," *Journal of Sport History* 49, no. 1 (Spring 2022): 1–19.

5. "Football," *Norfolk Journal and Guide*, November 27, 1926, 14.

6. Pamela Grundy and Susan Shackelford, *Shattering the Glass: The Remarkable History of Women's Basketball* (New York: New Press, 2005); Jennifer H. Landsbury, *A Spectacular Leap: Black Women Athletes in Twentieth-Century America* (Fayetteville: University of Arkansas Press, 2014); and Brad Austin, *Democratic Sports: Men's and Women's College Athletics During the Great Depression* (Fayetteville: University of Arkansas Press, 2015).

7. Ronald L. Heineman, *Harry Byrd of Virginia* (Charlottesville: University of Virginia Press, 1996); J. Douglas Smith, *Managing White Supremacy: Race, Politics, and Citizenship in Jim Crow Virginia* (Chapel Hill: University of North Carolina Press, 2002); Pippa Holloway, *Sexuality, Politics, and Social Control in Virginia, 1920–1945* (Chapel Hill: University of North Carolina Press, 2006); Peter Wallerstein, *Blue Laws and Black Codes: Conflicts, Courts, and Change in Twentieth Century Virginia* (Charlottesville: University of Virginia Press, 2004); Peter Wallerstein, *Race, Sex, and the Freedom to Marry: Loving v. Virginia* (Lawrence: University of Kansas Press, 2014); and Clayton McClure Brooks, *The Uplift Generation: Cooperation Across the Colorline in*

Early Twentieth Century Virginia (Charlottesville: University of Virginia Press, 2017).

8. Raymond Gavins, *Perils and Prospects of Southern Black Leadership: Gordon Blaine Hancock, 1884–1970* (Durham, NC: Duke University Press, 1977); Henry Lewis Suggs, *P. B. Young, Newspaperman: Race, Politics, and Journalism in the New South* (Charlottesville: University of Virginia Press, 1989); Dianne Swann Wright, *Claiming Family and Freedom in the New South* (Charlottesville: University of Virginia Press, 2002); Ann Alexander Field, *Race Man: The Rise and Fall of "Fighting Editor" John Mitchell, Jr.* (Charlottesville: University of Virginia Press, 2002); Gertrude Woodruff Marlowe, *A Right Worthy Grand Mission: Maggie Lena Walker and The Quest for Black Economic Empowerment* (Washington, DC: Howard University Press, 2003); Daniel B. Thorp, *Facing Freedom: An African American Community in Virginia From Reconstruction to Jim Crow* (Charlottesville: University of Virginia Press, 2017); Charlene Butts Ligeon, *Fearless: How a Poor Virginia Seamstress Took on Jim Crow, Beat the Poll Tax and Changed Her City Forever* (Bellevue, NE: Smallwood Charlotte Press, 2018); and Margaret Edds, *We Face the Dawn: Oliver Hill, Spottswood Robinson, and the Legal Team That Dismantled Jim Crow* (Charlottesville: University of Virginia Press, 2018).

9. Jaime Schultz, "Contesting the Master Narrative: The Arthur Ashe Statue and Monument Avenue in Richmond, Virginia," *International Journal of the History of Sport* 28, no. 8–9 (May 2011): 1235–51; Arthur Ashe and Arnold Rampersad, *Days of Grace: A Memoir* (New York: Knopf, 1993); Eric Allen Hall, *Arthur Ashe: Tennis and Justice in the Civil Rights Era* (Baltimore, MD: Johns Hopkins University Press, 2016); and Raymond Arsenault, *Arthur Ashe: A Life* (New York: Simon & Schuster, 2018); Clay Shampe and Thomas R. Garrett, *Baseball in Portsmouth, Virginia* (Charleston, SC: Arcadia Publishing, 2004); Peter Stewart and Thomas R. Garrett, *The Legacy Renewed, Football and Foreman Field: Norfolk Division—Old Dominion University* (Kitty Hawk, NC: Outer Banks Press, 2009); Lou Campanelli and Dave Newsome, *Dare to Dream: How James Madison University Became Coed and Shocked the Basketball World* (Charlottesville: University of Virginia Press, 2015); Peter C. Stewart, *Early Professional Baseball in Hampton Roads, A History, 1884–1928* (Jefferson, NC: McFarland & Company Press, 2010); Peter C. Stewart, *American Sports and the Great War: College, Military and Professional Athletics, 1916–1919* (Jefferson, NC: McFarland & Company Press, 2021); Nancy L. Struna, "The Formalizing of Sport and the Formation of an Elite: The Chesapeake Gentry, 1650–1720s, *Journal of Sports History* 13, no. 3 (Winter 1986): 212–34; Robert H. Gudmestad, "Baseball, the Lost Cause, and the New South in Richmond, Virginia, 1883–1890," *Virginia Magazine of History and Biography* 106, no. 3 (Summer 1998): 267–300; John S. Watterson, "Football at the University of Virginia, 1951–1961: A Perfect Gridiron Storm," *Journal of Sport History* 34, no. 3 (Fall 2007): 375–87; Ronald A. Smith, "The William and Mary Athletic Scandal of 1951: Governance and the Battle for Academic and Athletic Integrity," *Journal of Sport History* 34, no. 3 (Fall 2007): 353–73; and Josh Howard, "A Good Base Ball Club Is a Splendid Advertisement to a Town: Baseball and the New South in Clifton Forge, Virginia," *Virginia Magazine of History and Biography* 124, no. 3 (2016): 186–215.

10. Earl Lewis, *In Their Own Interest: Race, Class and Power in Twentieth-Century Norfolk* (Berkeley: University of California Press, 1991), 90.

11. Patrick B. Miller, "Muscular Assimilation: Sport and the Paradoxes of Racial Reform," in Charles K. Ross, ed., *Race and Sport: The Struggle for Equality On and Off the Field* (Jackson: University Press of Mississippi, 2004), 146–82.

12. Robert Pruter, *The Rise of American High School Sports and the Search for Control, 1880–1930* (Syracuse, NY: Syracuse University Press, 2013); Fuzzy Woodruff, *A History of Southern Football, 1890–1928* (Walter M. Brown Publishing, 1928); Henry "Zipp" Newman, *The Impact of Southern College Football* (Kearney, NE: Morris Publishing Company, 1969); Leo Andrew Doyle, "Causes Won, Not Lost: Football and Southern Culture, 1892–1983" (PhD diss., Emory University, 1998); John Sayle Watterson, *College Football: History, Spectacle, Controversy* (Baltimore, MD: Johns Hopkins University Press, 2000); and Andrew McIlwaine Bell, *The Origins of Southern College Football: How An Ivy League Game Became a Dixie Tradition* (Baton Rouge: Louisiana State University Press, 2020).

13. Miller, "Muscular Assimilation," 146–82.

14. Scott N. Brooks and Dexter Blackman, "African Americans and the History of Sports—New Perspectives," *Journal of African American History* 96, no. 4 (October 2011): 441–47; Amy Bass, "State of the Field: Sports History and the 'Cultural Turn,'" *Journal of American History* 101, no. 1 (June 2014): 148–72; Amari Rose Davis, "New Directions in African American Sports History: A Field of One's Own," *Journal of African American History* 96, no. 1 (Fall 2021): 183–88; Lane Demas, *Integrating the Gridiron: Black Civil Rights and American College Football* (New Brunswick, NJ: Rutgers University, 2010); Charles H. Martin, *Benching Jim Crow: The Rise and Fall of the Color Line in Southern College Sports, 1890–1980* (Chapel Hill: University of North Carolina Press, 2010); Samuel G. Freedman, *Breaking the Line: The Season in Black College Football That Transformed the Sport and Changed the Course of Civil Rights* (New York: Simon & Schuster, 2014); and Donald Spivey, *Racism, Activism, and Integrity in College Football: The Bates Must Play Movement* (Durham, NC: Carolina Academic Publishing, 2021).

15. Edwin Bancroft Henderson, *The Negro in Sports* (Washington, DC: Associated Publishers, 1939); A. S. "Doc" Young, *Negro Firsts in Sports* (Chicago: Johnson Publishing Co., 1963); Ocania Chalk, *Black College Sport* (New York: Dodd, Mead & Company, 1976); Daniel A. Nathan, ed., *Rooting for the Home Team: Sports, Community, and Identity* (Urbana: University of Illinois Press, 2013); Scott Ellsworth, *The Secret Game: A Wartime Story for Courage, Change, and Basketball's Lost Triumph* (New York: Little, Brown and Company, 2015); David K. Wiggins and Ryan Swanson, eds., *Separate Games: African American Sport Behind the Walls of Segregation* (Fayetteville: University of Arkansas Press, 2016); Harry Edwards, *Revolt of the Black Athlete: 50th Anniversary Edition* (Urbana: University of Illinois Press, 2017); Douglas Hartmann, *Race, Culture, and Revolt of the Black Athlete: The 1968 Olympic Protests and Their Aftermath* (Chicago: University of Chicago Press, 2004); Charles K. Ross, ed., *Race and Sport: The Struggle for Equality On and Off the Field* (Jackson: University Press of Mississippi, 2004); Raymond Schmidt, *Shaping College Football: The Transformation of an American Sport, 1919–1930* (Syracuse, NY: Syracuse University Press, 2007), 134–53; Demas, *Integrating the Gridiron*; Thomas Aiello, *Bayou Classic: The Grambling-Southern Football Rivalry* (Baton Rouge: Louisiana State University Press, 2010); Thomas Aiello, *The Kings of Casino Park: Black Baseball in the Lost Season of*

1932 (Tuscaloosa: University of Alabama Press, 2011); and Freedman, *Breaking the Line*; and Damion L. Thomas, *Globetrotting: African American Athletes and Cold War Politics* (Urbana: University of Illinois Press, 2017).

16. Hassan Kwame Jeffries, "Fields of Play: The Mediums through which Black Athletes Engaged in Sports in Jim Crow Georgia," *Journal of Negro History* 86, no. 3 (Summer 2001): 264; Rob Fink, *Football at Historically Black Colleges and Universities in Texas* (College Station: Texas A&M University Press, 2019), 3; Derrick White, *Blood, Sweat, and Tears: Jake Gathers, Florida A&M, and the History of Black College Football* (Chapel Hill: University of North Carolina Press, 2019), 7; Michael Hurd, *Black College Football, 1892–1992: One Hundred Years of History, Education, and Pride* (Virginia Beach, VA: Donning Co., Publishing, 1993); Nelson George, *Elevating the Game: Black Men and Basketball* (New York: Harper Collins Publishing, 1995); Mark Ribowski, *A Complete History of the Negro Leagues, 1884 to 1955* (New York: Birch Lane Press, 1995); Neil Lanctot, *Negro League Baseball: The Rise and Ruin of a Black Institution* (Philadelphia: University of Pennsylvania Press, 2004); and Michael Hurd, *Thursday Night Lights: The Story of Black High School Football in Texas* (Austin: University of Texas Press, 2017).

Chapter 1

1. "Football Friday," *Norfolk Virginia-Pilot*, November 16, 1900, 8. For more on how sports settled Southern debates about traditionalism versus modernism, see Pamela Grundy, *Learning to Win: Sports, Education, and Social Change in Twentieth Century North Carolina* (Chapel Hill: University of North Carolina Press, 2003); and Ted Ownby, *Subduing Satan: Religion, Recreation, and Manhood in the Rural South, 1865–1920* (Chapel Hill: University of North Carolina Press, 2014).

2. "Football To-Day Between Two Colored Teams," *Norfolk Virginian-Pilot*, November 29, 1900, 6.

3. Fred M. Alexander, *Education for the Needs of the Negro in Virginia* (Washington, DC: Southern Education Foundation, 1943), 64–65.

4. W. Fitzhugh Brundage, *Lynching in the New South: Georgia and Virginia, 1800–1930* (Urbana: University of Illinois Press, 1993); "Jim Crow Car," *Richmond Times*, December 27, 1899, 4; Charles E. Wynes, *Race Relations in Virginia* (Lanham, MD: Rowman & Littlefield, 1971), 5; and Alexander, *Education for the Needs of the Negro in Virginia*, 56–80.

5. Plummer B. Young Sr., "The Value of the Press," 13–14, speech in the 1926 CIAA Bulletin, Union Archives.

6. C. Vann Woodward, *Origins of the New South, 1877–1913* (Baton Rouge: Louisiana State University Press, 1951); and Edward L. Ayers, *The Promise of the New South: Life After Reconstruction* (Oxford, UK: Oxford University Press, 1992).

7. The most complete academic histories on the Negro Leagues are Lanctot, *Negro League Baseball*; Roberta J. Newman and Joel Nathan Rosen, *Black Baseball, Black Business: Race Enterprise and the Fate of the Segregated Dollar* (Jackson: University Press of Mississippi, 2015). Histories on Black organizationalism are C. Eric Lincoln and Lawrence H. Mamiya, *The Black Church in the African American Experience* (Durham, NC: Duke University Press, 1990); Evelyn Brooks Higginbotham, *Righteous Discontent: The Women's Movement in the Black Baptist Church, 1880–1920*

(Cambridge, MA: Harvard University Press, 1994); Kevin Gaines, *Uplifting the Race: Black Leadership, Politics, and Culture in the Twentieth Century* (Chapel Hill: University of North Carolina Press, 1996), xiv; Eric Arnson, *Brotherhoods of Color: Black Railroad Workers and the Struggle for Racial Equality* (Cambridge, MA: Harvard University Press); Jacqueline M. Moore, *Booker T. Washington, W. E. B. Du Bois, and the Struggle for Racial Uplift* (Wilmington, DE: Rowman & Littlefield, 2003); Michele Mitchell, *Righteous Propagation: African Americans the Politics of Racial Destiny After Reconstruction* (Chapel Hill: University of North Carolina Press, 2004); and Tamara L. Brown, Gregory S. Parks, and Clarenda M. Phillips, eds., *African American Fraternities and Sororities: The Legacy and the Vision* (Lexington: University of Kentucky Press, 2010).

8. Adam Fairclough, *Teaching Equality: Black Schools in the Age of Jim Crow* (Athens: University of Georgia Press, 2001), 3.

9. Archie G. Richardson, *The Development of Negro Education in Virginia, 1831–1970* (Richmond, VA: Phi Delta Kappa, 1976), ii and 7.

10. William T. Alderson, "The Freedmen's Bureau and Negro Education in Virginia," *North Carolina Historical Review* 29, no. 1 (January 1952): 64–90.

11. James D. Anderson, *The Education of Blacks in the South, 1860–1935* (Chapel Hill, University of North Carolina Press, 1988), 4–32; David Freedman, "African-American Schooling in the South Prior to 1861," *Journal of Negro History* 84, no. 1 (Winter 1999): 1–47; and Kay Ann Taylor, "Mary S. Peake and Charlotte L. Forten: Black Teachers During the Civil War and Reconstruction," *Journal of Negro Education* 74, no. 2 (Spring 2005): 124–37.

12. Richardson, *Development of Negro Education in Virginia,* 7; and Alexander, *Education for the Needs of the Negro in Virginia,* 110.

13. Alexander, *Education for the Needs of the Negro in Virginia,* 110; Howard N. Rabinowitz, "Half a Loaf: The Shift from White to Black Teachers in the Negro Schools of the Urban South, 1865–1890," *Journal of Southern History* 40, no. 4 (November 1974): 565–94; Anderson, *Education of the Blacks in the South,* 96–97; and Lester C. Lamon, "Black Public Education in the South, 1861—1920: By Whom, For Whom and Under Whose Control?" *Journal of Thought* 18, no. 3 (Fall 1983): 84.

14. Ullin Whitney Leavell, *Philanthropy in Negro Education* (Nashville, TN: George Peabody College for Teachers, 1930), 57–147.

15. Robert F. Engs, *Freedom's First Generation: Black Hampton, Virginia, 1861–1890* (New York: Fordham University Press, 1979), 44–65; and William A. Link, *A Hard Country and Lonely Place: Schooling, Society, and Reform in Rural Virginia, 1870–1920* (Chapel Hill: University of North Carolina Press, 2018).

16. Wynes, *Race Relations in Virginia,* 127; and Luther P. Jackson, *A History of the Virginia Teachers Association* (Norfolk, VA: Guide Publishing, 1937).

17. James T. Moore, "Black Militancy in Readjuster Virginia, 1879–1883," *Journal of Southern History* 41, no. 2 (May 1975): 172; and Leigh Alexandra Soares, "A Bold Promise: Black Readjusters and the Founding of Virginia State University" (MA thesis, Duke University, 2010).

18. Lyman Beecher Brooks, *Upward Bound: A History of Norfolk State University* (Washington, DC: Howard University Press, 1983).

19. Wynes, *Race Relations in Virginia,* 4–5.

20. Soares, "A Bold Promise," 1–38; Francis Ashton Thurman, "The History of Saint Paul's College, Lawrenceville, Virginia, 1888–1959" (PhD diss., Howard University, 1979); Adolph H. Grundman, "Northern Baptists and the Founding of Virginia Union University: The Perils of Paternalism," *Journal of Negro History* 63, no. 1 (January 1978): 26–41; and Ralph Reavis, "Virginia Seminary: A Tangible Symbol of Opposition to White Paternalism and Commitment to Self-Reliance" (PhD diss., University of Virginia, 1989).

21. Bruce Alain Brown, "Justice, Patience, Reason: The Writings of Virginius Dabney on Matters of Race" (MA thesis, The College of William and Mary, 1987), 11; Wynes, *Race Relations in Virginia*, 123–34; and Anderson, *Education of Blacks in the South*, 96–97.

22. Anderson, *Education of Blacks in the South, 1865–1935*, 96–180; and Linda B. Pincham, "A League of Willing Workers: The Impact of Northern Philanthropy, Virginia Estelle Randolph and the Jeanes Teachers in Early Twentieth-Century Virginia," *Journal of Negro Education* 74, no. 2 (Spring, 2005): 112–23.

23. James S. Russell, "Rural Economic Progress of the Negro in Virginia," *Journal of Negro History* 11, no. 4 (October 1926): 556–62; Virginia Writer's Project, *The Negro in Virginia* (New York: Hastings House, 1940); and Marshall W. Fishwick, The Negro in Twentieth Century Virginia, *Negro History Bulletin* 12, no. 8 (May 1949): 182–84.

24. J. Douglas Smith, *Managing White Supremacy: Race, Politics, and Citizenship in Jim Crow Virginia* (Chapel Hill: University of North Carolina Press, 2002), 107–29.

25. Dr. J. W. Barco, vice president of Virginia Union University, "The Functioning and Meaning of the Colored Intercollegiate Athletic Association," speech found in the 1937 CIAA Bulletin, 28–30, Union Archives.

26. P. B. Young, "Forward," 1936 CIAA Bulletin, Union Archives; Article II of the Constitution of the Colored Intercollegiate Athletic Association, in Edwin B. Henderson and Garnet C. Wilkinson, eds., *Official Handbook: Interscholastic Athletic Association of Middle Atlantic States* (New York: American Sports Publishing Company, 1912), 115; and Charles H. Williams, director of physical education at Hampton Institute, "A Quarter of A Century in Negro Organized Athletics," speech found in the 1936 CIAA Bulletin, 11–3, Union Archives; and P. B. Young, "Forward," the 1936 CIAA Bulletin, Union Archives.

27. Edwin B. Henderson, head of department of Physical Training in D.C. Public Schools, "The New Deal and College Athletics," speech found in the 1934 CIAA Bulletin, 7–9, Union Archives.

28. "Hampton Incidents," *Southern Workman* 30, no. 1 (January 1901): 779.

29. "Personal Notes," *Southern Workman* 32, no. 12 (December 1903): 603; William A. Aery, "Student Life at Hampton," *Southern Workman* 39, no. 6 (June 1910): 344.

30. Mrs. Charles Bartlett Dyke, "The Beginnings of Citizenship," *Southern Workman* 29, no. 2 (February 1, 1900): 93.

31. "At Home and Field," *Southern Workman* 40, no. 1 (January 1911): 59.

32. "Hampton Incidents," *Southern Workman* 36, no. 1 (January 1907): 53; Charles H. Williams, "Twenty Years' Work of the CIAA," 1–4, essay published in the 1932 CIAA Bulletin, Union Archives; Fisher, ed., *Virginia Union and Some of*

Her Achievements, 67; and "Hampton Strong For Inter-Class Sports," *Norfolk Journal and Guide,* January 17, 1925, 4.

33. "Growth of the Football Classic," *Norfolk Journal and Guide,* December 6, 1924, 12.

34. Senior Class of Virginia Union University, *The Panther: Virginia Union 1928 School Yearbook,* Yearbook Collection, Union Archives, 67.

35. "Football the Most Popular Varsity Sport at State," *Norfolk Journal and Guide,* July 26, 1930, 7.

36. "Football," *Norfolk Journal and Guide,* November 27, 1926, 14.

37. "Entertainment Given to the Poor," *Norfolk Landmark* 36, no. 31 (January 1893): 1.

38. "Suffolk Social," *Norfolk Virginian* 49, no. 107 (March 1895): 3.

39. "Hampton Incidents," *Southern Workman* 30, no. 1 (January 1901): 54–55.

40. "Athletics," *Southern Workman* 41, no. 5 (May 1912): 298.

41. "Athletics," *Southern Workman* 46, no. 2 (February 1917): 120.

42. Thomas L. Puryear, CIAA President, "A Well Balanced Athletic Program," 2–3, speech in the 1927 CIAA Bulletin, Union Archives.

43. "Sez Ches," *Pittsburgh Courier,* March 16, 1940, 16.

44. "Personal Notes," *Southern Workman* 36, no. 12 (December 1907): 699; Jane Porter Barrett, "Social Settlement For Colored People," *Southern Workman* 41, no. 9 (September 1912): 518; "Forty-Nine Years of Hampton Institute," *Norfolk Journal and Guide,* May 12, 1917, 4; "Hampton Strong For Inter-Class Sports," *Norfolk Journal and Guide,* January 17, 1925, 4; and "Athletics At Union," *Norfolk Journal and Guide,* January 21, 1922, 5.

45. "Hampton Incidents," *Southern Workman* 30, no. 1 (January 1901): 55.

46. Grundy and Shackleford, *Shattering the Glass,* 10–11.

47. "Athletic Notes," *Baltimore Afro-American,* February 26, 1910, 4.

48. Frank A. Young, "The World of Sports," *Chicago Defender,* October 26, 1912, 26.

49. "St. Paul Awards Maddux Prize," *Norfolk Journal and Guide,* July 7, 1923, 4.

50. "Gymnasium Exhibition Rendered at Hampton," *Baltimore Afro-American,* April 1, 1916, 2; Grundy and Shackleford, *Shattering the Glass,* 12.

51. "News and View of Women," *Baltimore Afro-American,* November 2, 1907, 6.

52. "Feminine News Notes," *Baltimore Afro-American,* December 21, 1907, 3.

53. "Hampton Incidents," *Southern Workman* 39, no. 12 (December 1910): 701; and "Hampton Incidents," *Southern Workman* 40, no. 11 (November 1911): 659.

54. "New Years Day," *Southern Workman* 44, no. 2 (February 1915): 119; "Growth of the Football Classic," *Norfolk Journal and Guide,* December 6, 1924, 12.

55. R. R. Wright Jr., "Forty Years of Negro Progress," *Southern Workman* 36, no. 3 (March 1907): 159; "Athletics and Entertainments," *Southern Workman* 40, no. 1 (January 1911): 58; "Athletics," *Southern Workman* 41, no. 1 (January 1912): 57.

56. "Athletics," *Southern Workman* 41, no. 5 (May 1912): 298.

57. "Football," *Southern Collegian* 6, no. 1 (April 1874): 2.

58. "Football," *Tazewell Church Valley News,* January 24, 1890, 20.

59. "Morgantown," *Wheeling Sunday Register,* March 22, 180, 2.

60. "Football Season Is Now Open," *Harrisonburg Evening News,* October 4, 1907, 6.

61. "Here Is a New Game," *Norfolk Virginian,* March 4, 1896, 8.

62. Hoke Smith, "The Resources and Development of the South," *North American Review* 159, no. 453 (August 1894): 129–36; and George F. Milton, "Note on the Recent Industrial Crisis at the South," *Sewanee Review* 2, no. 2 (February 1894): 227–38.

63. Patrick B. Miller, "The Manly, the Moral, and the Proficient: College Sport in the New South," *Journal of Sports History* 24, no. 3 (Fall 1997): 285–316; and Bell, *Origins of Southern College Football,* 2.

64. Charles H. Williams, "Twenty Years' Work of the CIAA," 1, essay published in the 1932 CIAA Bulletin, Union Archives; George, *Elevating the Game;* and White, *Blood, Sweat, and Tears,* 26.

65. "Football," *Baltimore Afro-American,* October 17, 1925, 9.

66. Williams, "Twenty Years' Work of the CIAA," 1–4; and C. H. Williams, "John Lyman Whitehead": Tributes to Messers Whitehead, Washington and Burr, speech in the 1958 CIAA Bulletin, Union Archives.

67. Martin, *Benching Jim Crow,* 1–3; Bell, *Origins of Southern College Football,* 1–20; Miller, "The Manly, the Moral, and the Proficient," 285–316; "South Carolina," *Richmond Daily Dispatch,* May 2, 1877, 10; "The Clemson Agricultural College," an ad in *Richmond Daily Dispatch,* May 11, 1877, 14; "Presbyterian College of South Carolina," ad found in the *Richmond Daily Dispatch,* June 7, 1877, 1; Thomas Aiello, *Hoops: A Cultural History of Basketball in America* (New York: Rowman & Littlefield, 2021), 54; Dates of the Beginning of Intercollegiate Competition in the Various Sports at Each Institution, found in Edgar S. Kiracofe, "An Historical Study of Athletics and Physical Education in the Standard Four-Year Colleges in Virginia," *Secondary Education in Virginia: University of Virginia Record* XVI, no. 9 (March 1932): 27 and 30.

68. "Social Events," *Richmond Dispatch,* June 20, 1886, 8.

69. "Editorial Notes and Comments," *Presbyterian of the South,* October 22, 1913, 9; Kiracofe, "Athletics and Physical Education in Virginia," 24–36, quote on 28; David Y. Thomas, "Political Science in Southern Universities," *Sewanee Review* 16, no. 4 (October 1908): 466–71; O. D. Foster, "In Southern Universities," *Christian Education* 8, no. 6 (March 1925): 265–66; Curtis H. Walker, "The Social Sciences in Southern Colleges and Universities," *Social Forces* 7, no. 2 (December 1928): 230–34; Grundy, *Learning to Win,* 16–21; and Luther L. Bernard, "The Teaching of Sociology in Southern Colleges and Universities," *American Journal of Sociology* 23, no. 4 (January 1918): 491–515.

70. Watterson, *College Football,* 40–53; and Bell, *Origins of Southern College Football,* 5.

71. Kiracofe, "An Historical Study," 27 and 30, 31; "Permanent Officials for College Athletics," *Richmond Times-Dispatch,* January 14, 1908, 7; Schmidt, *Shaping College Football,* 8–25; B. M. Ingrassia, "Public Influence Inside the College Walls: Progressive Era Universities, Social Scientists, and Intercollegiate Football Reform," *Journal of Gilded Age and Progressive Era* 10, no. 1 (January 2011): 59–88; and Watterson, *College Football,* 80–120. This VIAA was different from the VIAA that Black Virginians created.

72. One of the first times the phrase "gentlemen's agreement" was used to describe racial segregation in athletics was the 1913 case where the University of Kansas

refused to honor a game contract against the University of Nebraska because Nebraska refused to bench their lone Black player, named Clinton Ross. For more, see "Says Kansas Will Play," *Lincoln Nebraska State Journal*, October 28, 1913, 3. For examples and exceptions to the gentlemen's agreement, see Charles Martin, *Benching Jim Crow*, chapters 1 and 2.

73. "The Colored College Athlete," *Crisis Magazine* 2, no. 3 (July 1911): 115–19; "Social Uplift," *Crisis Magazine* 5, no. 1 (November 1912): 8; "A Counselor," *Crisis Magazine* 10, no. 1 (May 1915): 14; and "Our Graduates," *Crisis Magazine* 12, no. 3 (July 1916): 123; "Men of the Month," *Crisis Magazine* 11, no. 2 (December 1915): 70; "Along the Color Line," *Crisis Magazine* 10, no. 6 (October 1915): 271; "Men of the Month," *Crisis Magazine* 15, no. 5 (March 1918): 229–30; "The Horizon," *Crisis Magazine* 13, no. 2 (December 1916): 92; and "The Horizon," *Crisis Magazine* 13, no. 4 (January 1917): 191; "The Looking Glass," *Crisis Magazine* 13, no. 5 (March 1917): 237 and 249; "The Horizon," in the *Crisis Magazine* 14, no. 6 (October 1917): 315; "The Horizon," *Crisis Magazine* 15, no. 5 (January 1918): 14; "The Horizon," *Crisis Magazine* 16, no. 2 (June 1918): 87; "The Horizon," *Crisis Magazine* 18, no. 3 (July 1919): 150; "The Horizon," *Crisis Magazine* 14, no. 1 (May 1917): 42; David K. Wiggins, *Glory Bound: Black Athletes in White America* (Syracuse, NY: Syracuse University Press, 1997), 223–24; and David K. Wiggins, "With All Deliberate Speed: High School Sports, Race, and *Brown v. Board of Education*," *Journal of Sports History* 37, no. 3 (Fall 2010): 329–46.

74. "Mohawk Indian Conference," *Southern Workman* 25, no. 11 (November 1896): 224.

75. Martin, *Benching Jim Crow*, 1–26; "The Horizon," *Crisis Magazine*, Vo.23, no. 2 (December 1921): 85; "Along the Color Line," *Crisis Magazine* 7, no. 2 (December 1913): 63; "Along the Color Line," *Crisis Magazine* 7, no. 3 (January 1914): 117 and 131; "Along the Color Line," *Crisis Magazine* 7, no. 3 (January 1914): 117 and 131; "Our Future Leaders," *Crisis Magazine* 10, no. 3 (July 1915): 141; and "The Colored College Athlete," *Crisis Magazine* 2, no. 3 (July 1911): 115–19.

76. "Western Indian School Notes," *Southern Workman* 28, no. 10 (October 1899): 395; and "Christmas Day at Hampton Institute," *Southern Workman* 28, no. 12 (December 1899): 478.

77. "Hampton Incidents," *Southern Workman* 32, no. 12 (December 1903): 633; and quote on "Hampton Incidents, November 15-December 15," *Southern Workman* 34, no. 1 (January 1905): 57.

78. "Hampton Incidents, November 15-December 15," *Southern Workman* 33, no. 1 (January 1904): 56.

79. "Personal Notes," *Southern Workman* 32, no. 12 (December 1903): 603.

80. "A Campaign of Education," *Richmond Times-Dispatch*, April 28, 1904, 4.

81. Aiello, *Hoops*, 33–34; and Oriard, *Reading Football*, 160–61 and 229.

82. "A Quiet House," *Staunton Vindicator*, April 4, 1879, 1.

83. Oriard, *Reading Football*, 190.

84. Hurd, *Black College Football*, 12, and 27; and Williams, "Twenty Years' Work of the CIAA," 1–4.

85. Williams, "Twenty Years' Work of the CIAA"; and "Forty-Nine Years of Hampton Institute," *Norfolk Journal and Guide*, May 12, 1917, 4.

86. "St. Paul Awards Maddux Prize," *Norfolk Journal and Guide*, July 7, 1923, 4.

87. John H. Denison, "Hampton's Founder and Ideals," *Southern Workman* 32, no. 2 (March 1903): 168.

88. John S. Watterson, "The Gridiron Crisis of 1905: Was It Really a Crisis," *Journal of Sports History* 27, no. 2 (Summer 2000): 291–98; Watterson, *College Football*, 27; Guy M. Lewis, "Theodore Roosevelt's Role in the 1905 Football Controversy," *Research Quarterly* 40, no. 4 (Winter 1967): 717–24; Roberta J. Park, "From Football to Rugby—and Back: The University of California-Stanford Response to the 'Football Crisis of 1905,'" *Journal of Sports History* 11, no. 3 (Winter 1984): 5–40; Ronald Smith, "Harvard and Columbia and a Reconsideration of the 1905–6 Football Crisis," *Journal of Sports History* 8, no. 3 (Winter 1981): 5–19; John S. Watterson III, "Political Football: Theodore Roosevelt, Woodrow Wilson and the Gridiron Reform Movement," *Presidential Studies Quarterly* 25, no. 3 (Summer 1995): 555–64; Christopher C. Meyers, "Unrelenting War on Football: The Death of Richard Von Gammon and the Attempt to Ban Football in Georgia," *Georgia Historical Quarterly* 93, no. 4 (Winter 2009): 388–407; John S. Watterson, "The Death of Archer Christian: College President and the Reform of College Football," *Journal of Sports History* 22, no. 3 (Summer 1995): 149–67; and James Mennell, "The Service of Football Program of World War I: Its Impact on the Popularity of the Game," *Journal of Sports History* 16, no. 3 (Winter 1989): 248.

89. Williams, "Twenty Years' Work of the CIAA," 1–4.

90. "Barbarism Creates Barbarism," *Southern Workman* 32, no. 9 (September 1903): 403.

91. "Athletic News," *Southern Workman* 45, no. 2 (February 1916): 131.

92. John Brown Watson, "Football in Southern Negro Football," *Voice of the Negro* 4, no. 4 (May 1907): 165–66, and S. H. Archer, "Football in Negro Colleges," *Voice of the Negro* 3, no. 3 (March 1906): 198–205.

93. Quotes from Williams, Secretary of the CIAA, "Twenty Years' Work of the CIAA," 1–5 and 22; and Charles H. Williams, "Goals to Be Achieved in the Next Twenty-five Years," 26–28, The 1937 CIAA Bulletin, Union Archives.

94. Williams, "Twenty Years' Work of the CIAA," 1.

95. Charles H. Williams, director of physical education at Hampton Institute, "A Quarter of a Century in Negro Organized Athletics," 11–13, speech found in the 1936 CIAA Bulletin, Union Archives.

96. Constitution of the Colored Intercollegiate Athletic Association, Article VI—Athletic Contests, Section II (a): Prosetying and Eligibility, in First Annual CIAA Bulletin (1923), Union Archives.

97. Gaines, *Uplifting the Race*, xiv; and Moore, *Booker T. Washington, W. E. B. Du Bois, and the Struggle for Racial Uplift*; and Mitchell, *Righteous Propagation*.

98. Dr. Frank Coleman, Department of Physics and chairman of the Board of Athletic Control of Howard University, "The CIAA," 2, in 1933 CIAA Bulletin, Union Archives.

99. Lawrence, "The Purpose of the CIAA," 13–14.

100. Dr. J. W. Barco, vice president of Virginia Union University, "The Functioning and Meaning of the Colored Intercollegiate Athletic Association," 28–29, in 1937 CIAA Bulletin, Union Archives.

101. Booker T. Washington, "Teamwork: Speech to Students at Tuskegee Institute," October 17, 1915, reprinted in *Southern Workman* 44, no. 15 (December 1915): 651.

102. Williams, "A Quarter of A Century in Negro Organized Athletics," 11–13.

103. Williams, "Twenty Years' Work of the CIAA," 1–4; David K. Wiggins and Chris Elzey, "Creating Order in Black College Sports: The Lasting Legacy of the Colored Intercollegiate Athletic Association," in Wiggins and Swanson, eds., *Separate Games*, 147; Cavil, "Early Athletic Experiences at HBCUs" in Billy Hawkins et al., *The Athletic Experience at Historically Black Colleges and Universities: Past, Present, and Persistence* (New York: Rowman & Littlefield, 2015), 26; P. B. Young, "Forward," 1936 CIAA Bulletin, Union Archives; and quote in Williams, "A Quarter of A Century in Negro Organized Athletics," 11–13.

104. W. A. Rogers, president of the CIAA, "A Review of the 1922 Season in the CIAA," 5, First Annual Bulletin of the CIAA, Union Archives.

105. Constitution of the Colored Intercollegiate Athletic Association, Article III—Membership, found in The First Annual CIAA Bulletin, Union Archives; Dwight Oliver Wendell Holmes, *The Evolution of the Negro College* (New York: Columbia University Press, 1934); Editorial Comment: Eight Years of Rating of Negro Schools and Colleges by the Southern Association: An Evaluation, *Journal of Negro Education* 8, no. 1 (January 1939): 1–8.

106. Williams, "A Quarter of a Century in Negro Organized Athletics," 11–13.

107. Professor Frank Coleman, "Text of Addresses at CIAA 24th Annual Meeting," 7–8, 1935 CIAA Bulletin, Union Archives.

108. Charles H. Williams Hall of Fame Profile, Virginia Sports Hall of Fame Webpage, undated.

109. W. A. Rogers, president of CIAA and Virginia N&I professor, "Review of the Season of 1923 in Athletics," 5–9, 1924 CIAA Bulletin, Union Archives.

110. Stan Becton, "CIAA Championships by School," in "HBCU Football Championship History," NCAA Black College Football Webpage, February 27, 2023.

111. All Time CIAA Men's Basketball Champions, in CIAA Basketball Championships Webpage, undated.

112. List of Affiliated CIAA Press, in 1933 CIAA Bulletin, Union Archives.

113. "A Talk by President to the Hampton Students," *Southern Workman* 24, no. 3 (March 1, 1895): 50.

114. "Work of Expert Athletic Leader," *Norfolk Journal and Guide*, November 18, 1916, 7.

115. "A Great Month," *Norfolk Journal and Guide*, September 11, 1926, 12.

116. Charles H. Williams, "High Standards for Athletics," *Norfolk Journal and Guide*, March 26, 1921, 8.

117. "Athletics," *Southern Workman* 41, no. 3 (March 1912): 189; "Athletics," *Southern Workman* 44, no. 4 (April 1915): 251; "Town Tops," *Norfolk Journal and Guide*, December 16, 1916, 5.

118. "Athletics," *Southern Workman* 45, no. 12 (December 1916): 703.

119. "Athletics," *Southern Workman* 47, no. 1 (January 1918): 41.

120. The CIAA Gives Information to the Public, a summary of the Robert Dean Miller Case of 1924, 6–8, in 1924 CIAA Bulletin, Union Archives.

121. Article VI, Section II-A "Eligibility" for CIAA Competition, in Minutes of the Eighteenth Annual CIAA Meeting, 1929 CIAA Bulletin, Union Archives; and Williams, "Twenty Years' Work of the CIAA," 3. Saint Paul's was exempt from the eligibility rules because it was the only junior college in the conference. Student athletes could play CIAA sports with Saint Paul's and transfer to another CIAA school with full eligibility if they received their diploma. For more, see Williams, "Twenty Years' Work of the CIAA," 3.

122. "Unpublished History of Football and Baseball," *Norfolk Journal and Guide,* February 3, 1923, 8.

123. Benjamin Washington, Secretary Eastern Board of Officials, "The Evolution of Officiating," 37–39, in 1937 CIAA Bulletin, Union Archives.

124. "Scared," *Norfolk Landmark* 6, no. 18 (April 1876): 4.

125. H. A. Taylor, Football Coach at St. Paul's College, "Great Interest in Athletics," 9–10, speech found in the 1926 CIAA Bulletin, Union Archives.

126. "Unpublished History of Football and Baseball," *Norfolk Journal and Guide,* February 3, 1923, 8; and "Athletics and Gymnastics," *Southern Workman* 45, no. 6 (June 1916): 365.

127. "The Great Negro State Fair, Raleigh, NC," *Norfolk Journal and Guide,* October 24 to 28, 1916, 5; "West High Will Play Monarch Tuesday," *Norfolk Journal and Guide,* October 7, 1916, 8; "West High And Monarchs in Tie Game," *Norfolk and Journal and Guide,* October 14, 1916, 8; "Footballitia," *Norfolk Journal and Guide,* September 29, 1923, 7; "Webb to Coach the Virginia Stars," *Norfolk Journal and Guide,* September 29, 1923, 7; and "The Cause of Failure of Local Independent Football Clubs," *Norfolk Journal and Guide,* February 10, 1923, 8.

128. "Peninsular Basketball Association Organized," *Norfolk Journal and Guide,* December 3, 1921, 8; and "Popular Club Has Reunion," *Norfolk Journal and Guide,* August 25, 1923, 3.

129. "Great Revival At Roanoke," *Norfolk Journal and Guide,* October 21, 1916, 1; "Roanoke, VA," *Norfolk Journal and Guide,* November 4, 1916, 4; "Portsmouth," *Norfolk Journal and Guide,* December 9, 1916, 2; "Attucks Athletic Club has Great Opening," *Norfolk Journal and Guide,* September 10, 1921, 8; "Suffolk Sunbeams Playing in Big League Style," *Norfolk Journal and Guide,* September 10, 1921, 8; "Alpha AC of Portsmouth Will Play Adelphia AC of Richmond at Va. Union," *Norfolk Journal and Guide,* October 21, 8; "Prospects Bright for Athletics," *Norfolk Journal and Guide,* October 8, 1921, 8; "West High School Succumbs to YMCA Onslaughts," *Norfolk Journal and Guide,* November 25, 1916, 8; "Lexington vs. Charlottesville," *Lexington Gazette,* November 2, 1904, 9; "From the Press Box," *Norfolk Journal and Guide,* January 10, 1925, 4; and "Newport News Y Quint Makes Inevitable Record," *Norfolk Journal and Guide,* April 4, 1925, 4.

130. "Lynchburg," *Richmond Daily Dispatch,* August 31, 1877, 1; "Football Match," *Norfolk Landmark* 10, no. 12 (April 1878): 1; "Norfolk Local News," *Norfolk Landmark* 41, no. 108 (November 1895): 1; "YMCA Notes," *Roanoke Times,* May 4, 1899, 3; "A.L.I," *Alexandria Gazette,* December 19, 1899, 3; "Local Brevities," *Alexandria Gazette,* March 19, 1900, 3; "Getting Ready for Football Season," *Newport Daily News,* September 2, 1905, 11; and "The Football Season," *Norfolk Virginian,* September 9, 1897, 3.

131. "Harrison High Loses to Settlers AC," *Norfolk Journal and Guide,* April 9, 1921, 8; "Lincoln Plays Roanoke Team," *Norfolk Journal and Guide,* March 4, 1922, 8; "Unpublished History of Football and Baseball," *Norfolk Journal and Guide,* February 3, 1923, 8; "Unpublished History of Football and Baseball," *Norfolk Journal and Guide,* February 10, 1923, 8; and "Harrison Complains," *Norfolk Journal and Guide,* September 27, 1924, 5.

132. Henderson and Wilkinson, *Official Handbook,* 73–88; "Central Athletic Association," *Baltimore African-American,* October 5, 1901, 5.

133. "Athletic Notes," *Baltimore Afro-American,* November 12, 1910, 4.

134. "Basket Ball: Girls' Basketball Teams Take Notice," *Philadelphia Tribune,* November 21, 1914, 7.

135. "YWCA," *Norfolk Journal and Guide,* September 27, 1924, 2; "Scores Between Y Union High, 14–1," *Norfolk Journal and Guide,* March 13, 1926, 4.

136. "Roanoke, Va.," *Norfolk Journal and Guide,* February 19, 1921, 4; "Jno. J. Smallwood School," *Norfolk Journal and Guide,* January 21, 1922, 5; "Union Hi Girls in Post Season Basket Game," *Norfolk Journal and Guide,* May 10, 1924, 5.

137. "Football Has the Right of Way," *Norfolk Journal and Guide,* October 25, 1924, 12.

138. Composite and Characteristics for Urban and Rural Districts of Virginia, 1910 and 1920, US Census for the Commonwealth of Virginia, 25–27; *Education for the Needs of the Negro in Virginia,* 82–85; and Ayers, *Promise of the New South,* 70–80.

139. Alexander, *Education for the Needs of the Negro in Virginia,* 41.

140. "The Cause of failure of Local Independent Football Clubs," *Norfolk Journal and Guide,* February 10, 1923, 8; "Community Center in Active Program," *Norfolk Journal and Guide,* October 20, 1923, 1; and Alexander, *Education for the Needs of the Negro in Virginia,* 39.

141. "Popular Club Has Reunion," *Norfolk Journal and Guide,* August 25, 1923, 3.

142. "City to Have First Class Football Team," *Norfolk Journal and Guide,* August 25, 1923, 7; "Why Not Big League Ball for Norfolk," *Norfolk Journal and Guide,* January 19, 1924, 6; "Norfolk Football Teams Merge," *Norfolk Journal and Guide,* September 29, 1923, 7; "Comment on Local Sports," *Norfolk Journal and Guide,* February 23, 1924, 5; "A Slant Over the Gridiron Season," *Norfolk Journal and Guide,* January 3, 1925, 5; "The Gridiron Outlook," *Norfolk Journal and Guide,* August 1, 1925, 4; "Norfolk Athletic Club Has Prospect of Promising Team," *Norfolk Journal and Guide,* October 2, 1926, 4; and "Recreation of Norfolk," *Norfolk Journal and Guide,* April 23, 1927, 3.

143. "From the Press Box," *Norfolk Journal and Guide,* February 14, 1931, 6; and Anderson, *Education of Blacks in the South,* 186–247.

144. Richardson, *Development of Negro Education in Virginia,* 9–22; and Alexander, *Education for the Needs of the Negro in Virginia,* 158.

145. Henderson and Wilkinson, *Official Handbook,* 17–40; "Twenty-Two to Nothing," *Baltimore Afro-American,* November 30, 1901, 1; and "The Foot Ball Game," *Baltimore Afro-American,* November 29, 1902, 8.

146. Pruter, *Rise of American High School Sports and the Search for Control,* 283–84; Martha H. Verbrugge and Drew Yingling, "The Politics of Play: The Struggle over Racial Segregation and Public Recreation in Washington, DC, 1945–1950," *Washington*

History 27, no. 2 (Fall 2015): 56–69; and David K. Wiggins, "Edwin Bancroft Henderson: Physical Educator, Civil Rights Activist, and Chronicler of African American Athletes," *Research Quarterly for Exercise and Sport* 70, no. 2 (June 1999): 91–112.

147. Pruter, *Rise of American High School Sports and the Search for Control*; Henderson and Wilkinson, *Official Handbook*, quotes found first on page 5, second quote on page 73, 115–25, 150–70, and 173–74; and Tikia K. Hamilton, "The Cost of Integration: The Contentious Career of Garnet C. Wilkinson," *Washington History* 30, no. 1 (Spring 2018): 50–60.

148. "School Activities: Booker T. Washington High School," *Norfolk Journal and Guide*, January 21, 1922, 5.

149. "Interstate High School Meets in Washington," *Norfolk Journal and Guide*, December 12, 1925, 5.

150. "John T. West and Henderson Normal Game A Tie," *Norfolk Journal and Guide*, November 4, 1916, 8; "Christiansburg Institute Defeats Bluefield Institute" November 25, 1916, p.1; "Booker T. Routs IC Norcom in First Test," *Norfolk Journal and Guide*, November 4, 1922, 8; "Dunbar High Eleven Rapidly Developing," *Norfolk Journal and Guide*, September 29, 1923, 7; "Dunbar High Eleven Rapidly Developing," *Norfolk Journal and Guide*, September 29, 1923, 7; "Fighting Bookers Make Unique Football Record," *Norfolk Journal and Guide*, December 25, 1926, 4; and "Open Letter From Principal Thomas," *Norfolk Journal and Guide*, December 12, 1915, 16.

151. "B.T. Claims Unfair Tactics at Washington," *Norfolk Journal and Guide*, November 10, 1923, 4; and "Refutes Booker T.'s Charge of Bias," *Norfolk Journal and Guide*, November 24, 1923, 6.

152. "Anderson Fitting School," advertisement found in *Richmond Daily Dispatch*, May 31, 1877, 8; and "Improvements at Bingham School," *Richmond Daily Dispatch*, September 3, 1877, 10.

153. *The Alleghenian*, 1909 Yearbook for Clifton Forge High School, Library of Virginia, 65–67; Steven G. Meeks and Earl C. Leake, *Highlights of Earlysville High School, 1906–1936* (Meeks Enterprise, Inc., 1987), 64; *The Alecko*, 1928 Yearbook for Alexandria High School, Library of Virginia, p.60; *Recall*, 1917 Yearbook for Augusta Military Academy, library of Virginia, pp.94–113; and *The Arrow*, 1919 Yearbook for Cape Charles High School, Library of Virginia, 43–44.

154. "Football," *Alexandria Gazette*, November 24, 1884, 3; and "First Football," *Richmond Times-Dispatch*, January 14, 1908, 7.

155. "Challenge," *Accomack Peninsula Enterprise*, February 27, 1891, 2.

156. "Episcopal High School," *Alexandria Gazette*, June 23, 1887, 2.

157. Principal William H. Kamble, "Staunton Male Academy: A Preparatory School for Young Boys and Men," paid advertisement in the *Central Presbyterian*, August 12, 1885, 8.

158. "Football," *Washington Post*, November 21, 1886, 2; "A Game of Football," *Washington Post*, November 28, 1882, 2; "Football," *Washington Post*, October 7, 1887, 2; "Alexandria," *Washington Post*, November 13, 1887, 2; "Alexandria," *Washington Post*, November 24, 1887, 4; "Football Games," *Washington Post*, November 26, 1888, 2; "The Jefferson Football Team," *Washington Post*, November 22, 1887, 2; "The Game of Football," *Washington Post*, November 24, 1885, 2; Gunmestad,

"Baseball, the Lost Cause," 267–300; Niels, "Flag-Waving Wahoos," 461–88; and "Basketball," *Alexandria Gazette*, January 11, 1900, 3; and "Tennessee," *Presbyterian of the South*, April 1, 1914, 13.

159. J. A. Mangan, *Athleticism in the Victorian and Edwardian Public School: The Emergence and Consolidation of an Educational Ideology* (New York: Routledge, Taylor, and Francis, 1981); Tony Money, *Manly and Muscular Diversions: Public Schools in the Nineteenth-Century Sporting Revival* (London: Bristol Classic Press, 2001); Axel Bundgaard, *Muscle and Manliness: The Rise of Sport in American Boarding Schools* (Syracuse, NY: Syracuse University Press, 2005) and Pruter, *Rise of American High School Sports and the Search for Control*, 3–101.

160. "The Game of Football," *Washington Post*, November 24, 1885, 2; "A Football League," *Washington Post*, November 27, 1889, 1; and "State Schools Are to Compete Soon," *Richmond Times-Dispatch*, February 4, 1917, 29.

161. Michael Oriard, "Football Town Under Friday Night Lights: High School Football and American Dreams" in Nathan, ed., *Rooting for the Home Team*, 68–79.

162. *Handbook of the Virginia High School Literary and Athletic League, 1921–1923* (Charlottesville: University of Virginia, 1923), 1.

163. "Football," *Baltimore Afro-American*, November 7, 1925, 13.

164. "Booker T. Routs I. C. Norcom in First Test," *Norfolk Journal and Guide*, November 4, 1922, 8; and "Footballitia," *Norfolk Journal and Guide*, September 29, 1923, 7; "About Being Definite," *Norfolk Journal and Guide*, December 12, 1925, 4; "Interstate High School Conference Meets in Richmond," December 10, 1927, 6; "Thyme Is Voted Membership, Union Out," *Norfolk Journal and Guide*, December 15, 1928, 6; and "High School Conference Accepts Three New Members at Richmond Sessions; Thyme Gets Trophy," *Norfolk Journal and Guide*, December 21, 1929, 6. The nine Virginia members of the ISHAA were Petersburg's Peabody High School, Portsmouth's I. C. Norcom, Manassas Industrial Institute, Suffolk's Nansemond Institute, Richmond's Armstrong High School, Hampton's Union High School, Williamsburg High School, Norfolk's St. Joseph's School and Booker T., and Chase City's Thyme Institute.

165. "Turns Out Winners," *Norfolk Journal and Guide*, December 12, 1925, 5; "Fighting Bookers Make Unique Football Record," *Norfolk Journal and Guide*, December 25, 1926, 4; "Businessmen Banquet High School Eleven," *Norfolk Journal and Guide*, December 26, 1925, 2; "The High School Association," *Norfolk Journal and Guide*, August 22, 1925, 5; "Washington High School Team," *Norfolk Journal and Guide*, December 5, 1925, 14; "Interstate High School Meets in Washington," *Norfolk Journal and Guide*, December 12, 1925, 5; "Brilliant Rise of the Fighting Bookers Most Outstanding Feature," *Norfolk Journal and Guide*, December 12, 1925, 8; "School Notes," *Norfolk Journal and Guide*, October 7, 1922, 4; "Thyme Is Voted Membership, Union Out," *Norfolk Journal and Guide*, December 15, 1928, 4; and "New Principal of Booker T Pledges to Endeavor to Keep High Standard," *Norfolk Journal and Guide*, July 2, 1922, 1.

166. C. W. Reynold, principal of Booker T. Washington High School in Norfolk, Virginia to *Crisis Magazine*, December 8, 1926, W. E. B. Du Bois Papers (MS 312). Special Collections and University Archives, University of Massachusetts Amherst Libraries; and "The High School Association," *Norfolk Journal and Guide*, August 22,

1925, 5; and "When the South's Finest High School Football Team was Feted," *Norfolk Journal and Guide*, December 26, 1931, 9.

167. Henderson and Wilkinson, eds., *Official Handbook*, 13.

168. "The Virginia High School Football Championship," *Norfolk Journal and Guide*, December 24, 1927, 7; "Fourth Annual Virginia State Interscholastic Meet to be in Virginia State College Gym," *Norfolk Journal and Guide*, February 14, 1931, 6; "VA High Schools Form Association," *Norfolk Journal and Guide*, March 16, 1929, 3; and "VA Scholastic Conference to Get Under Way," *Norfolk Journal and Guide*, September 21, 1929, 9. The VIAA's founding members were Lynchburg's Dunbar High School, Norfolk's and Staunton's Booker T. Washington High School, Roanoke's Addison High School, Richmond's Armstrong High School, Harrisonburg's Effinger High School, Newport News's Huntington High School, Williamsburg's James City County Training School, Petersburg's Peabody High School, and Hampton's Union High School (later named George P. Phenix).

169. Arthur P. Davis, "Reports of the Vice Presidents," 9–10, report in the 1936 CIAA Bulletin, Union Archives.

170. "Western Division VA. State Asso'N Meets in Danville," *Norfolk Journal and Guide*, December 22, 1934, 14.

171. "Virginia High Schools Organize Own State Athletic Association," *Baltimore Afro-American*, March 18, 1933, 17.

172. Arthur P. Davis, "Reports of the Vice Presidents," 9–10.

173. "Panthers to Play Ky State Here Feb.3," *Norfolk Journal and Guide*, January 24, 1942, 21.

174. Sixty Attend CIAA Coaches-Officials Conference at Hampton, 4, 1933 CIAA Bulletin, Union Archives; The Hampton Institute Coaching School and List of Persons Present at CIAA Football Rules Interpretation Meeting Held at Hampton Institute, September 8, 1934, 13, 1935 CIAA Bulletin, Union Archives; "First Coaching School Meets With Success," *Norfolk Journal and Guide*, September 15, 1934, 14; and George Singleton, Report of the Second Annual Basketball Coaches, Officials, and Captains Conference Meet," 1937 CIAA Bulletin, Union Archives. High school coaches in attendance at coaching clinics were J. Q. Adams of Armstrong High School in Washington, DC, E. R. Archer of Booker T. Washington in Norfolk, R. D. Armstrong of Rocky Mount High School in North Carolina, H. A. Black of E. E. Smith High School in Fayetteville, North Carolina, E. D. Burnett of Tarboro High School in Tarboro North Carolina, Adbella J. Campbell of Mt. Garland Training School in Mt. Garland, Virginia, G. W. Clarke of George P. Phenix High School in Hampton, A. S. Gaither of Henderson Institute of Henderson, North Carolina, H. R. Harris of Charlotte Training School of Charlotte Courthouse, Virginia, R. L. Harris of Simmons High School in Oak Hill, West Virginia, C. M. Hill of Phenix High School in Hampton, J. L. Hunter of Armstrong High in Washington, DC, R. O. Karnagy of Wilson High School in Wilson North Carolina, C. C. Lewis of Downingtown Industrial School of Fort Valley, Georgia, J. O. Robinson of Covey Institute of Williamsburg Virginia, J. C. Tonsler of Genoa High School in Bluefield, West Virginia, W. G. White of St. Joseph High School in Norfolk, F. A. Williams of Henderson Institute in Henderson, North Carolina, R. A. Brooks of South Carolina A&M College of Aiken, South Carolina, Porter James of

A&M Institute in Normal Alabama, and H. D. Martin of Miner Teachers' College in Washington, DC.

175. Lawrence, "The Purpose of the CIAA," 13–14; Gideon E. Smith, assistant director of Athletics at Hampton Institute, "What the Coach Can Do To Develop Clean Sport," 7–11, First Annual Bulletin of the CIAA, Union Archives; Benjamin Washington, secretary of the Eastern Board of Officials, "The Evolution of Officiating," 37–39; and E. B. Henderson, president of the Affiliated Board of Officials, "Joint Report of the Approved Boards of Officials," 10 and 52, speeches and reports in the 1937 CIAA Bulletin, Union Archives.

176. Dean H. R. Jefferson of Virginia State College, "The American Coaches Association," 31, 1938 CIAA Bulletin, Union Archives.

177. Thomas C. Jervay, "CIAA Fourth Annual Conference of Football Coaches, Officials and Captains," 1936 CIAA Bulletin, Union Archives.

Chapter 2

1. "Community Center in Active program, *Norfolk Journal and Guide*, October 20, 1923, 1; and "Norcom Rests Hopes on Good Lines," *Norfolk Journal and Guide*, September 12, 1925, 4.

2. "Keep the Sport Clean and Manly," *Norfolk Journal and Guide*, November 4, 1922, 8.

3. I refer to the decade between the outbreak of World War I and the onset of the Great Depression as the World War I era.

4. Oriard, *Reading Football*, 56–133; Michael Oriard, *King Football: Sport and Spectacle in the Golden Age of Radio and Newsreels, Movies, and Magazines, the Weeklies and the Daily Press* (Chapel Hill: University of North Carolina Press, 2001), 24–39; and Schmidt, *Shaping College Football.*

5. White, *Blood, Sweat, and Tears*, 29.

6. "The Colored College Athlete," *Crisis Magazine* 2, no. 3 (July 1911): 115–19; William G. Jordan, *Black Newspapers & America's War For Democracy, 1914–1920* (Chapel Hill: University of North Carolina Press, 2001); and D'Weston Haywood, *Let Us Make Men: The Twentieth Century Black Press and a Manly Vision for Racial Advancement* (Chapel Hill: University of North Carolina Press, 2017).

7. Henry Louis Gates Jr., "The Trope of a New Negro and the Reconstruction of the Image of the Black," *Representation*, no. 24 (Autumn 1988): 131–38.

8. Alain Locke, eds., *The New Negro: An Interpretation* (New York: Albert and Charles Boni, Inc., 1925): 3–16.

9. Gregory Holmes Singleton, "Birth, Rebirth, and the "New Negro" of the 1920s," *Phylon* 43, no. 1 (1st Qtr., 1982), 30–31; Chad L. Williams, "Vanguards of the New Negro: African American Veterans and Post-World War I Racial Militancy," *Journal of African American History* 92, no. 3 (Summer 2007), 348; Cornelius L. Bynum, "The New Negro and Social Democracy during the Harlem Renaissance, 1917–37," *Journal of the Gilded Age and Progressive Era* 10, no. 1 (January 2011): 92–93; Jonathan S. Coit, "'Our Changed Attitude': Armed Defense and the New Negro in the 1919 Chicago Race Riot," *Journal of the Gilded Age and Progressive Era* 11, no. 2 (April 2012): 225–27.

10. "Editorial," *Crisis Magazine* 13, no. 3 (January 1917): 111.

11. Nathan Cardon, "The South's "New Negroes" and African American Visions of Progress at the Atlanta and Nashville International Expositions, 1895–1897," *Journal of Southern History* 80, no. 2 (May 2014): 287–93; Andrew J. Rosa, "New Negroes on Campus: St. Clair Drake and the Culture of Education, Reform, and Rebellion at Hampton Institute," *History of Education Quarterly* 53, no. 3 (August 2013): 206; and Gabriel A. Briggs, *The New Negro in the Old South* (New Brunswick, NJ: Rutgers University Press, 2015), 1–8.

12. Tuire Valkeakari, "New Negro Men, World War I, and African American Masculinity in Guy Johnson's "Standing at the Scratch Line," *MELUS* 39, no. 4 (Winter 2014): 51.

13. Suggs, *P. B. Young, Newspaperman*, 25–35.

14. Suggs, *P. B. Young, Newspaperman*, 37; and Field, *Race Man*, 188–89.

15. "Football Has the Right of Way," *Norfolk Journal and Guide*, October 25, 1924, 12.

16. "Physical Education," *Massachusetts Teacher* 3, no. 11 (November 1850): 342–48; Bell, *Origins of Southern College Football*, 37–38; Aiello, *Hoops*, 2–10, 33–48; Luther Hasley Gulick, "Team Games and Civic Loyalty," *School Review* 14, no. 9 (November 1906): 676–78; Luther Hasley Gulick, "Organized Play," *Journal of Education* 71, no. 14 (April 1910): 370–71; and Oliver S. Jones, "Morality in College Athletics," *North American Review* 160, no. 462 (May 1895): 638–40.

17. D. C. Barrow, "Honor Thy Father and Thy Mother," a speech given to Hampton Institute Students, recorded in the *Southern Workman* 36, no. 5 (May 1907): 303.

18. "Football Has the Right of Way," *Norfolk Journal and Guide*, October 25, 1924, 12.

19. Martin Summers, *Manliness and Its Discontents: The Black Middle Class and the Transformation of Masculinity, 1900–1930* (Chapel Hill: University of North Carolina Press, 2004); Marlon B. Ross, *Manning the Race: Reforming Black Men in the Jim Crow Era* (New York: New York University Press, 2004).

20. Field, *Race Man*, 33; Briggs, *The New Negro in the Old South*, 35–52; Henry Lewis Suggs, ed., *The Black Press in the South, 1865–1979* (Westport CT: Greenwood Press, 1983), viii–ix and 15; Emma Lou Thornbrough, "American Negro Newspapers, 1880–1914," *Business History Review* 40, no. 4 (Winter, 1966): 467–90.

21. White, *Blood, Sweat, and Tears*, 27–28; Haywood, *Let Us Make Men*, 3; Frankie Hutton, *The Early Black Press in America, 1827–1860* (Westport, CT: Greenwood Press, 1993); Patrick Rael, *Black Identity & Black Protest in the Antebellum North* (Chapel Hill: University of North Carolina Press, 2002); and Van Gosse, *The First Reconstruction: Black Politics in America from Revolution to Civil War* (Chapel Hill: University of North Carolina Press, 2021). The first Black news article involving Black sports was published by the *Baltimore Afro-American* in September 1895. This conclusion was drawn through numerous keyword searches of the Black newspaper database from the Library of Virginia.

22. "The Football Craze," *Chicago Defender*, January 22, 1910, 1.

23. "We Live to Learn," *Chicago Defender*, November 12, 1921, 10.

24. "Basket Ball Injures Women," *Chicago Defender*, November 4, 1911, 2.

25. "Fiddling While Rome Burns," *Baltimore Afro-American*, December 22, 1922, 16.

26. "The Football Games," *Pittsburgh Courier*, December 4, 1926, 16.

27. Gideon E. Smith, assistant physical director of Hampton Institute, "Football as a Character Builder," 15–16, 1924 CIAA Bulletin, Union Archives.

28. "The Football Craze," *Chicago Defender*, January 22, 1910, 1.

29. "Sportboard Reflections," *Norfolk Journal and Guide*, January 5, 1924, 7, reprinted August 9, 1924, 4; and "Sportboard Reflections," *Norfolk Journal and Guide*, March 8, 1924, 4.

30. US World War II Draft Registration Cards, 1942, National Archives at St. Louis; St. Louis, Missouri; Record Group Title: Records of the Selective Service System; Record Group Number: 147; and "Hampton Incidents," *Southern Workman* 39, no. 11 (November 1910): 639.

31. Gideon Edward Smith Hall of Fame Profile, Hampton Athletic Hall of Fame Webpage, 2009; and Franklin Hughes and David Pilgrim, "Gideon E. Smith," biographical profile, Jim Crow Museum of Racist Memorabilia Webpage, Ferris State University, September 2016.

32. "Shaw Forfeits to Hampton," *Richmond Planet*, November 18, 1922, 11.

33. "Hampton Incidents," *Southern Workman* 39, no. 12 (December 1910): 701; "Hampton Incidents," *Southern Workman* 40, no. 12 (December 1911): 726; "Hampton Incidents," *Southern Workman* 41, no. 12 (December 1912): 720; "Athletics," *Southern Workman* 43, no. 12 (December 1914): 706; "Athletic News," *Southern Workman* 44, no. 12 (December 1915): 695; and "Athletic News," *Southern Workman* 45, no. 2 (February 1916): 132.

34. "Gideon Smith of Hampton Institute Criticizes Prevalent Forfeiture of Games," *Richmond Planet*, December 2, 1922, 1 and 8.

35. "Hampton Downs Petersburg," *Richmond Planet*, November 24, 1917, 3.

36. "Hampton Beats Shaw," *Richmond Planet*, February 16, 1918, 8.

37. "Hampton Defeats Howard," *Richmond Planet*, February 23, 1918, 9.

38. "Gideon Smith of Hampton Institute Criticizes Prevalent Forfeiture of Games," *Richmond Planet*, December 2, 1922, 1 and 8.

39. "Howard Defeats Hampton," *Richmond Planet*, November 27, 1920, 5.

40. "Hampton Forfeits Game to The Union Eleven," *Richmond Planet*, December 4, 1920, 2

41. Jesse Coope, "Gymnastic Games," *Southern Workman* 33, no. 2 (February 1904): 81–86; "Athletics," *Southern Workman* 41, no. 5 (May 1912): 298; and "Open Air Schools," *Southern Workman* 40, no. 4 (April 1911): 200.

42. "Athletics and Gymnastics," Southern Workman 45, no. 6 (June 1916): 365; Charles H. Williams, "High Standards for Athletics," *Norfolk Journal and Guide*, March 26, 1921, 8; and "Hampton Quint Begins Grind," *Norfolk Journal and Guide*, December 13, 1924, 3.

43. "Importance of Athletics," *Southern Workman* 44, no. 5 (May 1915): 302; and "Championship Track and Field Will Bring Great Aggregation," *Richmond Planet*, April 1, 1922, 3; "Hampton's Foot Ball Outlook This Time the Brightest in Years," *Norfolk Journal and Guide*, September 27, 1924, 4; and Charles H. Williams, "High Standards for Athletics," *Norfolk Journal and Guide*, March 26, 1921, 8.

44. "Hampton's Foot Ball Outlook This Time the Brightest in Years," *Norfolk Journal and Guide*, September 27, 1924, 4.

45. Aiello, *Hoops*, 24.

46. Oriard, *Reading Football*, 189–276.

47. "St. Paul Closes Brilliant Season," *Richmond Planet*, December 18, 1920, 2; and "Hampton Defeats St. Paul," *Richmond Planet*, October 15, 1921, 3.

48. Presentation of Founder C. R. Frazier of Saint Paul's College, 45, 1956 CIAA Bulletin, Union Archives.

49. "Football Notes," *Richmond Planet*, October 14, 1922, 9.

50. "Seminary Swamps Biddle," *Richmond Planet*, November 25, 1922, 8.

51. "Union Defeats Hampton," *Richmond Planet*, November 17, 1917, 8

52. "An All-Star Colored Eleven," *Richmond Planet*, December 29, 1917, 11.

53. W. A. Rogers, President of CIAA, "Loyalty," 9, 1926 CIAA Bulletin, Union Archives.

54. "Football Has the Right of Way," *Norfolk Journal and Guide*, October 25, 1924, 12.

55. Plummer B. Young Sr., "The Value of the Press," 13–14.

56. "Sportboard Reflections," *Norfolk Journal and Guide*, January 12, 1924, 6; "Sportboard Reflections," *Norfolk Journal and Guide*, March 8, 1924, 4; "Sportboard Reflections," *Norfolk Journal and Guide*, March 22, 1924, 4; "Sportboard Reflections," *Norfolk Journal and Guide*, April 5, 1924, 4; "Sportboard Reflections," *Norfolk Journal and Guide*, January 25, 10, 1925, 4; "Sportboard Reflections," *Norfolk Journal and Guide*, February 21, 1925, 4; "Sportboard Reflections," *Norfolk Journal and Guide*, September 12, 1925, 4; "Sports Reflections," *Norfolk Journal and Guide*, July 18, 1925, 4; and Plummer B. Young Sr., "The Value of the Press," 13–14.

57. "Sportboard Reflections," *Norfolk Journal and Guide*, January 5, 1924, 7, reprinted in the August 9, 1924, 4.

58. "Football Has the Right of Way," *Norfolk Journal and Guide*, October 25, 1924, 12.

59. Death Certificate for James M. Harrison, January 8, 1940, Virginia Department of Health, Virginia Death Records, 1912–2014, Richmond Virginia, found in ancestry (website) Virginia Death Records; 1880 US Federal Census, Census Place: Norfolk, Virginia, Roll 1381, Family History Film 1255381, Page 290A, Enumeration District 68, ancestry (website) ; Norfolk City Directory, 1895, p.207, US City Directories, 1822–1995, ancestry (website) ; "The Sons of Freemen," *Norfolk Virginian*, October 10, 1896, 2; James M. Harrison Registration Card, Norfolk (Independent City), Virginia, Roll 1984907, Draft Board 2, World War I Draft Registration Cards, 1917–1918, ancestry (website).

60. "A Game of Baseball," *Norfolk Virginian*, June 4, 1899, 3; and Wallerstein, *Blue Laws and Black Codes*, 65.

61. "Unpublished History of Football and Baseball," *Norfolk Journal and Guide*, April 14, 1923, 8; "Unpublished History of Football and Baseball," *Norfolk Journal and Guide*, April 7,1923, 10; "Unpublished History of Football and Baseball," *Norfolk Journal and Guide*, February 10, 1923, 8; and "Unpublished History of Football and Baseball," *Norfolk Journal and Guide*, April 28, 1923, 10.

62. 1910 US Federal Census, Norfolk Ward 2, Norfolk (Independent City), Virginia, ancestry (website); 1920 US Federal Census, Norfolk Monroe Ward, Norfolk (Independent City), Virginia, Roll T625_1903, Page 26B, Enumeration District 120, ancestry (website); and 1930 US Federal Census, Norfolk, Norfolk (Independent

City), Virginia, Roll 2471, Page 5A, Enumeration District 75, Image 607.0, ancestry (website). For records of local divorces, see the "Legal Notices in the Circuit Court of Norfolk" section of the *Journal and Guide* between 1910 and 1930.

63. "Unpublished History of Football and Baseball," *Norfolk Journal and Guide*, March 10, 1923, 10.

64. "Unwritten History of Local Athletics," *Norfolk Journal and Guide*, February 12, 1923, 1.

65. Henry Lewis Suggs, "P. B. Young of The *Norfolk Journal and Guide*: A Booker T. Washington Militant, 1904–1928," *Journal of Negro History* 64, no. 4 (Autumn, 1979): 365–76; and H. Lewis Suggs, "Black Strategy and Ideology in the Segregation Era: P. B. Young and the *Norfolk Journal and Guide*, 1910–1954," *Virginia Magazine of History and Biography* 91, no. 2 (April 1983), 161–90.

66. "Old Norfolkian Wishes to Refresh Mr. J.M. Harrison's Memory," *Norfolk Journal and Guide*, March 3, 1923, 8.

67. "Unpublished History of Football and Baseball," *Norfolk Journal and Guide*, February 3, 1923, 8.

68. "Unpublished History of Football and Baseball," *Norfolk Journal and Guide*, February 24, 1923, 8; Death Record for Samuel Henry Harrison, Virginia Deaths and Burials Index, 1853–1917, FHL Film Number 2048590, ancestry (website); Death Record for Louisa Harrison, Virginia Deaths and Burial Index, FHL Film Number 32984, ancestry (website); and "Unpublished History of Football and Baseball," *Norfolk Journal and Guide*, March 31, 1923, 10.

69. "Unpublished History of Football and Baseball," *Norfolk Journal and Guide*, February 10, 1923, 8; "Unpublished History of Football and Baseball," *Norfolk Journal and Guide*, February 24, 1923, 8; "Unpublished History of Football and Baseball," *Norfolk Journal and Guide*, March 3, 1923, 8; and Engs, *Freedom's First Generation*, 13, 165–66.

70. "The Public Pulse: The Only Efficient Formula," *Norfolk Journal and Guide*, August 4, 1923, 8.

71. "Unpublished History of Football and Baseball," *Norfolk Journal and Guide*, March 3, 1923, 8.

72. "Unpublished History of Football and Baseball," *Norfolk Journal and Guide*, February 24, 1923, 8; "Old Norfolkian Wishes to Refresh Mr. J.M. Harrison's Memory," *Norfolk Journal and Guide*, March 3, 1923, 8; and "Unpublished History of Football and Baseball," *Norfolk Journal and Guide*, February 10, 1923, 8.

73. "Unpublished History of Football and Baseball," *Norfolk Journal and Guide*, February 24, 1923, 8.

74. "Unpublished History of Football and Baseball," *Norfolk Journal and Guide*, February 17, 1923, 8.

75. "The Public Pulse: The Only Efficient Formula," *Norfolk Journal and Guide*, August 4, 1923, 8.

76. "Unpublished History of Football and Baseball," *Norfolk Journal and Guide*, February 17, 1923, 8.

77. "Unpublished History of Football and Baseball," *Norfolk Journal and Guide*, March 31, 1923, 10.

78. "Unpublished History of Football and Baseball," *Norfolk Journal and Guide*, February 3, 1923, 8.

79. "Unpublished History of Football and Baseball," *Norfolk Journal and Guide*, April 21, 1923, 10.

80. "Unpublished History of Football and Baseball," *Norfolk Journal and Guide*, February 17, 1923, 8.

81. "Football Has the Right of Way," *Norfolk Journal and Guide*, October 25, 1924, 12.

82. "Negro and the Press," *Norfolk Journal and Guide*, October 23, 1926, 14.

83. Charlotte G. O'Kelly, "Black Newspapers and the Black Protest Movement: Their Historical Relationship, 1827–1945," *Phylon* 43, no. 1 (1st Qtr., 1982): 7 and 14; and E. Franklin Frazier, *Black Bourgeoisie* (New York: Free Press, 1957), chapter 8.

84. "Gentlemen and Football," *Chicago Defender*, November 21, 1925, A10; and "The Football Classic," *Pittsburgh Courier*, December 5, 1925, 16.

85. White, *Blood, Sweat, and Tears*, 28; Oriard, *King Football*, 38; William I (Bill) Gibson, sports editor of the *Baltimore Afro-American*, "Intercollegiate Athletics and the Public Press, An Analysis," 5–6, speech in the 1933 CIAA Bulletin, Union Archives; Plummer B. Young Sr., "The Value of the Press," 13–14.

86. Thomas L. Puryear, CIAA President, "The Influence of the Press," 4–5, speech found in the 1927 CIAA Bulletin, Union Archives.

87. Richard N. Dixon, captain-elect, Virginia State College 1937 Football Team, "What Athletic Competition Has Meant to Me," 1937 CIAA Bulletin, Union Archives.

88. Theodore H. Smith, football coach at St. Paul Normal and Industrial School, "Ethics in Coaching," p.16, the 1936 CIAA Bulletin, Union Archives.

89. W. M. Whitehead, head of the Department of Physical Education at St. Paul's Normal School, "Coordination of Athletics," the 1934 CIAA Bulletin, Union Archives.

90. Gideon E. Smith, assistant director of athletics at Hampton Institute, "What the Coach Can Do to Develop Clean Sport," 7–11, First Annual Bulletin of the CIAA, Union Archives.

91. P. B. Young, editor of the *Norfolk Journal and Guide*, "Forward," 1936 CIAA Bulletin, Union Archives.

92. Alain Locke, "Enter the New Negro," *Survey Graphic* 3 (March 1925): 631–34.

93. Campbell C. Johnson, YMCA Board of Athletic Control, "Observations," 3, 1933 CIAA Bulletin, Union Archives.

94. Quote in Professor George G. Singleton of Virginia State College, "President's Address" May 15, 1943, CIAA 1943 Bulletin, Union Archives.

95. Otis E. Troupe, quarterback at Morgan State College, "The Athlete in Competition," 1935 CIAA Bulletin, Union Archives.

96. Theodore H. Smith, football coach at St. Paul Normal and Industrial School, "Ethics in Coaching," 16, 1936 CIAA Bulletin, Union Archives.

97. Dr. John W. Barco, vice president of Virginia Union University, "The Functioning and Meaning of the Colored Intercollegiate Athletic Association," 28–29, 1937 CIAA Bulletin, Union Archives.

98. Charles H. Williams, "Twenty Years' Work of the CIAA," 1, 1932 CIAA Bulletin, Union Archives.

99. Smith, "What the Coach Can Do to Develop Clean Sport," 7–11.

100. Winston Douglass, director of Athletics at St. Paul's College, "The Advantage of Athletics to Athletes," 8–10, 1925 CIAA Bulletin, Union Archives.

101. "Va. State High School Stars Feted," *Norfolk Journal and Guide,* April 9, 1938, 17.

102. Professor Arthur P. Chippey of St Augustine College, "What Should Physical Education and Athletic Department Contribute to the Education of College Youth," 1937 CIAA Bulletin, Union Archives.

103. Douglass, "The Advantage of Athletics to Athletes," 8–10.

104. Smith, "What the Coach Can Do to Develop Clean Sport," 7–11.

105. Douglass, "The Advantage of Athletics to Athletes," 8–10.

106. U. S. Young, "The Influence of The Coach," 7–8, 1925 CIAA Bulletin, Union Archives.

107. Smith, "Ethics in Coaching," 16.

108. Gideon E. Smith, "Better Sportsmanship in Football," 14, 1927 CIAA Bulletin, Union Archives.

109. Smith, "Better Sportsmanship in Football," 14.

110. Smith, "What the Coach Can Do to Develop Clean Sport," 7–11.

111. U. S. Young, "The Influence of The Coach," 7–8, 1925 CIAA Bulletin, Union Archives.

112. Smith, "What the Coach Can Do to Develop Clean Sport," 7–11.

113. Douglass, "The Advantage of Athletics to Athletes," 8–10.

114. Smith, "What the Coach Can Do to Develop Clean Sport," 7–11.

115. Edward P. Hunt, "Inducing Athletes to Enter Institutions," 5–6, 1926 CIAA Bulletin, Union Archives.

116. Thomas L. Puryear, CIAA president, "Superlative Sportsmanship," 5, 1927 CIAA Bulletin, Union Archives.

117. Winston Douglass, director of Athletics at St. Paul's College, "The Advantage of Athletics to Athletes," 8–10.

118. Smith, "Football as a Character Builder," 15–16.

119. Smith, "Ethics in Coaching," 16.

120. Smith, "What the Coach Can Do to Develop Clean Sport," 7–11.

121. Smith, "Football as a Character Builder," 15–16.

122. J. H. Lawrence, director of Athletics at Virginia Seminary and College, "The Purpose of the CIAA," 13–4, 1924 CIAA Bulletin, Union Archives.

123. Gideon E. Smith, "Betting on Football Games," 15, 1926 CIAA Bulletin, Union Archives.

124. Everett W. Johnson, executive of West Chester Community Chest, Clarence F. Jones, police officer in Philadelphia, and A. B. Ballard, assistant director of Wissahickon Boys Club, "The College Athlete's Place in the Community," 21–24, speeches in the 1938 CIAA Bulletin, Union Archives.

125. "Attucks Athletic Club Has Great Opening," *Norfolk Journal and Guide,* September 10, 1921, 8.

126. "The Moral and Physical Development of the Man of the Future, Aim of the Norfolk Boys' Club," *Norfolk Journal and Guide,* October 3, 1925, 7.

127. "The Influence of the Boys' Club on the Youth of Norfolk City," *Norfolk Journal and Guide,* March 5, 1927, 6.

128. "Sportboard Reflections," *Norfolk Journal and Guide,* August 9, 1924, 4.

Chapter 3

1. "Dunbar Hi Takes State Title Back Home," *Norfolk Journal and Guide*, March 22, 1930, 7.

2. "Dunbar Wins All-State Cage Championship," *Norfolk Journal and Guide*, March 26, 1932, 12; "High School Conference Meets," *Norfolk Journal and Guide*, December 16, 1933, 16; and "Interscholastic Plays Limited to Five Sports," *Norfolk Journal and Guide*, April 7, 1934, A15.

3. "From the Press Box," *Norfolk Journal and Guide*, February 14, 1931, 6.

4. Charles H. Williams, "Twenty Years' Work of the CIAA," essay published in the 1932 CIAA Bulletin, Union Archives.

5. Vernon Johns, president of Virginia Seminary and College, to Professor Charles H. Williams of Hampton Institute, September 18, 1931, Annual Report of the CIAA Eligibility Committee, December 1930–32, 23, 1933 CIAA Bulletin, Union Archives.

6. Afternoon Session of the CIAA Annual Meeting, December 13, 1929, 5, 1930 CIAA Bulletin, Union Archives.

7. Charles Herbert Thompson, "The History of the National Basketball Tournament for Black High School," (PhD diss., at Louisiana State University, 1980); Oriard, *King Football*; and White, *Blood, Sweat, and Tears*, chapter 4.

8. David George Surdam, *Wins, Losses, and Empty Seats: How Baseball Outlasted the Great Depression* (Lincoln: University of Nebraska Press, 2011); and Austin, *Democratic Sports*.

9. Cheryl Lynn Greenberg, *To Ask for an Equal Chance: African Americans in the Great Depression* (New York: Rowman & Littlefield Publishers, 2010).

10. Mark Naison, *Communists in Harlem During the Depression: The Origins and Impact of America's Black Left* (Urbana: University of Illinois Press, 1983); Joe William Trotter Jr., *From a Raw Deal to a New Deal?: African Americans, 1929–1945* (New York: Oxford University Press, 1996); Mark Solomon, *The Cry Was Unity: Communists and African Americans, 1917–1936* (Jackson: University Press of Mississippi, 1998); Lashawn Harris, "Running with the Reds: African American Women and the Communist Party during the Great Depression," *Journal of African American History* 94, no. 1 (Winter 2009): 21–43; John A. Kirk, "The NAACP Campaign For Teachers' Salary Equalization: African American Women Educators and the Early Civil Rights Struggle," *Journal of African American History* 94, no. 4 (Fall 2009): 520–32; Bruce Beezer, "Black Teachers' Salaries and the Federal Courts Before *Brown v. Board of Education*: One Beginning for Equity," *Journal of Negro Education* 55, no. 2 (Spring 1986): 200–13; Edgar A. Toppin, "Walter White and the Atlanta NAACP's Fight for Equal Schools," *History of Education Quarterly* 7, no. 1 (Spring 1967): 3–21; Scott Baker, "Testing Equality: The National Teacher Examination and the NAACP's Legal Campaign to Equalize Teachers' Salaries in the South, 1936–63," *History of Education Quarterly* 35, no. 1 (Spring 1995): 49–64; Jon Hale, "'The Development of Power Is the Main Business of the School': The Agency of Southern Black Teacher Associations from Jim Crow Through Desegregation," *Journal of Negro Education* 87, no. 4 (Fall 2018): 444–59; Barbara J. Shircliffe, "Rethinking *Turner v. Keefe*: The Parallel Mobilization of African-American and White Teachers in Tampa, Florida, 1936–1946," *History of Education Quarterly* 52, no. 1 (February 2012): 99–136; Caroline Emmons, "Not a Single Battle but Rather a Real War: The Fight to Equalize

Teachers' Salaries in Florida in the 1930s and 1940s," *Florida Historical Quarterly* 81, no. 4 (Spring 2003): 418–35; and Keneshia N. Grant, *The Great Migration and the Democratic Party: Black Voters and the Realignment of American Politics in the 20th Century* (Philadelphia: Temple University Press, 2020).

11. Smith, *Managing White Supremacy*; and Brooks, *Uplift Generation.*

12. Doxey A. Wilkerson, "The Negro School Movement in Virginia: From "Equalization" to "Integration," *Journal of Negro Education* 29, no. 1 (Winter 1960): 17–29; Benjamin Muse, *Virginia's Massive Resistance* (Bloomington: University of Indiana Press, 1961); Robbins L. Gates, *The Making of Massive Resistance: Virginia's Politics of Public School Desegregation, 1954–1956* (Chapel Hill: University of North Carolina Press, 1964), 1–24; Robert A. Pratt, *The Color of Their Skin: Education and Race in Richmond, Virginia, 1954–89* (Charlottesville: University of Virginia Press, 1992); Alexander S. Leidholdt, *Standing Before the Shouting Mob: Lenoir Chambers and Virginia's Massive Resistance to Public School Integration* (Tuscaloosa: University of Alabama Press, 1997); Wallenstein, *Blue Laws and Black Codes*; Jeffrey E. Littlejohn and Charles H. Ford, *Elusive Equality: Desegregation and Resegregation in Norfolk's Public Schools* (Charlottesville: University of Virginia Press, 2012); Brian J. Daugherity, *Keep on Keeping On: The NAACP and the Implementation of Brown v. Board of Education in Virginia* (Charlottesville: University of Virginia Press, 2016); Jill Ogline Titus, *Brown's Battleground: Students, Segregationists, and the Struggle for Justice in Prince Edward County, Virginia* (Chapel Hill: University of North Carolina Press, 2011); Julian Maxwell Hayter, *The Dream Is Lost: Race, Voting Rights, and the Politics of Race in Richmond, Virginia* (Lexington: University of Kentucky Press, 2017); and Edds, *We Face the Dawn.*

13. Edwin B. Henderson, Head of Department of Physical Training in DC Public Schools, "The New Deal and College Athletics," 1934 CIAA Bulletin, Union Archives.

14. "From the Press Box," *Norfolk Journal and Guide*, January 24, 1931, 6.

15. "From the Press Box," *Norfolk Journal and Guide*, January 17, 1925, 5; "Sports Reflections," *Norfolk Journal and Guide*, January 24, 1925, 4.

16. Quotes "Facilities For Athletics Needed At High School," *Norfolk Journal and Guide*, April 11, 1925, 4; "State Teachers Make Plea for the Rural Child," *Norfolk Journal and Guide*, December 15, 1928, 9; and "From the Press Box," *Norfolk Journal and Guide*, June 1, 1929, 6.

17. Alexander, *Education for the Negro in Virginia*, 48.

18. Alexander, *Education for the Negro in Virginia*, 1.

19. Alexander, *Education for the Negro in Virginia*, 46–95.

20. Annual Report of the Superintendent of Public Instruction of the Commonwealth of Virginia with Accompanying Documents, School Year 1936–1937, Bulletin of the Virginia State Board of Education XX, no. 3 (September 1937): 13–20.

21. Alexander, *Education for the Negro in Virginia*, 109–62; Edward E. Recay, "Provisions for Negroes in Rural Areas," *Southern Workman* LXV, no. 8 (August 1936): 235–42.

22. Annual Report of the Superintendent of Public Instruction of the Commonwealth of Virginia with Accompanying Documents, School Year 1936–1937, 21.

23. Table LVII: Indices of Progress of Negro Education in Virginia, 1906–1939, found in Alexander, *Education for the Negro in Virginia*, 162–63.

24. *Daily Press* editorial, "Negro Education," *Southern Workman* LXV, no. 10 (October 1936): 308.

25. Alexander, *Education for the Negro in Virginia*, 46.

26. "Virginia and Education," *Norfolk Journal and Guide*, January 23, 1932, 6.

27. "Normal and Industrial Institute, One of The Land Grant Colleges for Negroes in American," *Norfolk Journal and Guide*, August 21, 1926, 7.

28. Anderson, *Education of Blacks in the South*, 110; Pincham, "A League of Willing Workers," 112–23; and Jackson, *Virginia Teachers Association*.

29. Alexander, *Education for the Negro in Virginia*, 49.

30. Isaac Fisher, "Virginia State Teachers Ass'N Counts Milestone," *Southern Workman* 67, no. 1 (January 1938): 23–24; Annual Report of the Superintendent of Public Instruction of the Commonwealth of Virginia with Accompanying Documents, School Year 1936–1937, 22.

31. J. Rupert Picott, "Desegregation of Higher Education in Virginia," *Journal of Negro Education* 27, no. 3 (Summer 1958): 324–31.

32. Alexander, *Education for the Negro in Virginia*, 36.

33. Alexander, *Education for the Negro in Virginia*, 1.

34. Meeting of the Virginia Teachers Association, recorded in the *Southern Workman* 59, no. 1 (January 1930): 12.

35. "Calls Newport News High School Interracial Venture," *Norfolk Journal and Guide*, December 17, 1932, 5.

36. "Southern Association Approval Puts Local High School in Front Rank," *Norfolk Journal and Guide*, December 17, 1932, 4; and "2 Virginia High Schools Get Southern Ass'n Approval," *Norfolk Journal and Guide*, December 24, 1932, 4.

37. Annual Report of the Superintendent of Public Instruction of the Commonwealth of Virginia with Accompanying Documents, School Year 1936–1937, 21 and 71. The accredited high schools were Roanoke's Lucy Addison High School, Charlotte County's Training School, Richmond's Armstrong High School, Christiansburg Institute, Lynchburg's Dunbar High School; Burkeville's Ingleside Fee Memorial Institute, Petersburg's Peabody High School, and Hampton's Phenix High School, along with Huntington and Booker T. Washington.

38. "Addison, One of The Outstanding High Schools in the South," *Norfolk Journal and Guide*, June 10, 1933, 10; "Hi Harris Football Ace Principal of Training School," *Norfolk Journal and Guide*, September 30, 1933, 20; and Marvin T. Chiles, "A Period of Misunderstanding: Reforming Jim Crow in Richmond, Virginia," *Virginia Magazine of History and Biography* 129, no. 3 (Fall 2021): 244–78.

39. David T. Ray, assistant coach of Johnson C. Smith University, "Response to the Welcome Address," 1937 CIAA Bulletin, Union Archives.

40. "Opposition to Colored Beach," *Norfolk Journal and Guide*, January 4, 1930, 1; "Readers Say," *Norfolk Journal and Guide*, January 25, 1930, 6; and "Playgrounds, Athletic Field, Swimming Pool," *Norfolk Journal and Guide*, December 23, 1933, 14.

41. "Norfolk's Christmas Gift to Her Negro Citizens," *Norfolk Journal and Guide*, January 4, 1930, 6

42. "Only 1 Member of Council Opposed It," *Norfolk Journal and Guide*, January 18, 1930; "Delay Now Seen As Probably in Beach Project," *Norfolk Journal and Guide*, February 1, 1930, 1; "City Council Takes the High Road," *Norfolk Journal and Guide*,

February 1, 1930, A2; and "Plantation Beach, New Shore Resort For Colored of Norfolk," *Norfolk Journal and Guide*, April 19, 1930, 2.

43. Shircliffe, "Rethinking *Turner v. Keefe*," 99–136; Irvin D. S. Winsboro and Abel A. Bartley, "Race, Education, and Regionalism: The Long and Troubling History of School Desegregation in the Sunshine State," *Florida Historical Quarterly* 92, no. 4 (Spring 2014): 725–27; Charles W. McKinney Jr, "Multiple Fronts: The Struggle for Black Educational and Political Equality in Wilson, North Carolina, 1941—1953," *North Carolina Historical Review* 88, no. 1 (January 2011): 1–39; Leander L. Boykin, "The Status and Trends of Differentials Between White and Negro Teachers' Salaries in the Southern States, 1900–1946," *Journal of Negro Education* 18, no. 1 (Winter 1949): 40–47; James L. Leloudis II, "School Reforms in the New South: The Women's Association for the Betterment of Public Schools in North Carolina, 1902–1919," *Journal of American History* 69, no. 4 (March 1983): 886; Carl V. Harris, "Stability and Change in Discrimination against Black Public Schools: Birmingham, Alabama, 1871–1931," *Journal of Southern History* 51, no. 3 (August 1985), 375; John R. Wennersten, "The Black School Teacher in Maryland, 1930's," *Negro History Bulletin* 38, no. 1 (April/May 1975): 370–73; Jon Hale, "The Fight Was Instilled in Us," High School Activism and The Civil Rights Movement in Charleston," *South Carolina Historical Magazine* 114, no. 1 (January 2013): 9–10; and Caroline Emmons, "Not a Single Battle but Rather a Real War: The Fight to Equalize Teachers' Salaries in Florida in the 1930s and 1940s," *Florida Historical Quarterly* 81, no. 4 (Spring 2003): 418–35.

44. "Interscholastic Plays Limited to Five Sports," *Norfolk Journal and Guide*, April 7, 1934, A15.

45. Alexander, *Education for the Negro in Virginia*, 1.

46. Thomas Calhoun Walker, *Lawyer Walker of Gloucester* (Williamsburg, VA: College of William and Mary Special Collection, undated).

47. Walker, *Lawyer Walker of Gloucester*, chapter XVI.

48. "Local Relief Situation for Negroes Is Less Acute," *Norfolk Journal and Guide*, December 14, 1935, 18.

49. Annual Report of the Superintendent of Public Instruction of the Commonwealth of Virginia with Accompanying Documents, School Year 1936–1937.

50. "Athletic Fields Approve for Norfolk," Norfolk Journal and Guide, December 16, 1933, 1.

51. "Newport News PWA School Projects Rejected," *Norfolk Journal and Guide*, August 31, 1935, 3; "WPA Withdraws Job Offered Johnson," *Norfolk Journal and Guide*, November 9, 1935, A2; "Failure To Take Up WPA Offer May Cost Richmond $1500,000," *Norfolk Journal and Guide*, May 2, 1936, 13; "WPA Project Funds Go Round But None Come Here," *Norfolk Journal and Guide*, June 27, 1936, 12; "Council Defers Action on Reported PWA School Grant," *Norfolk Journal and Guide*, November 7, 1936, 12; and "Project in Lynchburg Remains Uncertain," *Norfolk Journal and Guide*, March 20, 1937, 11.

52. Ronald L. Heinemann, *Depression and New Deal in Virginia: The Enduring Dominion* (Charlottesville: University of Virginia Press, 1983).

53. Kari Frederickson, *Dixiecrat Revolt and the End of the Solid South, 1932–1968* (Chapel Hill: University of North Carolina Press, 2001).

54. Suggs, *P. B. Young, Newspaperman*, 77–81.

55. Suggs, *P. B. Young, Newspaperman,* 50–51.

56. Suggs, *P. B. Young, Newspaperman,* 72 and 82.

57. Martha H, Swain, "The Harrison Education Bills, 1936–1941," *Mississippi Quarterly* 31, no. 1 (Winter 1977): 122.

58. John M. Gandy, president of Virginia State College to the National Education Association, February 18, 1937, reprinted in C. H. Thompson, "Editorial Comment: The Harrison-Black-Fletcher Bill Makes Its Debut," *Journal of Negro Education* 6, no. 2 (April 1937): 129–33; "Leaders Urge School Aid Bill Changes," *Norfolk Journal and Guide,* February 27, 1937, 1; and "Revised School Aid Bill Drafted," *Norfolk Journal and Guide,* March 13, 1937, 1.

59. "Byrd and Darden Get New School for Portsmouth," *Norfolk Journal and Guide,* July 11, 1936, 12; "Norcom School Faces Serious Overcrowding," *Norfolk Journal and Guide,* September 5, 1936, 5; "WPA Project For Recreation," *Norfolk Journal and Guide,* April 24, 1937, A2; "WPA Officials At Opening of Center," *Norfolk Journal and Guide,* July 10, 1937, A15; "Ten Thousand Colored People on WPA in Virginia," *Norfolk Journal and Guide,* July 17, 1937, 13; "Mrs. J.D. Rockefeller, Jr., Gives $50,000 to School," *Norfolk Journal and Guide,* December 24, 1938, 11; "Early Report On Barraud Park Plan Expected," *Norfolk Journal and Guide,* October 17, 1936, 1; "To Begin Construction on Gymnasium Project July 11," *Norfolk Journal and Guide,* July 9, 1938, 12; "City Plans to Develop Barraud Park," *Norfolk Journal and Guide,* December 3, 1938, 20; "WPA Officials Approve Gym Project for Norfolk," *Norfolk Journal and Guide,* May 21, 1938, 12; "Lack of Equipment May Delay Opening of New Schools," *Norfolk Journal and Guide,* August 29, 1936, 5; "Dedicate New High School Structure," *Norfolk Journal and Guide,* June 19, 1937, A2; "New Middlesex County High School Dedicated," *Norfolk Journal and Guide,* September 2, 1939, 11; "Suffolk to Get New 36,587 High School," *Norfolk Journal and Guide,* November 12, 1938, 10; "Ten Thousand Colored People on WPA in Virginia," *Norfolk Journal and Guide,* Jul 17, 1937, 13; "Nearly Four Million Given in the South By WPA," *Norfolk Journal and Guide,* September 11, 1937, A9; "Additional Sports," *Norfolk Journal and Guide,* December 23, 1939, 17.

60. Jesse A. Reynolds, History of WPA Recreation (Washington, DC: Work Progress Administration, 1947).

61. Annual Report of the Superintendent of Public Instruction of the Commonwealth of Virginia with Accompanying Documents, School Year 1936–1937, 13.

62. "$15,000 Is Raised to Build School," *Norfolk Journal and Guide,* January 29, 1938, 14.

63. Edwin B. Henderson, head of Department of Physical Training in DC Public Schools, "The New Deal and College Athletics," 7–9, 1934 CIAA Bulletin, Union Archives.

64. Arthur P. Davis, "Reports of the Vice Presidents," 1935 CIAA Bulletin, Union Archives.

65. Edwin B. Henderson, head of Department of Physical Training in DC Public Schools, "The New Deal and College Athletics," 7–9, 1934 CIAA Bulletin, Union Archives.

66. "Virginia N& I.I. Arrives at Full Status of College," *Norfolk Journal and Guide,* March 15, 1930, 2.

67. "To Reorganize High School Association," *Norfolk Journal and Guide*, March 16, 1940, 16; Edgar Allen Toppin, *Loyal Sons and Daughters: Virginia State University, 1882 to 1992* (New York: Pictorial Heritage Publishing, Co., 1992). The collection of historian Luther Porter Jackson holds a litany of organizational papers that detail Virginia State's place as the center for Black dynamism in the twentieth century. Many of the statewide Black organizations dealing with issues ranging from welfare to voting rights often met at Virginia State and these meetings were run by Virginia State professors. For more, see the Luther Porter Jackson Papers held at Virginia State University Archives, Petersburg, Virginia.

68. Copy of Virginia State College for Negroes Public Works Administration Request, Docket #1808 in Hawkins, Delafield, and Longfellow Law Firm to Collins Deny, Jr., Esq., October 27, 1934, Folder: Virginia State College for Negroes Civil Works Projects, Public Works Administration, Virginia Board of Education Records.

69. Certain Acts Pertaining to the National Recovery Program, Extra Session of the General Assembly of Virginia, 1933, Folder: State Board of Education, Public Works Projects Files, 1934–36, Virginia Board of Education Records; and Director of Higher Education in Virginia to Thomas E. Massie, Legal Division of Public Works Administration, March 7, 1934, Folder: State Board of Education, Public Works Projects Files, 1934–36, Library of Virginia.

70. Denny & Valentine Law Firm to Honorable Abram P. Staples, Attorney General, October 30, 1934, Folder: Virginia State College For Negroes Civil Works Projects, Public Works Administration, Virginia Board of Education Records; and Governor's Certificate for Virginia State College For Negroes Bonds, March 9, 1934, Folder: Virginia State College For Negroes Civil Works Projects, Public Works Administration, Virginia Board of Education Records.

71. Extract from the minutes of the state board of education of Virginia, July 27, 1935, Folder: Virginia State College For Negroes Civil Works Projects, Public Works Administration, Virginia Board of Education Records.

72. "High School Conference Meets," *Norfolk Journal and Guide*, December 16, 1933, 16.

73. "Virginia High School Conference Opens Next Week," *Norfolk Journal and Guide*, September 23, 1933, A16.

74. "Dopesters Says Can't Repeat in State High School Tourney," *Norfolk Journal and Guide*, March 10, 1934, 12.

75. "New Va High School Ass'N To Be Fixture," *Norfolk Journal and Guide*, March 10, 1934, 12.

76. "From the Press Box," *Norfolk Journal and Guide*, March 25, 1933, 12; "Basketball Coaches Form Plans For Sectional Cage Associations in Virginia," *Norfolk Journal and Guide*, January 16, 1937, 17; and "They Vie For Highest Honors at the Eleventh Annual Va. State Basketball," *Norfolk Journal and Guide*, March 19, 1938, 17.

77. "Stage Set for SIAA Basketball Tourney," *Norfolk Journal and Guide*, February 25, 1933, 12; "Southside Association Makes Plans For Basketball Season," *Norfolk Journal and Guide*, October 14, 1933, 17; "St. Paul Host To SIAA Tournament," *Norfolk Journal and Guide*, March 3, 1934, 12; "Dunbar Retains VA State Honors," *Norfolk Journal and Guide*, March 17, 1934, 13; "Coming Basketball Tourneys," *Norfolk Journal and Guide*, March 2, 1935, 14; "Baby Pirates Win Cage Title," *Norfolk Journal*

and Guide, March 21, 1936, 14; "SIAA Tournament," *Norfolk Journal and Guide*, February 27, 1937, 15; "From the Press Box," *Norfolk Journal and Guide*, March 12, 1938, 16; "St. Paul High, Phenix Wins District Title," *Norfolk Journal and Guide*, March 11, 1939, 18; and "14 Teams to Play In SIAA Tourney at St. Paul's on February 24," *Norfolk Journal and Guide*, February 24, 1940, 17.

78. "NC State High School Meet March 6–7," *Norfolk Journal and Guide*, February 21, 1931, 6; "CIAA Tract Meet at Hampton May 16," *Norfolk Journal and Guide*, April 18, 1931, 12; and NC Prep School Makes Changes," *Baltimore Afro-American*, January 24, 1931, 19.

79. Thompson, "The History of the National Basketball Tournaments for Black High Schools," 45.

80. "According to Sirrah Semaj," *Chicago Defender*, February 21, 1931, 1.

81. "Plans for Annual High School Tourney," *Norfolk Journal and Guide*, February 1, 1941, 19; and "Armstrong in Nationals," *Norfolk Journal and Guide*, March 29, 1941, 14.

82. "State College Has Fathered Prep Game," *Norfolk Journal and Guide*, January 15, 1944, 10.

83. "From the Press Box," *Norfolk Journal and Guide*, September 23, 1944, 10.

84. "Attention: High School Athletic Conference," *Norfolk Journal and Guide*, December 16, 1944, 13; and "High School Conference to Resume Championships," *Norfolk Journal and Guide*, December 23, 1944, 12; "SIAL Holds Initial Meeting of Year," *Norfolk Journal and Guide*, November 11, 1950, D20.

85. "1945 High School Grid Schedule," *Norfolk Journal and Guide*, December 30, 1944, 10; and "Scholastic Athletic Conference," *Norfolk Journal and Guide*, December 8, 1945, 14.

86. "Reorganized League Gets New Name," *Norfolk Journal and Guide*, December 15, 1945, 15.

Chapter 4

1. Watterson, *College Football*, 39–99 and 143–286; Oriard, *King Football*, 101–25; Ronald A. Smith, *Play-By-Play: Radio, Television, and Big-Time College Sport* (Baltimore, MD: Johns Hopkins University Press, 2001), 119; J. Douglas Tomas, *Football U: Spectator Sports in the Life of the American University* (Ann Arbor: University of Michigan Press, 2003), 245–82; Schmidt, *Shaping College Football*, 174–233; Demas, *Integrating the Gridiron*, 49–71; and Kurt Edward Kemper, *Before March Madness: The Wars For the Soul of College Basketball* (Urbana: University of Illinois Press, 2020), 69–107.

2. Hurd, *Black College Football*; George, *Elevating the Game*; Aiello, *Bayou Classic*; Hawkins et al., *Athletic Experience at Historically Black Colleges and Universities*; Nathan, ed., *Rooting for The Home Team*; and White, *Blood, Sweat, and Tears*.

3. Williams, "A Quarter of a Century in Negro Organized Athletics," 11–13.

4. Annual Report of the CIAA Eligibility Committee from December 1930–December 1932, 18–27, report in the 1933 CIAA Bulletin; Reports of the 1932–1933 Committees, 21–26, report in the 1934 CIAA Bulletin, Union Archives.

5. CIAA eligibility rules exempted St. Paul's because they were the only junior college in the conference. Student athletes could play CIAA sports with St. Paul's and

transfer to another CIAA school with full eligibility if they received their diploma. This changed when St. Paul's became a four-year institution in 1944. For more, see Charles H. Williams, "Twenty Years' Work of the CIAA," 3.

6. Blanks for Brown, Princeton, and Tufts Games by the Harvard Athletic Association, Series 1A, General Correspondence, W. E. B. Du Bois Papers, Robert S. Cox Special Collections University Archives Research Center, University of Massachusetts at Amherst; Application Blank for the Harvard vs Brown Football Game 1919; Harvard Athletic Association Schedule of Football Games for the Season 1919; Game Blank for Tufts vs. Harvard Football Game 1919; Game Blank for Princeton vs Harvard Football Game 1919, W. E. B. Du Bois Papers, Robert S. Cox Special Collections University Archives Research Center, University of Massachusetts at Amherst.

7. Charles W. Eliot, "College Football," *Journal of Education* 61, no. 7 (February 1905): 171–72; and Watterson, *College Football*, 23–49.

8. Dan S. Green and Earl Smith, "W.E.B. DuBois and the Concepts of Race and Class," *Phylon* 44, no. 4 (4th Quarter, 1983): 262–72; and Adolph L. Reed Jr., "W.E.B. DuBois: A Perspective on the Bases of His Political Thought," *Political Theory* 13, no. 3 (August 1985): 431–56.

9. "Famous Colored Athletes," *Crisis Magazine* 2, no. 3 (July 1911): 1–44; Locke, ed., *New Negro*, 3–5; and Elliot M. Rudwick, "W. E. B. Du Bois in the Role of *Crisis* Editor," *Journal of Negro History* 43, no. 3 (July 1958): 214–40. The quote is on page 218.

10. "The Horizon" and "Along the Color Line" were the primary sections where football was covered in the *Crisis*; "The Horizon," *Crisis Magazine* 13, no. 2 (December 1916): 92; "The Colored College Athlete," *Crisis Magazine* 2, no. 3 (July 1911): 115–19; "Social Uplift," *Crisis Magazine* 5, no. 1 (November 1912): 8; "A Counselor," *Crisis Magazine* 10, no. 1 (May 1915): 14; "Our Graduates," *Crisis Magazine* 12, no. 3 (July 1916): 123; "Men of the Month," *Crisis Magazine* 11, no. 2 (December 1915): 70; and "The Horizon," *Crisis Magazine* 14, no. 1 (May 1917): 42; and David K. Wiggins, *Glory Bound*, 223–24.

11. "Along the Color Line," *Crisis Magazine* 10, no. 6 (October 1915): 271; "Men of the Month," *Crisis Magazine* 15, no. 5 (March 1918): 229–30; "The Horizon," *Crisis Magazine* 13, no. 2 (December 1916): 92; and "The Horizon," *Crisis Magazine* 13, no. 4 (January 1917): 191; "The Looking Glass," *Crisis Magazine* 13, no. 5 (March 1917): 237 and 249; "The Horizon," *Crisis Magazine* 15, no. 5 (January 1918): 14; "The Horizon," *Crisis Magazine* 16, no. 2 (June 1918): 87; and "The Horizon," *Crisis Magazine* 18, no. 3 (July 1919): 150.

12. "Along the Color Line," *Crisis Magazine* 3, no. 3 (January 1912): 99; "Vagaries of Prejudice," *Crisis Magazine* 2, no. 5 (September 1911): 187; "Along the Color Line," *Crisis Magazine* 3, no. 3 (January 1912): 99; "The Horizon," *Crisis Magazine* 23, no. 2 (December 1921): 85; "Along the Color Line," *Crisis Magazine* 7, no. 2 (December 1913): 63; "Along the Color Line," *Crisis Magazine* 7, no. 3 (January 1914): 117 and 131; and "Our Future Leaders," *Crisis Magazine* 10, no. 3 (July 1915): 141.

13. W. E. B. Du Bois, editor of the *Crisis*, to Prof. Paul W. L. Jones, teacher at Kentucky Normal and Industrial Institute in Frankfort, Kentucky, December 15, 1924, W. E. B. Du Bois Papers (MS 312), Special Collections and University Archives, University of Massachusetts Amherst Libraries, henceforth cited as Du Bois Papers; A

Resolution Recognizing Jackson Hall in Frankfort, Kentucky, 18 RS BR, 1963; W. E. B. Du Bois, editor of the *Crisis*, to Prof. Paul W. L. Jones, teacher at Kentucky Normal and Industrial Institute in Frankfort, Kentucky, December 15, 1924, Du Bois Papers; Paul W. L. Jones, teacher at Kentucky Normal and Industrial Institute in Frankfort, Kentucky to Dr. W. E. B. Du Bois, editor of the *Crisis*, December 17, 1924, Du Bois Papers; and W. E. B. Du Bois, editor of the *Crisis*, to Mr. P. W. L. Jones, December 24, 1924, Du Bois Papers; Paul W. L. Jones, teacher at Kentucky Normal and Industrial Institute in Frankfort, Kentucky to Dr. W. E. B. Du Bois, editor of the *Crisis*, December 28, 1924, Du Bois Papers; W. E. B. Du Bois, editor of the *Crisis*, to Mr. P.W.L. Jones, teacher at Kentucky Normal and Industrial Institute in Frankfort, Kentucky, November 7, 1925, Du Bois Papers; W. E. B. Du Bois, editor of the *Crisis*, , to Mr. P. W. L. Jones, teacher at Kentucky Normal and Industrial Institute in Frankfort, Kentucky, October 28, 1925, Du Bois Papers; R. S. Darnaby, secretary of the Athletic Committee at Tuskegee Institute in Tuskegee, Alabama to the Crisis Magazine, January 6, 1925, Du Bois Papers; J. F. Williams, Football Coach at Paul Quinn College in Waco, Texas, *Crisis Magazine*, January 5, 1925, Du Bois Papers; and W. E. B. Du Bois, editor of the *Crisis* to Mr. J. F. Williams of Paul Quinn College in Waco, Texas, January 15, 1925, Du Bois Papers.

14. Frank A. Young, "Football in the South Needs Housecleaning," *Chicago Defender*, December 14, 1929, 8.

15. Hurd, *Black College Football*, 165–66. In this section of Hurd's book, readers see that while the first Black national champions (a media-awarded prize, not an actual feat that could be accomplished) was awarded in 1920, and the first Black All-American team was first announced in 1927, the year 1929 was completely omitted. Hurd never explains this; rather he picks back up with listing the 1930 All-American team.

16. Smith, "Betting on Football Games," 15.

17. Howard J. Savage et al., "American College Athletics," report by the Carnegie Foundation for the Advancement of Teaching, 1929, chapter VII, 2; Watterson, *College Football*, 150–77; and Schmidt, *Shaping College Football*, 174–233.

18. George Streator, professor of mathematics and physics at Bennett College for Women in Greensboro, North Carolina to Dr. W. E. B. Du Bois, editor of the *Crisis Magazine*, April 28, 1930, Du Bois Papers.

19. George Streator, professor of mathematics and physics at Bennett College for Women in Greensboro, North Carolina to Dr. W. E. B. Du Bois, editor of the *Crisis Magazine*, August 2, 1930, Du Bois Papers.

20. George Streator, professor of mathematics and physics at Bennett College for Women in Greensboro, North Carolina to Dr. W. E. B. Du Bois, editor of the *Crisis Magazine*, April 28, 1930, Du Bois Papers.

21. Schmidt, *Shaping College Football*; Ingrassia, "Public Influence Inside the College Walls"; Watterson, *College Football*, 44–46; and Oriard, *King Football*, 67–70.

22. Thomas L. Puryear, dean of Men at Virginia Normal and Industrial Institute, "Eligibility and Professionalism," 23–26, speech in the 1924 CIAA Bulletin, Union Archives.

23. The CIAA Gives Information to the Public, a summary of the Robert Dean Miller Case of 1924, 6–8, found in 1924 CIAA Bulletin, Union Archives.

24. George W. Streator, "A Program for the CIAA," 8 and 24, essay in the 1932 CIAA Bulletin, Athletic Department, Union Archives.

25. George W. Streator, "Negro Football Standards," *Crisis Magazine* (March 1931): 85–86.

26. George W. Streator, "Football in Negro Colleges," *Crisis Magazine* (April 1932): 129–30; and "Football In Negro Colleges Razzed in Article By George W. Streator: Schools Grouped Into Good, Medium, and Bad Classes," *Norfolk Journal and Guide,* April 16, 1932, 12. Much of the *Crisis* article was reprinted in the *Journal and Guide.*

27. Becton, "CIAA Championships By School," chart found in "HBCU Football Championship History," NCAA Black College Webpage, February 27, 2023; "Training For Rural Leadership," *Southern Workman* 43, no. 5 (May 1914): 298; "Athletics and Gymnastics," *Southern Workman* 45, no. 6 (June 1916): 365; and "Athletics," *Southern Workman* 46, no. 1 (January 1917): 57.

28. George W. Streator, "Football in Negro Colleges," *Crisis Magazine* (April 1932): 129–30; and "Football In Negro Colleges Razzed in Article By George W. Streator: Schools Grouped Into Good, Medium, and Bad Classes," *Norfolk Journal and Guide,* April 16, 1932, 12. Much of the *Crisis* article was reprinted in the *Journal and Guide.*

29. Chas. H. Williams, physical education director at Hampton Institute in Hampton, Virginia to Dr. W. E. B. Du Bois, editor of the *Crisis Magazine,* March 25, 1932, Du Bois Papers.

30. "Streator Asked for Correction," *Baltimore Afro-American,* January 14, 1933, 16.

31. "Streator's Criticism Draw Sharp Reply from Hampton," *Norfolk Journal and Guide,* January 7, 1933, A12.

32. "Streator Asked for Correction," *Baltimore Afro-American,* January 14, 1933, 16.

33. "Too Much Laxity Writes Streator," *Baltimore Afro-American,* January 21, 1933, 17.

34. "Coach Disputes Football Critic," *Norfolk Journal and Guide,* April 23, 1932, 13; and "Aw Nerts," *Norfolk Journal and Guide,* April 30, 1932, 13.

35. Streator, "Football in Negro Colleges," 129.

36. "Rotten Athletics in Schools Alleged," *Baltimore Afro-American,* April 2, 1932, 21; "National Code of Ethics Needed," *Norfolk Journal and Guide,* February 28, 1931, 6; and "Football in Negro Colleges Razzed in Article by George W. Streator: Schools Grouped into Good, Medium, and Bad Classes," *Norfolk Journal and Guide,* April 16, 1932, 12.

37. "From the Press Box," *Norfolk Journal and Guide,* April 9, 1932, 12.

38. "With Our Schools: Why Not Abolish Football," *Atlanta Daily World,* April 8, 1932, 6; and "Abolish College Football Southern Teacher Suggests," *Baltimore Afro-American,* April 16, 1932, 14.

39. "Streator OK," *Norfolk Journal and Guide,* May 7, 1932, 12.

40. "Ike Richmond, Hampton Yearling Unleash Sparkling Attacks," *Norfolk Journal and Guide,* October 8, 1932, 12.

41. "Hi Harris Named Captain of 1932 Team," *Norfolk Journal and Guide,* October

1, 1932, 12; and "Ike Richmond," *Norfolk Journal and Guide*, October 8, 1932, 12; and Tom Young, "VA State Takes the Lead in CIAA," *Norfolk Journal and Guide*, October 22, 1932, 12.

42. Report of the Chairman of the Committee to Investigate the Richmond Case, 35, report in the 1933 CIAA Bulletin, Union Archives.

43. President J. B. Watson of Arkansas State College to Mr. L. H. Foster of Virginia State College, November 18, 1932, 19–20, 1933 CIAA Bulletin, Union Archives.

44. Annual Report of the CIAA Eligibility Committee, December 1930–32, 20–21, 1933 CIAA Bulletin, Union Archives.

45. Bill Gibson, "The Richmond Case or Block That Kicker," *Baltimore Afro-American*, December 24, 1932, 16.

46. A Copy of Arkansas State College Football Roster 1931, 24; J. B. Watson to Chas. H. Williams, October 18, 1932, 22, letter forwarded as Chas. H. Williams to CIAA Eligibility Committee, October 18, 1932, found in Annual Report of the CIAA Eligibility Committee, December 1930–32, 1933 CIAA Bulletin, Union Archives.

47. Remarks of Mr. G. E. Smith of Hampton Institute, undated, 25, in Annual Report of the CIAA Eligibility Committee, December 1930–32, 1933 CIAA Bulletin, Union Archives.

48. "Reinstates Richmond," *Norfolk Journal and Guide*, December 17, 1932, 12; Article III: Membership, in Annual Report of the CIAA Eligibility Committee, December 1930–32, 26, 1933 CIAA Bulletin, Union Archives.

49. Linda B. Pincham, "A League of Willing Workers: The Impact of Northern Philanthropy, Virginia Estelle Randolph and the Jeanes Teachers in Early Twentieth-Century Virginia," *Journal of Negro Education* 74 (Spring 2005): 112–23; and Luther P. Jackson, *A History of the Virginia Teachers Association* (Norfolk, VA: Guide Publishing Co., 1937).

50. Thomas Jesse Jones, *Negro Education: A Study of the Private and Higher School for Colored People in the United States* (Washington, DC: United States Department of the Interior, 1916), 16; Table LVII: Indices of Progress of Negro Education in Virginia, 1906–1939, found in Fred M. Alexander, *Education for the Negro in Virginia* (Washington, DC: John F. Slater Fund, Inc., 1943), 162–63.

51. James D. Anderson, *The Education of Blacks in the South, 1860–1935* (Chapel Hill: University of North Carolina Press, 1988), 110–47; Adam Fairclough, *Teaching Equality: Black Schools in the Age of Jim Crow* (Athens: University of Georgia Press, 2001), 1–19; and Bobby L. Lovett, *America's Historically Black Colleges: A Narrative History, 1837–2009* (Macon, GA: Mercer University Press, 2011), 42–96.

52. Dwight Oliver Wendell Holmes, *The Evolution of the Negro College* (New York: Columbia University Teachers College Press, 1934); and "Editorial Comment: Eight Years of Rating of Negro Schools and Colleges by the Southern Association: An Evaluation," *Journal of Negro Education* 8 (January 1939): 1–8.

53. George Streator, "Bennett College for Women," *Chicago Defender*, March 13, 1932, 4.

54. Bill Gibson, "The Richmond Case or Block That Kicker," *Baltimore Afro-American*, December 24, 1932, 16; and A. Stephen Stephan, "The Negro Public College in Arkansas," *Journal of Negro Education* 31 (Summer 1962): 5–9.

55. Lovett, *America's Historically Black Colleges*, 54; Historical Overview of the University of Arkansas at Pine Bluff, University of Arkansas at Pine Bluff Webpage, 2005, 1–7.

56. Watson, "Football in Southern Negro Football," *Voice of the Negro* 4, no. 4 (May 1907): 165–66.

57. Fairclough, *Teaching Equality*, 20–40; Lewis K. McMillan, "Negro Higher Education as I Have Known It," *Journal of Negro Education* 8 (January 1939): 9–18.

58. "Reinstates Richmond," *Norfolk Journal and Guide*, December 17, 1932, 12.

59. Annual Report of the CIAA Eligibility Committee, December 1930–32, 19, 1933 CIAA Bulletin, Union Archives.

60. "Reinstates Richmond," *Norfolk Journal and Guide*, December 17, 1932, 12.

61. For the expansion of the Eligibility Committee in the CIAA after 1932, see CIAA Bulletin, 1932–1935, Athletic Department Records, AR-005, Box 1 of 3, Union Archives.

62. Annual Report of the CIAA Eligibility Committee, December 1939 to December 1940, 23, 1941 CIAA Bulletin, Union Archives.

63. "Wilberforce Placed on Probation for One Year," *Baltimore Afro-American*, January 12, 1935, 21.

64. Watterson, *College Football*, 158–83.

65. Becton, "CIAA Championships by School," chart found in "HBCU Football Championship History," NCAA Black College Football Webpage, February 27, 2023; and "Joe Taylor to the College Football Hall of Fame," *Hampton University News* webpage, January 7, 2019.

66. "Experts Believe Globetrotters Best," *Negro History Bulletin* 17, no. 6 (March 1954): 142.

67. "Union to Face Globetrotters Friday Night," *Norfolk Journal and Guide*, March 8, 1941, 13; "Score Tied Eight Times as Trotters Shade Union," *Baltimore Afro-American*, March 15, 1941, 21; and "Globetrotters Nose Union," *Norfolk Journal and Guide*, March 15, 1941, 12.

68. George, *Elevating the Game*; Martin, *Benching Jim Crow*; Milton S. Katz, *Breaking Through: John B. McLendon, Basketball Legend and Civil Rights Pioneer* (Fayetteville: University of Arkansas Press, 2010); Ellsworth, The Secret Game; Wiggins and Elzey, "Creating Order in Black College Sports," 145–48; Jim Junot, "The Forgotten Champion," Virginia Union University Men's Tennis Webpage, October 25, 2010; "Globetrotters Helped Shape VUU History," *Richmond Times Dispatch*, September 19, 2019, online article; Fred Jeter, "Remembering VUU's Glory Days as NCAA Champions," *Richmond Free Press*, March 26, 2020, n.p.; Kemper, *Before March Madness*, 3; and Aiello, *Hoops*.

69. Niklas Thomas and Till Neuhaus, "Shut Up and Dribble: Fractured Race Relations in the NBA in Times of (Perceived) Corporate Crisis," *Jam It! Fractured States of America*, no. 6 (May 2022): 132–54.

70. Jim Junot, "Barco-Stevens Hall: 80 Years of History," *Virginia Union Sports News* webpage, May 1, 2019.

71. Black Fives Foundation webpage, undated.

72. H. D. Martin, "How to Introduce and Popularize Basketball in the Schools," 12–13, speech in the 1924 CIAA Bulletin, Union Archies.

73. Thomas L. Puryear, CIAA President, "A Well Balanced Athletic Program," 1–2, speech in the 1927 CIAA Bulletin, Union Archives.

74. Senior Class of Virginia Union University, *The Panther*: Virginia Union 1928 School Yearbook, Yearbook Collection, Virginia Union University.

75. "Coach Hucles Once Offered Grays Contract," *Norfolk Journal and Guide*, May 3, 1941, 13; Jim Junot, "The Story of Henry Hucles," *Virginia Union University Athletic News* Webpage, December 14, 2010; Senior Class of Virginia Union University, *The Panther*: Virginia Union 1928 School Yearbook, Yearbook Collection, Virginia Union University; Noman C. Keith, chairman of the board of trustees at Springfield College, Springfield, Massachusetts to Mr. Henry B. Hucles Jr., associate professor of history and P.E. at Virginia Union, July 18, 1968, Folder 5, Box 1, Henry Boyd Hucles Jr., Collection, Union Archives; "Former Panthers Honor 'Their Boy'" undated clipping, Folder 4: Box 1, MS-0046, Henry Boyd Hucles Jr. Collection, Union Archives; and Untitled undated clipping, Folder 9, Box 1,MS-0046, Henry Boyd Hucles Jr. Collection, Union Archives.

76. Arthur P. Davis, "Reports of the Vice Presidents," 9–10, 1935 CIAA Bulletin, Union Archives.

77. Junot, "Barco-Stevens Hall: 80 Years of History."

78. Charles H. Williams, secretary-treasurer, "The CIAA," 1, 1928 CIAA Bulletin, Union Archives.

79. R. C. Crutchfield Jr., basketball coach of Hampton Institute, "Basketball in the Colored Intercollegiate Athletic Association, 1936," 44, 1937 CIAA Bulletin, Union Archives.

80. H. R. Jefferson, "Basketball in the Colored Intercollegiate Athletic Association—1938," 50, 1938 CIAA Bulletin, Union Archives.

81. Honorable Joseph H. Rainey, Pennsylvania State Athletic Commission, "The Negro Athlete as a Goodwill Ambassador," 25, 1938 CIAA Bulletin, Union Archives.

82. Minutes of the Executive Council 1937 Meetings at Lincoln University, 14, 1938 CIAA Bulletin, Union Archives.

83. Charles H. Williams, "Goals to Be Achieved in the Next Twenty-five Years," 26–27, 1937 CIAA Bulletin, Union Archives.

84. Introduction to the 1930 CIAA Bulletin, 1, 1930 CIAA Bulletin, Union Archives.

85. Martin, *Benching Jim Crow*, 27–71; and Kemper, *Before March Madness*, 3.

86. "SEZ Ches," *Pittsburgh Courier*, March 26, 1938, 16.

87. "In This Corner," *New York Amsterdam*, March 19, 1938, 16; "Long Island U to Oppose Sepains," *Philadelphia Tribune*, March 17, 1938, 12; and "Long Island to Meet Both Union, Morgan," *Chicago Defender*, March 19, 1938, 8.

88. "When Panthers Score 59 Points, Followers of Jumpin' Jive Quintet," *Pittsburgh Courier*, February 10, 1940, 16.

89. "Former Panthers Honor 'Their Boy,'" undated clipping, Folder 4, Box 1, MS-0046, Henry Boyd Hucles Jr. Collection, Union Archives.

90. Jefferson, "Basketball in the Colored Intercollegiate Athletic Association—1938," 50; S. Russell Wilson of Bishop Payne Divinity School to the *Richmond Times-Dispatch* sports editor, reprinted in the *Richmond Times-Dispatch*, March 28, 1939, 12.

91. CIAA Basketball Records, 1938, 52, 1938 CIAA Bulletin, Union Archives; "Substitute Stars as Union Beats State, 46–39," *Norfolk Journal and Guide*, March 12, 1938, 16.

92. "In This Corner," *New York Amsterdam*, March 19, 1938, 16; "Long Island U to Oppose Sepains," *Philadelphia Tribune*, March 17, 1938, 12; and "Long Island to Meet Both Union, Morgan," *Chicago Defender*, March 19, 1938, 8.

93. "LIU Coach Would See Sepians in Garden," *Baltimore Afro-American*, April 2, 1938, 11.

94. "The Sports Broadcast," *Baltimore Afro-American*, April 9, 1938, 22.

95. "LIU Coach Would See Sepians in Garden," *Baltimore Afro-American*, April 2, 1938, 11.

96. "In This Corner," *New York Amsterdam*, March 19, 1938, 16.

97. "More Interracial Cage Frays Afoot," *New York Amsterdam News*, February 19, 1938, 14; and "Union Stopped by Harlem Senior Quintet, 39–27," *Baltimore Afro-American*, April 2, 1938, 23.

98. "Soupy Campbell, Former Rankin Ace, Star at Union," *Pittsburgh Courier*, February 25, 1939, 17; "Sez Ches," *Pittsburgh Courier*, March 16, 1940, 16; "Long Island U to Oppose Sepains," *Philadelphia Tribune*, March 17, 1938, 12; "Dolly King Not With LIU Team," *Baltimore Afro-American*, September 10, 1938, 23; and "Smitty's Port Purts," *Pittsburgh Courier*, September 10, 1938, 17; and "VA Union Tops Benezet Cage Team 44 to 35," *Chicago Defender*, January 10, 1938, 8. Wylie Campbell starred at Rankin High School in Pittsburgh, scoring 514 points in seventy-three career games. He earned dozens of scholarships from across the HBCU landscape but very few from northern white schools. Campbell chose Union after hometown Duquesne University rejected him due to his grades. He scored 1,006 points in seventy-nine career college games at Union. Campbell later played professional basketball for the Philadelphia Commandeurs and the New York Renaissance before settling down and becoming a youth basketball coach in Richmond after World War II.

99. "VA Union Paces CIAA Cagesters," *Atlanta Daily World*, February 14, 1939, 5; and "Long Island U. Blackbirds vs. Panthers," *New York Amsterdam News*, March 18, 1939, 18.

100. "The Sports Bugle," *Pittsburgh Courier*, March 30, 1940, 17; and "When Panthers Score 59 Points, Followers of Jumpin' Jive Quintet," *Pittsburgh Courier*, February 10, 1940, 16.

101. Official Ranking of CIAA Basketball Teams, 1940, 44, 1940 CIAA Bulletin, Union Archives; and "VA Union Paces CIAA Cagesters," *Atlanta Daily World*, February 14, 1939, 5.

102. "Union's Crack Quint Drills on Dirt Court," *Baltimore Afro-American*, January 6, 1940, 21; "Union 74, Morgan 49," *Baltimore Afro-American*, February 25, 1939, 23; "Union Meets State a Roanoke Monday," *Norfolk Journal and Guide*, March 4, 1939, 17; and "Must Decide CIAA Title with Pencil, Pad," *Atlanta Daily World*, March 7, 1939, 5.

103. "Xavier Plays White Five," *Atlanta Daily World*, March 17, 1939, 5; and "State Palace Open Nightly," *New York Amsterdam News*, March 18, 1939, 9.

104. "Long Island U. Blackbirds vs. Panthers," *New York Amsterdam News*, March

18, 1939, 18; and "Union's Crack Quint Drills on Dirt Court," *Baltimore Afro-American*, January 6, 1940, 21.

105. "Slants on Sports," *Atlanta Daily World*, March 31, 1939, 5.

106. "Va Union Ends Long Island Win Streak at 24!" *Atlanta Daily World*, March 30, 1939, 5.

107. VA Union vs VA State Program, October 31, 1942, Folder 91: Athletic Department Programs,

108. Virginia Union University Basketball Handbook, 1948, Folder Athletics Department, Basketball Programs, Athletic Department, Box 1 of 3, AR-0005, Union Archives.

109. Howard "Hunky" Hill, attorney at law, Gary, Indiana, to Dr. Ivan Fraser, chairman of the Hucles Fund, May 16, 1969, Folder 9, Box 1, MS-0046, Henry Boyd Hucles Jr., Collection, Union Archives.

110. "Former Panthers Honor 'Their Boy'" undated clipping, Folder 4, Box 1, MS-0046, Henry Boyd Hucles Jr., Collection, Union Archives.

111. "Va Union Ends Long Island Win Streak at 24!" *Atlanta Daily World*, March 30, 1939, 5.

112. "From the Press Box," *Norfolk Journal and Guide*, April 8, 1939, 18.

113. "SEZ Ches," *Pittsburgh Courier*, April 8, 1939, 16; "They Broke the Winning Streak," *Cleveland Call and Post*, April 13, 1939, 10; "Webber Thinks Union, Ky. State Were Equal of Long Island," *Atlanta Daily World*, April 15, 1939, 5; and "Yep, T'Was LIU Blackbirds That Went The Way of All Flesh Before Va Union," *New York Amsterdam News*, April 15, 1939, 18.

114. "Many Fans in Dark about Union Victory," *Baltimore Afro-American*, April 1, 1939, 22.

115. "Slants on Sports," *Atlanta Daily World*, April 4, 1939, 5; "When Panthers Score 59 Points, Followers of Jumpin' Jive Quintet," *Pittsburgh Courier*, February 10, 1940, 16; and "From the Press Box," *Norfolk Journal and Guide*, April 8, 1939, 18.

116. "VA Union Tops LIU, 36 to 28!" *New York Amsterdam News*, April 1, 1939, 18.

117. "Local Five Victorious Over Champs," *Richmond Times-Dispatch*, March 25, 1939, 14; and "From the Press Box," *Norfolk Journal and Guide*, April 8, 1939, 18.

118. "Slants on Sports," *Atlanta Daily World*, April 4, 1939, 5.

119. S. Russell Wilson of Bishop Payne Divinity School to the *Richmond Times-Dispatch* sports editor, and H. B. Hucles of Virginia Union University to the *Richmond Times-Dispatch* sports editor, reprinted in the *Richmond Times-Dispatch*, March 28, 1939, 12.

120. "Union Panthers Modest Despite Conquest of LIU Blackbirds," *Atlanta Daily World*, April 4, 1939, 5.

121. "Panthers Are Modest over Their Conquest of LIU," *Richmond Times-Dispatch*, March 28, 1939, 12.

122. J. L. Whitehead, *Secretary Treasurer, CIAA Bulletin 1940, Proceedings of the Twenty-Seventh Annual Meeting*, Folder: CIAA Bulletins, 1936–1938, 1940–41, Union Archives.

123. "Cage Tournament Idea Takes Form in CIAA," *Norfolk Journal and Guide*, September 28, 1940, 16; and "CIAA Votes Tournament Plan on Experimental Basis,"

Baltimore Afro-American, December 21, 1940, 19. Before 1940, the CIAA did not host a postseason basketball tournament to determine a conference champion. Thus, coaches and school presidents voted on who they felt was the best team. Total wins and quality of wins were taken into the equation, but league leadership always selected the winner.

124. "VA Union's Great Quint Declared CIAA Champs," *Pittsburgh Courier,* April 8, 1939, 16; and "Bill Robinson Trophy Given Union Team," *Norfolk Journal and Guide,* April 15, 1939, 17.

125. "From the Bench," *Baltimore Afro-American,* January 27, 1940, 19.

126. "Virginia Union First in Three Fields," *Norfolk Journal and Guide,* May 6, 1939, 12; and "Campbell, Glover bag 243 Each," *Atlanta Daily World,* April 4, 1939, 5.

127. "From the Press Box," *Norfolk Journal and Guide,* April 8, 1939, 18.

128. "Dream Team of VA Union Honored," *Atlanta Daily World,* April 30, 1940, 5; and "Vivat, Union Abat," *Philadelphia Tribune,* January 18, 1940, 11.

129. "I Cover the Eastern Front," *Chicago Defender,* February 10, 1940, 22.

130. Director James H. Rowland Sr., Bluefield State Teachers College, "Response to President Clark's Welcome Address," 18, 1941 Bulletin of the CIAA, Union Archives.

131. "CIAA Dream Team Is Praised by Writer," *Atlanta Daily World,* March 11, 1940, 5; and "When Panthers Score 59 Points, Followers of Jumpin' Jive Quintet," *Pittsburgh Courier,* February 10, 1940, 16.

132. "When Panthers Score 59 Points, Followers of Jumpin' Jive Quintet," *Pittsburgh Courier,* February 10, 1940, 16; "5,000 See Union Clinch CIAA Cage Championship," *Baltimore Afro-American,* March 9, 1940, 19; "CIAA's no. 1 Team Decided in Heated Battle," *Atlanta Daily World,* March 18, 1940, 5; "NC State Claims Title After Triumph Over Union," *Baltimore Afro-American,* March 16, 1940, 19; "Slants on Sports," *Atlanta Daily World,* March 16, 1940, 5; "Eagles Claim National Cage Honors," *Norfolk Journal and Guide,* March 16, 1940, 17; "Slants on Sports," *Atlanta Daily World,* March 18, 1940, 5; "CIAA's no. 1 Team Decided in Heated Battle," *Atlanta Daily World,* March 18, 1940, 5; and "The Sports Bugle," *Pittsburgh Courier,* March 30, 1940, 17; Henry B. Hucles, head coach of Virginia Union University, "Basketball in the CIAA-1940," 1940 Bulletin of the CIAA, Union Archives; "Union's Crack Quint Drills on Dirt Court," *Baltimore Afro-American,* January 6, 1940, 2; "Union Cagers Plan to Play Mexican Five," *Baltimore Afro-American,* November 18, 1939, 21; "Union Opens Season With 60–41 Win," *Norfolk Journal and Guide,* December 16, 1939, 19; "Va Union's Crack Cage Machine Set," *Atlanta Daily World,* December 19, 1939, 5; "Union 5 Trounces Waves, 52–24," *Norfolk Journal and Guide,* December 23, 1939, 17; "Union Wallops Morgan, 59–47," *New York Amsterdam News,* January 27, 1940, 18; "From the Bench," *Baltimore Afro-American,* January 27, 1940, 19; and "When Panthers Score 59 Points, Followers of Jumpin' Jive Quintet," *Pittsburgh Courier,* February 10, 1940, 16.

133. "All-CIAA Team to Test Union," *Baltimore Afro-American,* March 9, 1940, 19.

134. "Southerners Nuts over Much Talked of Union Dream Team," *Atlanta Daily World,* April 4, 1940, 5; and "When Panthers Score 59 Points, Followers of Jumpin' Jive Quintet," *Pittsburgh Courier,* February 10, 1940, 16.

135. Union University Panthers Record-Basketball, Press Release for the Week

of February 29, 1940, Folder 92: Athletic Department Public Relations; and "When Panthers Score 59 Points, Followers of Jumpin' Jive Quintet," *Pittsburgh Courier*, February 10, 1940, 16.

136. "Southerners Nuts Over Much Talked of Union Dream Team," *Atlanta Daily World*, April 4, 1940, 5.

137. "CIAA All-Stars Find Va Union Too Tough," *Atlanta Daily World*, March 18, 1940, 5.

138. "Panthers Set Pace for CIAA Cagers Last Year," *Baltimore Afro-American*, January 4, 1941, 20.

139. "LIU Coach Would See Sepians in Garden," *Baltimore Afro-American*, April 2, 1938, 11.

140. Carlson, *Making March Madness*, 6–7.

141. Martin, *Benching Jim Crow*, 70; and Kemper, *Before March Madness*, 3. The three major tournaments that emerged in the 1930s were the National Association of Intercollegiate Basketball Tournament (later the NAIA) in 1937, the National Invitational Tournament (NIT) in 1938, and the NCAA Tournament in 1939. Neither tournament had supremacy over the other, and multiple "national champions" emerged from these competing tournaments. It was not until the 1950s that the NCAA Tournament solely determined the national champion. The NIT tournament that the Dream Team sought admission to was the most prominent of the day.

142. "Sez Ches," *Pittsburgh Courier*, March 16, 1940, 16.

143. "Union Stymied in Effort to Get in NY Tourney," *Philadelphia Tribune*, February 29, 1940, 12.

144. "From the Press Box," *Norfolk Journal and Guide*, February 10, 1940, 19.

145. "Union Stymied in Effort to Get in NY Tourney," *Philadelphia Tribune*, February 29, 1940, 12; "Bar Race Teams from Garden Cage Tourney," *Atlanta Daily World*, February 23, 1940, 5.

146. "Bar Race Teams from Garden Cage Tourney," *Atlanta Daily World*, February 23, 1940, 5; and "I Cover the Eastern Front," *Chicago Defender*, March 16, 1940, 23.

147. "Union Stymied in Effort to Get in NY Tourney," *Philadelphia Tribune*, February 29, 1940, 12.

148. "Panthers Set Pace for CIAA Cagers Last Year," *Baltimore Afro-American*, January 4, 1941, 20.

149. "Union Panthers Booked to Meet Brooklyn College '5,'" *Norfolk Journal and Guide*, November 30, 1940, 18.

150. "Union Drops Lincoln In," *Philadelphia Tribune*, December 12, 1940, 13.

151. "Union, W.VA State to Play White Five," *Baltimore Afro-American*, February 24, 1940, 21; and "Delay Selection of Cage Teams," *Baltimore Afro-American*, March 9, 1940, 20.

152. "Va Union-Brooklyn Cage Game December 27 A 'Natural,'" *Chicago Defender*, December 21, 1940, 22; "Union-Brooklyn Tilt Scheduled for Gate," *Baltimore Afro-American*, December 7, 1940, 21; and Official Basketball Program, 1942, Folder: Athletics Department, Basketball Programs, Athletic Department, Box 1 of 3, AR-0005, Union Archives.

153. "Union Panthers Booked to Meet Brooklyn College '5,'" *Norfolk Journal and Guide*, November 30, 1940, 18.

154. "Virginia Union Five Turns Back Brooklyn College, 54–38," *New York Amsterdam News,* January 4, 1941, 15; Brooklyn College Loses: Routed by Virginia Union Five" *New York Times,* December 28, 1940, S23; "Confidently Yours," *New York Amsterdam News,* January 4, 1941, 14; "I Cover the Eastern Front," *Chicago Defender,* January 11, 1941, 22; "Virginia Union Five Turns Back Brooklyn College, 54–38," *New York Amsterdam News,* January 4, 1941, 15; and "Virginia Union Cagers Crush Brooklyn College," *Pittsburgh Courier,* January 4, 1941, 16.

155. Minutes of the Special Meeting of the Colored Intercollegiate Athletic Association Held at Virginia State College, Petersburg, Virginia, March 15, 1941, 15, 1941 CIAA Bulletin, Union Archives; and Report of the Eligibility Committee, December 1940–December 1941, 19–24, 1942 CIAA Bulletin, Union Archives.

156. Wiggins and Elzey, "Creating Order in Black College Sports," 147.

157. Kemper, *Before March Madness,* 69–107.

158. Report of the Eligibility Committee, December 1940–December 1941, 19–24, 1942 CIAA, Union Archives.

159. Dr. J. A. Moore, Virginia State and chairman to the Virginia AAU, undated, 16, in Minutes of the Special Meeting of the Colored Intercollegiate Athletic Association Held at Virginia State College, Petersburg, Virginia, March 15, 1941, 1941 CIAA Bulletin, Union Archives.

160. "Smith Turns Back Morgan," *Norfolk Journal and Guide,* March 12, 1942, 12; "Union Awarded CIAA Cage Title," *Norfolk Journal and Guide,* June 6, 1942, 14; "Souvenir Program: The Basketball Epic of 1941–1942," Folder Athletics Department, Basketball Programs, Athletic Department, Box 1 of 3, AR-0005; Alpha Eta Chapter of the Alpha Kappa Alpha Sorority Banquet, April 22, 1942, Folder 91: Athletic Department Programs; and "Union vs. All-Stars," *Norfolk Journal and Guide,* April 4, 1942, 13.

161. Official Rankings of CIAA Basketball Season, 1942, 36, 1942 CIAA Bulletin, Union Archives.

162. "Lincoln and Union Breaks Relations," *Philadelphia Tribune,* December 26, 1940, 9.

163. "Atlanta Sports Await Dream Game," *Atlanta Daily World,* January 2, 1941, 5; "Mad Trojans Smash Union's Title Hopes," *Norfolk Journal and Guide,* March 8, 1941, 15; "Panther Is Series with Kentucky," *Norfolk Journal and Guide,* January 31, 1942, 13; "Clark, Tuskegee Play Tomorrow," *Atlanta Daily World,* January 10, 1941, 5; and "Clark Cagers Upset Union," *Norfolk Journal and Guide,* January 11, 1941, 18.

164. "From the Press Box: Basketball Now Respected by Sports Lovers," *Norfolk Journal and Guide,* January 24, 1942, 12; "Sim Booker Gets Another Union Plug," *Norfolk Journal and Guide,* February 7, 1942, 13; and "Eagles Turn Tables on Union," *Norfolk Journal and Guide,* February 28, 1942, 12.

165. Martin, *Benching Jim Crow,* 53; and Ellsworth, *Secret Game,* 4 and 288–99.

166. "Slants on Sports," *Atlanta Daily World,* April 1, 1940, 5.

167. Watterson, *College Football,* 202–7; and Martin, *Benching Jim Crow,* 52–57.

168. "Morris Brown's Football Hopes Gloomy For Forthcoming Season," *Atlanta Daily World,* June 6, 1942, 5; "Memphis Proves Ideal to Host Southern Coaches," *Atlanta Daily World,* September 15, 1942, 5; and "Bishop Drops Football for Body Fitness," *Norfolk Journal and Guide,* September 19, 1942, 15.

169. Venable Bravid W. Harris, archdeacon for Colored Work, Diocese of Southern Virginia, and rector of Grace Protestant Episcopal Church in Norfolk, Virginia, "The Challenge of the Present Crisis," 17–18, 1943 CIAA Bulletin, Union Archives.

170. "United States Army, Navy, Air Corps, List Some of Nation's Foremost Sports Celebs," *Atlanta Daily World*, June 14, 1942, 8; and "Football Coaches, Officials Meet in Memphis September 12–13," *Atlanta Daily World*, August 23, 1942, 8.

171. "The Outlook for Football Is Dark," *Norfolk Journal and Guide*, May 23, 1942, 13.

172. Professor Clarence W. Davis of Minter Teachers College, "You Must Adjust," CIAA 1943 Bulletin, Union Archives.

173. Professor George G. Singleton of Virginia State College, "President's Address," May 15, 1942, 19–21, CIAA 1943 Bulletin, Union Archives.

174. "West Virginia Announces 1942 Grid Schedule," *Norfolk Journal and Guide*, August 29, 1942, 14; "Tuskegee Mentor Calls Gridders," Norfolk Journal and Guide, August 29, 1942, 14; "Clark Hopes in Skies as 1942 Grid Nears," *Atlanta Daily World*, August 30, 1942, 8; "Morris Brown Badly Riddled Two-Time National Champs Resume Football," *Atlanta Daily World*, August 30, 1942, 8; "South Atlantic Football Coaches, Officials Meet at Claflin, September 19," *Atlanta Daily World*, September 5, 1942, 5; "Memphis Proves Ideal to Host Southern Coaches," *Atlanta Daily World*, September 15, 1942, 5; "Southwest Conference Set for Big Football Season," *Atlanta Daily World*, September 21, 1942, 5; and "Norfolk Polytech, Miner Drop Football in EIAC," *Norfolk Journal and Guide*, September 26, 1942, 14.

175. "Athletic Programs Warned to Adjust Programs to War Crisis," *Norfolk Journal and Guide*, December 26, 1942, 15; and "CIAA to Continue Despite Handicap of War," *Norfolk Journal and Guide*, May 22, 1943, 14.

176. Professor George G. Singleton of Virginia State College, "President's Address," May 15, 1943, 19–21, CIAA 1943 Bulletin, Union Archives.

177. "From the Press Box," *Norfolk Journal and Guide*, January 30, 1943, 13.

178. "CIAA Considers Effect of War on Football Schedules," *Norfolk Journal and Guide*, May 23, 1942, 12.

179. "Stress Moral Aspects Urges Dr. Ellison," *Norfolk Journal and Guide*, September 26, 1942, 14; and "Honor CIAA Athletes in Service," *Norfolk Journal and Guide*, December 19, 1942, 14; and "CIAA Directors Determined to Carry On," *Norfolk Journal and Guide*, December 19, 1942, 14.

180. John W. Barco, "To CIAA Men in the Armed Services," CIAA 1943 Bulletin, Union Archives.

181. De Athletis, articles in honor of fallen CIAA alumni during World War II, CIAA 1943 Bulletin, Union Archives; "From the Press Box," *Norfolk Journal and Guide*, January 2, 1943, 15; and "CIAA Honors Athletes Killed in Services," *Norfolk Journal and Guide*, December 16, 1944, 12.

182. "CIAA Breaks Down Eligibility Code for Duration," *Norfolk Journal and Guide*, September 25, 1943, 13.

183. "From the Press Box," *Norfolk Journal and Guide*, October 16, 1943, 13; and "CIAA Breaks Down Eligibility Code for Duration," *Norfolk Journal and Guide*, September 25, 1943, 13.

184. "From the Press Box," *Norfolk Journal and Guide*, December 16, 1944, 12.

185. "From the Press Box," *Norfolk Journal and Guide*, October 16, 1943, 13.

186. "V. Union On Court Friday," *Norfolk Journal and Guide*, December 11, 1943, 12; "Panthers Offer to Play for War Fund Benefit," *Norfolk Journal and Guide*, January 24, 1942, 11; "Brown Bombers Want Relief Game with CIAA," *Norfolk Journal and Guide*, June 13, 1942, 15; "CIAA Calls Emergency Session To Consider Wartime Schedule Changes," *Norfolk Journal and Guide*, September 5, 1942, 14; "Virginia State, Morgan State Seen as Top CIAA Teams," *Norfolk Journal and Guide*, September 12, 1942, 14; "From the Press Box," *Norfolk Journal and Guide*, September 19, 1942, 15; and "From the Press Box," *Norfolk Journal and Guide*, December 4, 1943, 13.

187. "Two Colleges Cancel as CIAA Hold Session," *Norfolk Journal and Guide*, September 26, 1942, 14.

188. "Virginia State, Morgan State Seen as Top CIAA Teams," *Norfolk Journal and Guide*, September 12, 1942, 14; and "Two Colleges Cancel as CIAA Hold Session," *Norfolk Journal and Guide*, September 26, 1942, 14.

189. Professor George G. Singleton, Virginia State College and president of the CIAA, "Address of the President of the Association," 1944 CIAA Bulletin, Union Archives; and "A. And T. Challenges Morgan Eleven To A Showdown," *Norfolk Journal and Guide*, December 18, 1943, 12.

190. "High Schools Arrange Two Games Per Season," *Norfolk Journal and Guide*, October 12, 1942; and "From the Press Box," *Norfolk Journal and Guide*, January 23, 1943, 12.

191. J. A. Moore, Commissioner of VIAL Basketball, "Forward," 5, 1948 VIAL Bulletin, Folder: VA Interscholastic Athletic League, Box 1: AR0005: Athletic Department, Union Archives.

192. Author Unknown, "Behind Each Sport—Unknown Millions," 21 and 28, 1951 VIAL Bulletin, Union Archives.

193. "From the Press Box," *Norfolk Journal and Guide*, February 6, 1943, 12; "From the Press Box," *Norfolk Journal and Guide*, March 27, 1943, 13; and "From the Press Box," *Norfolk Journal and Guide*, January 15, 1944, 10.

194. "From the Press Box," *Norfolk Journal and Guide*, May 22, 1943, 15.

195. "From the Press Box," *Norfolk Journal and Guide*, March 27, 1943, 13.

196. J. A. Moore, commissioner of VIAL Basketball, "Forward," 5, 1948 VIAL Bulletin, Union Archives.

197. "High School Conference To Resume Championships," *Norfolk Journal and Guide*, December 23, 1944, 12. The schools who formalized the VIAA's relationship with the CIAA were Booker T. Washington and St. Emma of Rock Castle (private) of Norfolk, Lucy B. Addison of Roanoke, Armstrong and Maggie Walker of Richmond, Christiansburg Institute, Dunbar of Lynchburg, Huntington of Newport News, Jefferson of Charlottesville, Parker-Gray of Alexandria, Norcom of Portsmouth, Peabody of Petersburg, Phenix of Hampton, and Walker-Grant of Alexandria.

198. The first publication of the VIAL Bulletin was in 1948, with each member paying $2.00 for the publication and mass distribution of the bulletin. The only surviving copy that is widely accessible to researchers is in Folder: VA Interscholastic Athletic League, Box 1: AR0005: Athletic Department, Union Archives.

199. The President's Message to the VIAL, 5–6, Report of Commissioner of Basketball, 6, and Last Minute Meeting, 11–12, 1951 VIAL Bulletin, Union Archives.

200. J. A. Moore, Commissioner of VIAL Basketball, "Forward," 5, 1948 VIAL Bulletin, Union Archives.

201. Richard L. Armistead, Principal of Langston High School in Danville, Virginia, "Excepts President's Address," 11, 1948 VIAL Bulletin, Union Archives.

Chapter 5

1. "From the Press Box," *Norfolk Journal and Guide*, December 16, 1967, 12. Richmond native Warren Winston started at cornerback for the Indians of the College of William and Mary in 1968 (in 1978, the William and Mary athletics teams' nickname changed to "the Tribe"). John Rainey, Kent Merritt, Harrison Davis, Stanley Land, and John Dobbins also broke the gridiron color barrier at then in-state rivals University of Virginia and Virginia Polytechnic Institute and State University. Edgar Ausberry of James Madison University; Dennis Howard of Randolph-Macon College; Charlie Tyler of Virginia Military Institute, Carlton Mack of University of Richmond, Arthur Speaks of Old Dominion University, Frankie Allen of Roanoke College, and Charles McLeod of Virginia Commonwealth University all integrated the hardwood.

2. "From the Press Box," *Norfolk Journal and Guide*, March 28, 1970, B21.

3. John W. Haun et al., *The 25th Edition of the Virginia High School League Record Book* (Charlottesville: Virginia High School League, April 2022), 10 and 31.

4. "Conference to Honor Bennie Washington," *Norfolk Journal and Guide*, April 2, 1955, 23.

5. David K. Wiggins, "'The Future of College Athletics Is at Stake:' Black Athletes and Racial Turmoil on Three Predominantly White University Campuses, 1968–1972," *Journal of Sport History* 15, no. 3 (Winter 1988): 304–33; Chris Lamb, "'I Never Want to Take Another Trip Like This One': Jackie Robinson's Journey to Integrate Baseball," *Journal of Sport History* 24, no. 2 (Summer 1997): 177–91; Ursula McTaggart, "Writing Baseball into History: The *Pittsburgh Courier*, Integration, and Baseball in a War of Position," *American Studies* 47, no. 1 (Spring 2006): 113–32; Michael E. Lomax, "The African American Experience in Professional Football," *Journal of Social History* 33, no. 1 (Autumn 1999): 163–78; Gregory J. Kaliss, "Un-Civil Discourse: Charlie Scott, the Integration of College Basketball, and the 'Progressive Mystique,'" *Journal of Sport History* 35, no. 1 (Spring 2008): 98–117; S. Zebulon Baker, "'On the Opposite Side of the Fence': The University of Kentucky and the Racial Desegregation of the Southeastern Conference," *Register of the Kentucky Historical Society* 115, no. 4 (Autumn 2017): 561–610; Charles K. Ross, *Outside the Lines: African Americans and the Integration of the National Football League* (New York: New York University Press, 2001); Martin, *Benching Jim Crow*; Demas, *Integrating the Gridiron*; Freedman, *Breaking the Line*; David Kingsley Snell, *The Baron and the Bear: Rupp's Runts, Haskins's Miners, and the Season that Changed Basketball Forever* (Lincoln: University of Nebraska Press, 2016); Douglas Stark, *Breaking Barriers: A History of Integration in Professional Basketball* (Washington, DC: Rowman & Littlefield, 2018); Art Chansky, *Game Changers: Dean Smith, Charlie Scott, and the Era That Transformed a Southern College Town* (Chapel Hill: University of North Carolina Press, 2018); and Robert Jacobus, *Black Man in the Middle: Stories from the Integration of Texas Football* (College Station: Texas A&M University Press, 2019).

6. Eddie W. Morris, "The Contemporary Negro College and the Brain Drain,"

Journal of Negro Education 41, no. 4 (Autumn 1972): 309–19; Henry Lee Allen, "The Mobility of Black Collegiate Faculty Revisited: Whatever Happened to the 'Brain Drain'?" *Journal of Negro Education* 60, no. 1 (Winter 1991): 97–109; Jeanita W. Richardson and J. John Harris II, "Brown and Historically Black Colleges and Universities (HBCUs): A Paradox of Desegregation Policy," *Journal of Negro Education* 73, no. 3 (Summer 2004): 365–78; Rachel A. Woldoff, *White Flight/Black Flight: The Dynamics of Racial Change in an American Neighborhood* (Ithaca, NY: Cornell University Press, 2011); Robert W. Lake, *The New Suburbanites: Race and Housing in the Suburbs* (New York: Taylor & Francis Publishing, 2012); Bobby L. Lovett, *America's Historically Black Colleges: A Narrative History, 1837–2009* (Macon, GA: Mercer University Press, 2011), 199–203; Mehrsa Baradaran, *The Color of Money: Black Banks and the Racial Wealth Gap* (Cambridge, MA: Harvard University Press, 2017); Keeanga Yamahtta Taylor, *Race for Profit: How Banks and the Real Estate Industry Undermined Black Homeownership* (Chapel Hill: University of North Carolina Press, 2019); and Stacy Hawkins, "Reverse Integration: Centering HBCUs in the Fight for Education Equality," *Journal of Law and Social Change* 24, no. 3 (2021): 351–410.

7. Hawkins et al., *Athletic Experience at Historically Black Colleges and Universities*, 114.

8. Charles W. Johnson, "V for Virginia: The Commonwealth Goes to War," *Virginia Magazine of History and Biography* 100, no. 3 (July 1992): 365–98.

9. "From the Press Box," *Norfolk Journal and Guide*, February 6, 1943, 12; and "From the Press Box," *Norfolk Journal and Guide*, December 4, 1943, 13.

10. "Annual Coaching School Ends at Virginia State College," *Norfolk Journal and Guide*, July 19, 1947, 14.

11. Frank A. Young, "Football in the South Needs Housecleaning," *Chicago Defender*, December 14, 1929, 8; "Southerners Nuts Over Much Talked of Union Dream Team," *Atlanta Daily World*, April 4, 1940, 5; "Slants on Sports," *Atlanta Daily World*, April 1, 1940, 5; and "Clark Places Three, Union Two On All-American Cage Team," *Pittsburgh Courier*, April 6, 1940, 17; "When Panthers Score 59 Points, Followers of Jumpin' Jive Quintet," *Pittsburgh Courier*, February 10, 1940, 16; "CIAA Dream Team Is Praised by Writer," *Atlanta Daily World*, March 11, 1940, 5; "Between the Lines: Whence," *Norfolk Journal and Guide*, October 14, 1933, 6; "Between the Lines: Race Relations in North Carolina," *Norfolk Journal and Guide*, January 28, 1939, 8; Mal Nicholson of the *Virginian-Pilot* to Mr. Womble, executive secretary, September 28, 1965; Charles W. Womble, executive secretary to Mr. Mal Nicholson, *Virginian-Pilot*, September 30, 1965, Folder 13—VIA Press, 1965; Malverse Nicholson, Sports Department of the *Virginian-Pilot* to Mr. Charles Womble, executive secretary, July 28, 1966; Charles W. Womble, executive secretary to Mr. Malverse Nicholson, Sports Department at the *Virginian Pilot*, August 1, 1966, Folder #14—Press (Correspondence, etc.,), 1966–1967, Box 11, Virginia Interscholastic Association (VIA) Papers, Virginia State University Special Collections, Petersburg, Virginia. The Virginia Interscholastic Association Papers, all of which are located at Virginia State University, will be henceforth cited as VIA Papers.

12. "From the Press Box," *Norfolk Journal and Guide*, December 29, 1962, B20.

13. Martin, *Benching Jim Crow*; and Spivey, *Racism, Activism, and Integrity in College Football.*

14. Reports of Special Committee on Basketball, 48, the 1956 CIAA Bulletin, Union Archives; T. L. Hill, Report of the NAIA District Twenty-Nine, 67, G. G. Singleton, Report on the NCAA Delegation, 67–68, and H. R. Jefferson, Report of the National Athletic Steering Committee, 68–69, the 1957 CIAA Bulletin, Union Archives.

15. Demas, *Integrating the Gridiron*, 28–77; and Martin, *Benching Jim Crow*, 61–71.

16. "From the Press Box," *Norfolk Journal and Guide*, August 15, 1970, B21; and *The Lion*, Lincoln University Student Yearbook (website), 50.

17. Dr. Charles C. Hawkins, "Introduction of Mr. William T. Nunn," 1946–1947 CIAA Bulletin, Union Archives.

18. Paul J. Moore, president of the CIAA "President's Address to the Thirty-Seventh Annual Meeting of the CIAA," 1950 CIAA Bulletin, Union Archives.

19. "Joe Rainey Approves of Athletic Scholarships," *Baltimore Afro-American*, December 25, 1937, 18; Charles H. Williams, "Goals to be Achieved in the Next Twenty-five Years," 1937 CIAA Bulletin, Union Archives.

20. "College Presidents Move to Bar Athletic Scholarships," *Atlanta Daily World*, January 14, 1953, 5.

21. Panel Discussion on Aid to Athletes, 12–15, 1955 CIAA Bulletin, Union Archives.

22. Dr. C. R. Frazier, Head of Academic Department at Morgan State University, Report of the Committee to Aid Athletes, 41–42, 1956 CIAA Bulletin, Union Archives.

23. Dr. C. R. Frazier, "Report of the Committee to Aid Athletes," 1956 CIAA Bulletin, Union Archives; and Dr. Charles R. Frazier, Committee on Aid to Athletes, 76–77, 1957 CIAA Bulletin, Union Archives.

24. "CIAA Officials, Presidents Launch Joint Effort to Solve Scholarship, Aid to Athlete Problems," *Norfolk Journal and Guide*, March 31, 1956, 19.

25. "ACC's Use of Negro Players May Doom All-Negro Conferences," *Philadelphia Tribune*, February 5, 1963, 10.

26. "Whites Easily Integrated into Negro Colleges," *Chicago Defender*, November 14, 1962, 1.

27. "From the Press Box," *Norfolk Journal and Guide*, December 7, 1963, B22.

28. "From the Press Box," *Norfolk Journal and Guide*, November 29, 1958, 16.

29. "Seek White Players," *Cleveland Call and Post*, January 16, 1965, 12.

30. "From the Press Box," *Norfolk Journal and Guide*, December 7, 1963, B22.

31. "CIAA Has a White Cager," *Philadelphia Tribune*, January 25, 1966, 12; "Va Union, Va College Seek White Gridders," *Chicago Defender*, September 3, 1966, 17; and "First White Player at A&T," *Michigan Chronicle*, March 1, 1969, 2.

32. "Thorobreds Integrate Football Team," *Chicago Daily Defender*, September 30, 1964, 32; and "4 White Players Rattler Signees," *Atlanta Daily World*, April 29, 1970, 9.

33. "From the Press Box," *Norfolk Journal and Guide*, June 12, 1971, A20; "Norfolk State College Grid Team Is Changing with the Times," Norfolk State, *Norfolk Journal and Guide*, December 27, 1975, 16;

34. Quote "From the Press Box," *Norfolk Journal and Guide*, August 15, 1970, B21; "Spartans Sign First White Cager," *Norfolk Journal and Guide*, October 22, 1966, 13;

"VA Union May Be Next," *Norfolk Journal and Guide,* September 3, 1966, 25; and "From the Press Box," *Norfolk Journal and Guide,* August 15, 1970, 12.

35. "NCAA Sanctions Second Black College Bowl Game," *Norfolk Journal and Guide,* October 26, 1979, 16

36. "From the Press Box," *Norfolk Journal and Guide,* December 30, 1972, 13; "Road Openers to Test Cager," *Norfolk Journal and Guide,* November 26, 1977, 16; "Press Box," *Norfolk Journal and Guide,* October 13, 1978, 16; "From the Press Box," *Norfolk Journal and Guide,* December 30, 1972, 13; "Spartan's Opener William & Mary," *Norfolk Journal and Guide,* March 26, 1977, 16; "Road Openers to Test Cager," *Norfolk Journal and Guide,* November 26, 1977, 16; "Press Box," *Norfolk Journal and Guide,* October 13, 1978, 16; and "Virginia State Announces 1980 Football Schedule," *Norfolk Journal and Guide,* March 28, 1980, 13.

37. "Hires White Cage Coach," *Michigan Chronicle,* September 9, 1978, 1.

38. Daryl Bell, "No One Can Deny the Coaching Greatness of the White Shadow," *AndScape* (formerly known as the *Undefeated*) (website), October 13, 2016; CIAA Hall of Fame Profile for Dave Robbins of Virginia Union University (website), undated; and Autumn Childress, "Soul of RVA: A Look Inside VUU's Dominant Basketball Program and Coach Behind Team's Success," *ABC 8 News* (website), April 7, 2016.

39. Edwards, *Revolt of the Black Athlete,* quote on 5, and 38–75; Hartmann, *Race, Culture, and the Revolt of the Black Athlete;* and Martha Biondi, *The Black Revolution on Campus* (Berkeley: University of California Press, 2014).

40. "Peace Returns to USC Cage Team After Boycott by White Players," *Atlanta Daily World,* January 27, 1968, 5; "Black Players Strike Team," *Cleveland Call and Post,* November 14, 1970, 11; and "Calif Cagers Plan Boycott," *Chicago Defender,* December 26, 1970, 25.

41. "College Campus Very Lonely Place for Negro Athletes," *Philadelphia Tribune,* July 9, 1968, 3; "White Women Pose Problem for Athletes," *Cleveland Call and Post,* January 27, 1968, 3; and "Jim Brown Supports Suspended Syracuse 8," *Chicago Defender,* September 21, 1970, 29.

42. "Black Coach Suspends Eight White Players," *Michigan Chronicle,* December 13, 1969, A4.

43. "Why No Negro Football Coaches at American White Universities," *Daily Defender,* February 11, 1959, 22; and "Blacks Still Have Hard Time Getting a Non-Playing Job," *Philadelphia Tribune,* December 5, 1970, 18.

44. "White Athletes Face 'Being Different,'" *Michigan Chronicle,* April 25, 1970, A4.

45. Recommendations to the CIAA, 45, 1959 CIAA Bulletin, Union Archives.

46. E. H. McClenney, Address of Secretary of Presidents, 46, 1959 CIAA Bulletin, Union Archives.

47. J. E. Thompson, vice president of the Central District of the CIAA, Reports to the Vice President, 1, Resume of the Proceedings of the Forty-Eight Annual Meeting of the CIAA, March 24–26, 1960, 1960 CIAA Bulletin, Union Archives.

48. "Trouble in the CIAA?" *Norfolk Journal and Guide,* October 13, 1962, 13.

49. Joseph E. Thompson, Reports of the Central District of the CIAA, 45–46, 1959 CIAA Bulletin, Union Archives; "From the Press Box," *Norfolk Journal and*

Guide, April 4, 1970, 13; "Rich Television Deal May Loom for CIAA," *Norfolk Journal and Guide*, March 19, 1970, B10; and "The CIAA To Survive," *Norfolk Journal and Guide*, September 8, 1970, 5.

50. "From the Press Box," *Norfolk Journal and Guide*, April 29, 1972, B24.

51. Wiggins, "With All Deliberate Speed," 329–46; "NJ Schools Almost 100% Integrated," *Philadelphia Tribune*, May 17, 1949, 3; and James W. Miller, *Integrated: The Lincoln Institute and Vanished Tradition* (Lexington: University of Kentucky Press, 2017).

52. "Sees Interracial Games Challenge to Athletics," *Norfolk Journal and Guide*, March 23, 1946, 13; "DC Witnesses First Mixed Hi Game," *Baltimore Afro-American*, November 11, 1950, 17; John McNamara, *The Capital of Basketball: A History of DC Area High School Hoops* (Washington, DC: Georgetown University Press, 2019), 40; and Wendell A. Parriss, "Integration of Athletics in the District of Columbia Public High Schools," *Negro History Bulletin* 19, no. 1 (October 1955): 14–15.

53. "Carlisle's 1955 Integrated Team," Notable Kentucky African American Database (website), last modified November 29, 2023.

54. Peter L. Scamardo II, "Legend Reflects on How Corpus Christi Led Way to Integrate High School Football in Texas," *Corpus Cristi Caller Times* (website), November 25, 2019.

55. Todd Holcomb, "Notebook: 50th Anniversary of First Integrated Game," *Atlanta Journal and Constitution* (website), September 2, 2016.

56. "Epithets Hurled, Players Spat On," *Baltimore Afro-American*, February 9, 1946, 22; and Donald Roe, "From Desegregation to Resegregation: The Crisis in the District of Columbia Public School System, 1954–1962," *Black History Bulletin* 67, no. 1/4 (January-December 2004), 18–25.

57. Muse, *Virginia's Massive Resistance*; Gates, *Making of Massive Resistance*, 1–24; Pratt, *Color of Their Skin*, 1–32; Matthew D. Lassiter and Andrew B. Lewis, eds., *The Moderates' Dilemma: Massive Resistance to School Desegregation in Virginia* (Charlottesville: University of Virginia Press, 1998); James R. Sweeney, "Southern Strategies," *Virginia Magazine of History and Biography* 106, no. 2 (Spring 1998): 165–200; Leidholdt, *Standing Before the Shouting Mob*; Sara K. Eskridge, "Virginia's Pupil Placement Board and the Practical Applications of Massive Resistance, 1956–1966," *Virginia Magazine of History & Biography* 118, no. 3 (June 2010): 246–76; James R. Sweeney, ed., *Race, Reason, and Massive Resistance: The Diary of David J. Mays, 1954–1959* (Athens: University of Georgia Press, 2008); William P. Hustwit, *James J. Kilpatrick: Salesman for Segregation* (Chapel Hill: University of North Carolina Press, 2013); Littlejohn and Ford, *Elusive Equality*; Daugherity, *Keep on Keeping On*; and Titus, *Brown's Battleground*.

58. Miller, *Integrated*; and Phillip Hoose, *Attucks!: How Crispus Attucks Basketball Broke Racial Barriers and Jolted the World* (New York: Farrar, Straus and Giroux, 2018).

59. Virginia Interscholastic Association Executive Council Meeting in Virginia Hall Conference Room at Virginia State University, April 20, 1954, Folder #1: VIA Executive Committee Meetings, 1954–1955, Box #1, Series 1: Minutes and Annual Reports, VIA Papers.

60. Bound Volume of Legislative Council Meeting, June 1954 to June 1969, 9, Box #3, Series #1: Minutes and Annual Reports, VIA Papers, VSU Archives.

61. Minutes of the Executive Committee of the Virginia Interscholastic Association, Saturday, May 15, 1954, Folder #1: VIA Executive Committee Meetings, 1954–1955, Box #1, Series 1: Minutes and Annual Reports, VIA Papers.

62. Virginia Interscholastic Association Executive Council Meeting in Virginia Hall Conference Room at Virginia State College, May 14, 1954, Folder #1: VIA Executive Committee Meetings, 1954–1955, Box #1, Series 1: Minutes and Annual Reports; Annual Report, Virginia Interscholastic Association Division of Field Services, Virginia State College, Petersburg, Virginia, June 15, 1955, Folder #5, VIA Annual Report, 1954–1955, Box#4: Annual Reports, Series #1, Minutes and Annual Reports, VIA Papers.

63. Minutes of the Meeting of the Executive Committee of the Virginia Interscholastic Association at Hampton Institute, June 23, 1954, Folder #1: VIA Executive Committee Meetings, 1954–1955, Box #1, Series 1: Minutes and Annual Reports, VIA Papers.

64. Minutes of the Meeting of the Executive Committee of the Virginia Interscholastic Association, January 22, 1955, at 114 Foster Hall at Virginia State College, Folder #1: VIA Executive Committee Meetings, 1954–1955, Box #1, Series 1: Minutes and Annual Reports, Virginia Interscholastic Association Papers, Virginia State University; Annual Report, Virginia Interscholastic Association Division of Field Services, Virginia State College, Petersburg, Virginia, June 15, 1955, Folder #5, VIA Annual Report, 1954–1955, Box #4: Annual Reports, Series #1, Minutes and Annual Reports, VIA Papers.

65. Annual Report, Virginia Interscholastic Association Division of Field Services, Virginia State College, Petersburg, Virginia, June 15, 1955, Folder #5, VIA Annual Report, 1954–1955, Box#4: Annual Reports, Series #1, Minutes and Annual Reports, VIA Papers.

66. Virginia Interscholastic Association Executive Council Meeting in Virginia Hall Conference Room at Virginia State University, April 20, 1954, Folder #1: VIA Executive Committee Meetings, 1954–1955, Box #1, Series 1: Minutes and Annual Reports, VIA Papers.

67. Minutes of the Meeting of the Executive Committee of the Virginia Interscholastic Association, September 25, 1954, at Virginia State College, Folder #1: VIA Executive Committee Meetings, 1954–1955, Box #1, Series 1: Minutes and Annual Reports, VIA Papers.

68. Areas for Study, undated, Folder #10: The VIA Executive Committee Report, undated (probably 1960–61), Box #2, Series #1: Minutes and Annual Reports, VIA Papers.

69. Jackson, *Virginia Teachers Association*; and Adah L. Ward Randolph, "It Is Better to Light a Candle Than Curse the Darkness: Ethel Thompson Overby and Democratic Schooling in Richmond, Virginia, 1910–1958," *Journal of American Educational Studies Association* 48, no. 3 (May 2012): 220–43.

70. W. D. Scales, principal of Huntington High School in Newport News, Virginia to C. D. Paige, November 29, 1955, Folder #15: The VIA Protests (Member Schools), 1955–1956, Box#11, Series IV: Administrative Correspondence, VIA Papers.

71. Minutes of the Meeting of the Executive Committee of the Virginia Interscholastic Association, December 3, 1954, at 114 Foster Hall at Virginia State College,

Folder #1: VIA Executive Committee Meetings, 1954–1955, Box #1, Series 1: Minutes and Annual Reports, VIA Papers.

72. Minutes of the Meeting of the Executive Committee of the Virginia Interscholastic Association, January 22, 1955, at 114 Foster Hall at Virginia State College, Folder #1: VIA Executive Committee Meetings, 1954–1955, Box #1, Series 1: Minutes and Annual Reports, VIA Papers.

73. Minutes of the Meeting of the Executive Committee of the Virginia Interscholastic Association, February 19, 1955, in the Conference Room in Virginia Hall at Virginia State College, Folder #1: VIA Executive Committee Meetings, 1954–1955, Box #1, Series #1: Minutes and Annual Reports, VIA Papers.

74. Annual Report, Virginia Interscholastic Association Division of Field Services, Virginia State College, Petersburg, Virginia, June 15, 1955, Folder #5, VIA Annual Report, 1954–1955, Box#4: Annual Reports, Series #1, Minutes and Annual Reports, VIA Papers.

75. JA Hubbard, principal of Tazewell County High School to Mr. C. D. Page, executive secretary of VIA, March 19, 1955, Folder 2: Legislative Council Correspondence, 1954–1955, Box #3, Series #1: Minutes and Annual Reports, VIA Papers.

76. Minutes of the Meeting of the Executive Committee of the Virginia Interscholastic Association, Sunday, March 13, 1955 at Virginia State College, Folder #1: VIA Executive Committee Meetings, 1954–1955, Box #1, Series #1: Minutes and Annual Reports; C. D. Page to Mr. R. L. Rice, principal of James W. Johnson High School, Yorktown, Virginia, May 16, 1955, Folder #2: Legislative Council Correspondence, 1954–1955, Box #3, Series #1: Minutes and Annual Reports, VIA Papers. For more "protests" during the earliest days of the VIA, see Folder 15: The VIA Protests (Member Schools), 1955–1956, Box #11, Series IV: Administrative Correspondence, VIA Papers.

77. Bound Volume of Legislative Council Meeting, June 1954 to June 1969, 61–107, Box #3, Series #1: Minutes and Annual Reports, VIA Papers.

78. Annual Report, Virginia Interscholastic Association, 1958–1959, Folder #8, VIA Annual Report 1958–1959, Box #4: Annual Reports, Series#1: Minutes and Annual Reports, VIA Papers.

79. Bound Volume of Legislative Council Meeting, June 1954 to June 1969, 21, p. 61, Box #3, Series #1: Minutes and Annual Reports, VIA Papers.

80. Annual Report, Virginia Interscholastic Association, 1958–1959, Folder #8, VIA Annual Report 1958–1959, Box #4: Annual Reports, Series #1: Minutes and Annual Reports, VIA Papers.

81. Annual Report of Virginia Interscholastic Association, June 15, 1957, Folder #11: The VIA Annual Report, June 15, 1957, Box #2, Series #1: Minutes and Annual Reports, VIA Papers.

82. Annual Report, Virginia Interscholastic Association, 1958–1959, Folder #8, VIA Annual Report 1958–1959, Box #4: Annual Reports, Series #1: Minutes and Annual Reports, VIA Papers.

83. Annual Report VIA, 1960–61, Folder #12, The VIA Annual Report 1960–1961, Box #2, Series #1: Minutes and Annual Reports, VIA Papers.

84. Meeting of the Executive Committee and Northern District, Group I, March 25, 1961, Folder 3: The VIA Districts, a.d., Box #9, Series IV: Series IV: Administrative Correspondence, VIA Papers.

85. C. P. Hazzard, chairman of the Northern District, Group 1 of the VIA and principal of Luther Porter Jackson High School in Merrifield, Virginia to Mr. C. D. Paige, executive secretary, October 25, 1963, Folder 4: Group I Schools Correspondence, 1958–1964, Box #10, Series IV: Administrative Correspondence, VIA Papers.

86. Virginia Interscholastic Association, 1962–1963, Folder #11: VIA Annual Report, 1962–1963, Box #4: Annual Reports, Series #1: Series #1: Minutes and Annual Reports; Charles W. Womble, executive secretary of the VIA to Mr. H. A. Fleshmon, principal of George W. Carver Regional in Rapidan, Virginia, April 25, 1966, Folder #2: The VIA Coaches Conference Correspondence, 1961–1962, Series IV: Administrative Correspondence, VIA Papers.

87. Continued Decline, Reduced Operation Catalysts for Merger and Dissolution: The Final Annual Report of the Executive Secretary, Virginia Interscholastic Association, Submitted to the Legislative Council by Charles W. Womble, Executive Secretary, Folder #13: The VIA Final Annual Report, 1968–1969, Box #4: Annual Reports, Series #1: Minutes and Annual Reports, VIA Papers.

88. A. L. Scott, chairman of the Legislative Council and Charles W. Womble, executive secretary, Special Notice of the VIA, June 10, 1966, Folder #2: The VIA Coaches Conference Correspondence, 1961–1962, Series IV: Administrative Correspondence, VIA Papers.

89. "State of the VIA, 1967–1968: A Report to the Legislative Council of the Virginia Interscholastic Association," prepared by Charles W. Womble, executive secretary: report also called "VIA at the Crossroads" (Womble, February 1968), found in VIA Papers.

90. Charles W. Womble, executive secretary of VIA to Mr. D. C. Robinson, principal of JS Russell High School in Lawrenceville, VA, August 10, 1967, Folder #2: The VIA Coaches Conference Correspondence, 1961–1962, Series IV: Administrative Correspondence, VIA Papers; C. D. Paige, executive secretary of Group I to Schools in the Southern District of Group I, October 21, 1963, Folder #21: The VIA Schools in Southern Districts, Group 1, Box#11, VIA Papers.

91. S. M. Hawkins, athletic director of Lee M. Waid School, to District Committee, Group II, District V, February 28, 1963, Folder #9: The VIA, Group II Schools Information and Correspondence, 1958–1964, Box #10, Series IV, VIA Papers.

92. C. D. Harman, principal of Carver High School in Salem, Virginia to District III Principals, February 25, 1963; Maurice M. Robinson, principal of Carver-Price High School in Appomattox, Virginia to Mr. C. D. Paige, executive secretary, February 27, 1964, Folder #9, Box #10, Series IV, VIA Papers.

93. CD Paige, executive secretary to All Western District VIA Schools, March 9, 1964, Folder 4: Group I Schools Correspondence, 1958–1964, Box #10, Series IV, VIA Papers.

94. Womble, "State of the VIA, 1967–1968" and "VIA at the Crossroads" (February 1968), VIA Papers.

95. C. Wittman Banks Jr., member of the Danville Board of Officials to Mrs. Vera Murphy, Chairman of the Western District Group I of the VIA, Langston High School, Danville, Virginia, December 12, 1966, Folder #2: The VIA Coaches Conference Correspondence, 1961–1962, Series IV: Administrative Correspondence, VIA Papers.

96. James C. Nelson, director of Student Activities at Burton Heights High School in Williamsburg, Virginia to Mr. H. Colson Jackson, dean of Men at Virginia State College, April 16 1964, Folder 3: The VIA Correspondence (General), 1963–1964, Box #10, Series IV, Virginia Interscholastic Association Papers, Virginia State University; Elmore E. Rainey, principal of Peabody High School in Petersburg, Virginia to the Very Reverend Egbert J. Figaro, director and dean of St. Emma Military Academy in Powhatan, Virginia, November 8, 1967: fight happened at a football game October 20, 1967, Folder #2: The VIA Coaches Conference Correspondence, 1961–1962, Series IV: Administrative Correspondence, VIA Papers.

97. District IX, Group II Meeting at George Washington Carver High School in Chesapeake, Virginia, February 24, 1963, Folder 7: The VIA Meetings (Group II) 1960–1967, Box #10, Series IV; Minutes of the Northern District Group I of the VIA, December 16, 1963; CW Seay, principal of Dunbar High School in Lynchburg, Virginia to Mr. A.G. Tippitt, principal of Northside High School in Gretna, Virginia, March 20, 1964, Folder 3: The VIA Correspondence (General), 1963–1964, Box #11, Series IV, VIA Papers.

98. Continued Decline, Reduced Operation Catalysts for Merger and Dissolution: The Final Annual Report of the Executive Secretary, Virginia Interscholastic Association, Submitted to the Legislative Council by Charles W. Womble, executive secretary, Folder #13: The VIA Final Annual Report, 1968–1969, Box #4: Annual Reports, Series #1: Minutes and Annual Reports, VIA Papers.

99. Continued Decline, Reduced Operation Catalysts for Merger and Dissolution: The Final Annual Report of The Executive Secretary, Virginia Interscholastic Association, Submitted to the Legislative Council by Charles W. Womble, executive secretary, Folder #13: The VIA Final Annual Report, 1968–1969, Box #4: Annual Reports, Series #1: Minutes and Annual Reports, VIA Papers.

100. "From the Press Box," *Norfolk Journal and Guide*, February 10, 1968, 13.

101. "State of the VIA, 1967–1968: A Report to the Legislative Council of the Virginia Interscholastic Association," prepared by Charles W. Womble, executive secretary: report also called "VIA at the Crossroads," February 1968, Folder #23: Legislative Council Report, 1967–1968, Box #3, Series #1: Minutes and Annual Reports, VIA Papers.

102. Continued Decline, Reduced Operation Catalysts for Merger and Dissolution: The Final Annual Report of the Executive Secretary, Virginia Interscholastic Association, Submitted to the Legislative Council by Charles W. Womble, executive secretary, Folder #13: The VIA Final Annual Report, 1968–1969, Box #4: Annual Reports, Series #1: Minutes and Annual Reports, VIA Papers.

103. "From the Press Box," *Norfolk Journal and Guide*, July 1, 1967, 12.

104. "From the Press Box," *Norfolk Journal and Guide*, June 3, 1967, 12.

105. Statement of VIA-VHSL Joint Committee, undated, Folder #13: The VIA Final Annual Report, 1968–1969, Box #4: Annual Reports, Series #1: Minutes and Annual Reports, VIA Papers.

106. "VIA-VHSL Consolidate As Leagues Approve Merger," *Norfolk Journal and Guide*, March 29, 1969, 12; "Veteran Coach to Head State Athletic Program," *Norfolk Journal and Guide*, April 18, 1970, 1.

107. "Smith's VHSL Initial Coach," *Norfolk Journal and Guide*, May 30, 1970, 25.

108. "Tidewater Sports," *Norfolk Journal and Guide*, January 24, 1970, B20.

109. "From the Press Box," *Norfolk Journal and Guide*, February 28, 1970, 12.

110. "From the Press Box," *Norfolk Journal and Guide*, September 27, 1969, 12.

111. Haun et al., *The 25th Edition of the Virginia High School League Record Book*, 10 and 31.

112. "From the Press Box," *Norfolk Journal and Guide*, March 27, 1971, 13.

113. "From the Press Box," *Norfolk Journal and Guide*, November 18, 1967, 13.

114. Continued Decline, Reduced Operation Catalysts for Merger and Dissolution: The Final Annual Report of the Executive Secretary, Virginia Interscholastic Association, Submitted to the Legislative Council by Charles W. Womble, executive secretary, Folder #13: the VIA Final Annual Report, 1968–1969, Box #4: Annual Reports, Series #1: Minutes and Annual Reports, VIA Papers.

115. Charles I. Thurston, chairman of the VIA, Preface, undated, Folder #23: Legislative Council Report, 1967–1968, Box #3, Series #1: Minutes and Annual Reports, VIA Papers.

116. Continued Decline, Reduced Operation Catalysts for Merger and Dissolution: The Final Annual Report of the Executive Secretary, Virginia Interscholastic Association, Submitted to the Legislative Council by Charles W. Womble, executive secretary, Folder #13: the VIA Final Annual Report, 1968–1969, Box #4: Annual Reports, Series #1: Minutes and Annual Reports, VIA Papers.

117. Final Meeting of the VIA Executive Committee, August 5, 1969, Folder 12: the VIA Annual Report Correspondence, 1968–1969, Box #4, Series #1: Minutes and Annual Reports, VIA Papers.

118. Bound Volume of Legislative Council Meeting, June 1954 to June 1969, Box #3, Series #1: Minutes and Annual Reports, VIA Papers.

119. "Black Coach Quits Manual, Says Racial Bias Hurt Team," *Louisville Defender*, September 10, 1970, 1. "Community College's Black Coach Tenders Resignation," *Pittsburgh Courier*, October 3, 1970, 15.

120. "Dixie Team's Fight Song," *Norfolk Journal and Guide*, October 17, 1970, 15.

121. "Coaches Quit in Fuss Over Clinched Fist," *Michigan Chronicle*, March 21, 1970, 3.

122. "Boy Who Quit Team in Anger Slashes White Coach," *Norfolk Journal and Guide*, November 14, 1970, 2.

123. "Black and White Athletes," *Michigan Chronicle*, March 14, 1970, 2.

Coda

1. Kenn Rashad, "Division 1 HBCU Revenue Rankings," HBCU Sports (website), July 3, 2018.

2. Brianna Nargiso, "Why HBCUs Athletic Programs Have Not Reached Top Tier Status," Howard University News Service (website), undated.

3. Omer Yusuf, "Team Penny Captures Second Straight AAU National Title," *Commercial Appeal* (website), July 13, 2015; and Andrew Joseph, "An Animated Lebron Helped Coach His Son's AAU Team to a National Championship," USA Today (website), July 22, 2018.

4. Billy Hawkins, "The Black Student Athlete: The Colonized Black Body," *Journal of African American Men* 1, no. 3 (Winter 1995/96): 23–35; Andrew Zimbalist,

Unpaid Professionals: Commercialism and Conflict in Big-Time College Sports (Princeton, NJ: Princeton University Press, 1999); William C. Rhoden, *Forty Million Dollar Slaves: The Rise, Fall, and Redemption of the Black Athlete* (New York: Crown Publishing Group, 2006); and Billy Hawkins, *The New Plantation: Black Athletes, College Sports, and Predominantly White NCAA Institutions* (London: Palgrave MacMillan, 2010).

5. Steven J. Gaither, "HBCU One Step Closer to Bringing Home National Title," *HBCU Gameday* (website), March 20, 2022.

6. "Black Athletics Alive and Well," *Norfolk Journal and Guide*, July 16, 1977, 17.

7. Alex Poinsett, "The Brain Drain at Negro Colleges," *Ebony Magazine* 25, no. 12 (October 1970): 74–82.

8. "College Campuses, Educators Say," *Jet Magazine* 33, no. 21 (February 1968): 23; "Black Institutions Face Brain Drain," *Louisville Defender*, March 26, 1970, 9; Eddie W. Morris, "The Contemporary Negro College and the Brain Drain," *Journal of Negro Education* 41, no. 4 (Autumn, 1972): 309–19; Valorie Jo Bradley, "Ohio's Antioch College," *Jet Magazine* 34, no. 9 (June 1969): 21; "Black Professor Reverses White College Brain Drain," *Jet Magazine* 43, no. 2 (March 1973): 45.

9. "Quality of Faculty, Students, Seen Falling at Black Colleges," *Philadelphia Tribune*, May 30, 1970, 32; "Black Students and Parents Should Have More Faith in Black Colleges," *Philadelphia Tribune*, June 24, 1980, 5.

10. Nick Chiles, "HBCUs Graduate More Poor Students Than White Colleges," NPR (website), March 1, 2017; Walter R. Allen et al., "Historically Black Colleges and Universities: Honoring the Past, Engaging the Present, Touching the Future," *Journal of Negro Education* 76, no. 3 (Summer 2007): 263–80; and Mary Ellen Flannery, "HBCUs as Economic Engines of Upward Mobility," National Education Association (website), December 12, 2018.

11. Leon Wright Bey, "Impact of Desegregation on Selected Aspects of the Athletic Programs of Traditionally Black Institutions in the Central Intercollegiate Athletic Association," (PhD diss, Temple University, 1985), 1–24; "Black College Tidbits," *Louisville Defender*, February 12, 1981, 14.

12. "Dr. Chaoqun Ni Awared Grant to Study Faculty Mobility at Historically Black Colleges and Universities (HBCUs)," Information School at the University of Wisconsin (website), October 6, 2021; and Matt Kelly et al., "First steps in Identifying Academic Migration using Memento and Qasi-Canonicalization," *Web Archiving and Digital Libraries Workshop 2022 at the ACM/IEEE Joint Conference on Digital Libraries*, January 1, 2022.

13. "Black College Tidbits," *Call and Post*, September 13, 1980, 14.

14. "Tidbits," *Louisville Defender*, April 2, 1981, 14.

15. "Black College Tidbits," *New York Amsterdam*, January 5, 1980, 36.

16. "Sports Tidbits," *Louisville Defender*, September 11, 1980, 10; and "Black College Sports Tidbits," *Call and Post*, October 11, 1980, 16.

17. "Black College Tidbits," *Louisville Defender*, February 19, 1981, 16; "Black College Tidbits," *Norfolk Journal and Guide*, November 9, 1983, 15.

18. "Tidbits," *Louisville Defender*, April 16, 1981, 14.

19. "Black College Tidbits," *Norfolk Journal and Guide*, November 9, 1983, 15.

20. *National Collegiate Athletic Association v. Board of Regents of the University of Oklahoma* et al., 468 US 85, 104 S. Ct. 2948 (1984).

21. "Black College Tidbits," *Atlanta Daily World,* August 21, 1981, 5.

22. "Black College Tidbits," *Call and Post,* November 29, 1980, 13; "Tidbits," *Louisville Defender,* April 30, 1981, 21; and "Black College Tidbits," *Michigan Chronicle,* February 6, 1982, 1.

23. "Black College Sports: Lack of Promotion," *New York Amsterdam News,* January 26, 1980, 64.

24. "Black College Tidbits," *New York Amsterdam,* January 26, 1980, 62.

25. Dr. Charles A. Ray, Report of the CIAA Director of Publicity, 50, the 1959 CIAA Bulletin, Union Archives.

26. "Black College Tidbits," *Pittsburgh Courier,* July 25, 1981, 9.

27. "Black College Sports," *Pittsburgh Courier,* August 8, 1981, 9; "Rich Tradition Behind HU-NSU Rivalry," *Norfolk Journal and Guide,* October 14, 1992, 12; and "SC State vs Winston-Salem," *Baltimore Afro-American,* November 26, 1977, 7.

28. History of the Gold Bowl Classic, section in the 1993 Gold Bowl Classic Program, undated, 9, Folder: Football: Gold Bowl, AR-005, Athletics, Box 1, Athletic Department, Union Archives.

29. "Gold Bowl Plans in the Air," *Baltimore Afro-American,* December 15, 1979, 6; "Black College Sports," *Pittsburgh Courier,* January 17, 1981, 11; and "Black College Tidbits," *Norfolk Journal and Guide,* November 7, 1984, 13.

30. "What Ails Black College Athletics," *Norfolk Journal and Guide,* January 30, 1985, A3.

31. "The Black Student Athlete Examined," *Los Angeles Sentinel,* September 29, 1983, 4.

32. "African-American College Athletes: Debunking the Myth of the Dumb Jock," *Journal of Blacks in Higher Education,* no. 35 (Spring 2002): 36–40; Carlton Keith Harrison, "'Eagles Don't Fly with Sparrows': Self-Determination Theory, African American Male Scholar-Athletes and Peer Group Influences on Motivation," *Journal of Negro Education* 84, no. 1 (Winter 2015): 80–93; and Martin P. Smith et al., "The Historical Hypocrisy of the Black Student-Athlete," *Race, Gender & Class* 21, no. 1/2 (2013): 220–35.

33. "Black College Sports: NCAA Rule Racist," *Pittsburgh Courier,* February 5, 1983, 6.

34. "Most of College Football Players Disqualified Were Black," *Los Angeles Sentinel,* October 20, 1988, B3.

35. "Officials Meet on Proposal 48," *New York Amsterdam,* February 19, 1983, 48.

36. "Black College Tidbits," *Norfolk Journal and Guide,* November 30, 1983, 18.

37. "NCAA Prop 42 Nixes Prop 48," *Michigan Chronicle,* January 21, 1989, 4B.

38. "Black Schools Could Benefit Most From Proposition 48," *Pittsburgh Courier,* February 22, 1986, 6; "Black Schools Ponder Leaving The NCAA," *Pittsburgh Courier,* January 31, 1987, 5; and "NCAA or NAIA: Which is Better for Black Sports," *Norfolk Journal and Guide,* January 27, 1988, 4.

39. Scott Brooks, "High School Basketball Needs Its Own Commission," *Global Sports Matters*: Arizona State University Global Sport Institute (website), May 17, 2018; Milton W. Hinton Jr., "Minority Athletes Are Not Just for Schools' Show and Tell," NJ (website), May 6, 2018; Daniel J. Jones et al., "When the Mirage Fades: Black Boys Encountering Antiblackness in a Predominantly White Catholic High

School," *Race, Ethnicity, and Education* 22, no. 7 (July 2020): 958–77; and Angela Judge-Stasiak, "Special Admission: How College Sports Recruitment Favors White, Suburban Athletes," *International Journal of Educational Integrity* 18, no. 1 (December 2022): 1–4.

40. Krystal Beamon, "Racism and Stereotyping on Campus: Experiences of African American Male Student Athletes," *Journal of Negro Education* 83, no. 2 (Spring 2014): 121–34; and "Black Teams, White Coaches: Racial Inequality in Coaching of College Sports," *Journal of Blacks in Higher Education*, no. 63 (Spring 2009): 30–31.

41. Hawkins, "The Black Student Athlete"; and Krystal Beamon, "'I'm a Baller': Athletic Identity Foreclosure among African-American Former Student Athletes," *Journal of African American Studies* 16, no. 2 (June 2012): 195–208.

42. Ed Sherman, "Degrees Elude Black Athletes," *Chicago Tribune* (website), March 31, 1993; and Richard Lapchick, "College Grad Rates Slide," ESPN (website), December 23, 2020.

43. Kyle T. Mosley, "Deion Sanders: Confident HBCUs Can Compete Against FBS Programs," *Sports Illustrated* (website), September 18, 2021; Dante Pryor, "Changing the Narrative About HBCU Athletes," *Saturday Blitz* (website), May 21, 2021; Karhan Spearman, "The Future of HBCU Football," *Daily Dot* (website), October 6, 2021; "Money Woes, Declining Talent Plague HBCU Football," *USA Today* (website), May 26, 2014; Kevin Trahan, "Should Grambling State, Southern, and Other HBCUs Drop out of Division 1 Football?" *Vice* (website), May 12, 2016; Ray Glier, "Historically Black College Football Programs Struggling to Keep Up," *Al Jazeera America* (website), January 14, 2014; Tyler Tynes, "The Golden Age of Black College Football Lost to Integration," *The Ringer* (website), September 19, 2019; Shira Springer, "HBCUs and Their Role in Disrupting the College Sports Cartel," *WBUR* (website), October 13, 2017.

44. "Highland Springs Wins Class 5 State Football Championship After Victory Over Maury," *CBS News 6* (website), December 11, 2022.

45. Sean Robertson, "Highland Springs Wins State Football Title Again," *Richmond Free Press* (website), December 13, 2018; and "Table of Football Team Records for the Virginia High School League," found in Haun et al., *25th Edition of the Virginia High School League Record Book*, 12 and 30–32, copy provided to author by officials of the Virginia High School League, May 2022.

46. Fall 2020 Enrollment at Highland Springs High School in Henrico County, Virginia, statistics found in Virginia Department of Education School Quality Profiles (website).

47. Gary Orfield, *Dismantling Desegregation: The Quiet Reversal of Brown v. Board of Education* (New York: Free Press, 2001); Gary Orfield and Erica Frankenberg, *Educational Delusions?: Why Choice Can Deepen Inequality and How to Make Schools Fair* (Berkeley: University of California Press, 2013); Toby L. Parcel and Andrew J. Taylor, *The End of Consensus: Diversity Neighborhoods and the Politics of Public School Assignments* (Chapel Hill: University of North Carolina Press, 2015); and Genevieve Seigel-Hawley, *When the Fences Come Down: Twenty-First Century Lessons from Metropolitan School Desegregation* (Chapel Hill: University of North Carolina Press, 2016).

48. Marvin Chiles, "Our Metropolitan Separations: The Case for Metropolitan Public Schools in the Commonwealth of Virginia," *Journal of Race and Policy* 16, no. 1

(Winter 2022): 59–80; and James E. Ryan, *Five Miles Away, A World Apart: One City, Two Schools, and the Story of Educational Opportunity in Modern America* (Oxford, UK: Oxford University Press, 2016).

49. "Longtime AAU Member/Volunteer Remembered," Tribute to P. K. Martin on the AAU Boys Basketball Website, January 13, 2021, AAU Boys Basketball Webpage, accessed December 10, 2023; "Elks Club Hoop Shoot Winner Announced," *Roanoke Times* (website), January 28, 1993, accessed January 12, 2024; Will Goldsmith, "Can J.R. Reynolds Make It Happen," *C-Ville Magazine* (website), March 13, 2007, accessed February 2, 2024; John D. Cramer, "Purified Water Has Its Price," *Roanoke Times*, July 27, 1998, 1; Greg Esposito, "Close Ties Help Team Final Success," *Roanoke Times*, April 12, 2001, 75; and AAU 1989 Girls' and Boys' Basketball Handbook, Amateur Athletic Union (AAU) Archives in Lake Buena Vista, Florida.

50. Hall of Fame Profile for Sonny Hill, Philadelphia Sports Hall of Fame (website), undated.

51. "Summer Hoops Program Brings Area Prominence," *Norfolk Journal and Guide*, August 19, 1992, 11; Profile for Marcellus Spencer "Boo" Williams, Virginia Changemakers (website), undated; and "Sponsor of Summer League Basketball: Meet Boo Williams," *Norfolk Journal and Guide*, March 20, 1991, 1.

52. "Rival AAU Organizations Have Success in Common," *Richmond Times-Dispatch*, July 9, 1989, E2.

53. "The Survivor—Tony Squire Has Kept Basketball Program Going for 20 Years," *Richmond Times-Dispatch*, July 30, 2008, C1.

54. "Geeches Create Places for Youth off the Street," *Richmond Times-Dispatch*, May 30, 1989, F1.

55. Paul Pogge, "Full Court Press: Problems Plaguing Youth Basketball in the United States and an Aggressive Plan to Attack Them," *University of Denver Sports and Entertainment Law* (website).

56. "AAU True to Ideals," *Pittsburgh Courier*, February 27, 1926, 12.

57. Scott N. Brooks, "City of Basketball Love: Philadelphia and the Nurturing of Black Males' Hoop Dreams," *Journal of African American History* 96, no. 4 (Fall 2011): 522–36; Gerald R. Gems, "Blocked Shot: The Development of Basketball in the African-American Community of Chicago," *Journal of Sport History* 22, no. 2 (Summer 1995): 135–48; And 1's Legendary History (website), undated; Joshua Wright, "Be Like Mike?: The Black Athlete's Dilemma, *Spectrum: A Journal on Black Men* 4, no. 2 (Spring 2016): 1–19; and Eva Bosenberg, "Who's Afraid of Shaq Attaq? Constructions of Black Masculinity and the NBA," *American Studies* 43, no. 4 (1998): 681–91.

58. Profile for Marcellus Spencer "Boo" Williams, Virginia Changemakers (website), undated; and "Sponsor of Summer League Basketball: Meet Boo Williams," *Norfolk Journal and Guide*, March 20, 1991, 1.

59. "Geeches Create Places for Youth off the Street," *Richmond Times-Dispatch*, May 30, 1989, F1.

60. "Squires Is Touchstone in Basketball World," *Richmond Times-Dispatch*, November 4, 1989, 18; "Right Turn on the Road to Stardom?" *Richmond Times-Dispatch*, June 23, 2006, E10.

61. "Free AAU Hoop Clinic," *Southside Sentinel*, January 30, 1997, B3.

62. "Summer Hoops Program Brings Area Prominence," *Norfolk Journal and Guide*, August 19, 1992, 11.

63. "Recruiting Ready to Press as AAU Tourney Begins," *Richmond Times-Dispatch*, April 7, 1994, C8.

64. "Shootout," *Richmond Free Press*, April 13, 1995, 13.

65. "Recruiting Ready to Press as AAU Tourney Begins," *Richmond Times-Dispatch*, April 7, 1994, C8.

66. "Squires Is Touchstone in Basketball World," *Richmond Times-Dispatch*, November 4, 1989, 18.

67. "Rival AAU Organizations Have Success in Common," *Richmond Times-Dispatch*, July 9, 1989, E2.

68. Dan Wetzel, "Former AAU Basketball Coach Says Those Wrapped Up in College Basketball Scandal Will Flip for Feds," *Yahoo News* (website), September 17, 2017.

69. Jed Hughes, "College Athletic Recruiting: AAU Basketball Corruption and Illegal Recruiting," *Bleacher Report* (website), July 10, 2012; and Mark Sclabach, "Feds Drop Charges Against AAU Basketball Program Director," *ABC News* (website), February 14, 2018.

70. Ricky O'Donnell, "The NCAA Is Wrong About Grassroots Basketball," *SB Nation* (website), September 12, 2018.

71. "DC Assault Co-Founder Curtis Malone Released from Prison," *NBC Sports* (website), May 21, 2020; "The Scheme," *Guardian* (website), March 21, 2020.

72. "Squires Challenge AAU Action," *Richmond Times-Dispatch*, December 22, 1991, D9; "Squire Penalty Reduced by AAU," *Richmond Times-Dispatch*, March 2, 1992, 22; and "Youth Program Penalized," *Richmond Times-Dispatch*, December 12, 1991, 31.

73. David Teel, "Curry-UNC: A Marriage of Circumstance," *Daily Press*, March 25, 1998, B1–B5; "Curry Dispels Rumors of His Decision," *Daily Press*, March 26, 1998, B5; and David Fairbank and David Teel, "The Life and Times of Basketball Guru Boo Williams," *Daily Press*, August 17, 1998, C1–C5.

74. "Shootout," *Richmond Free Press*, April 13, 1995, 13.

75. "Piranhas to Bring AAU Football to Suffolk," *Suffolk News-Herald*, June 28, 2011; "Virginia Vipers Play for a National Title," *ABC 8 News*, December 17, 2018; "Roanoke's Virginia Wolverines Play Football During COVID-19 Pandemic," *WRXR Fox News*, October 15, 2020; "Turning a Dream into Reality: Virginia Hellcats 8U Preps for Inaugural Season," *NBC 10 News*, April 18, 2021; "Central Va. Wolfpack U11 Wins AAU National Title," *ABC 13 News*, June 26, 2023; "Welcome to the Virginia Athletic Conference," Virginia AAU Webpage, undated; and Kenneth Gantt, "We Are American Youth Football Alliance," organizational webpage, undated.

Bibliography

Primary Source Documents and Public Documents

Newspapers and Magazines

Alexandria Gazette
Atlanta Daily World
Baltimore Afro-American
Chicago Defender
Chicago Tribune
Cleveland Call and Post
Crisis Magazine
Daily Defender
Daily Press
Ebony Magazine
Harrisonburg Evening News
Jet Magazine
Louisville Defender
Michigan Chronicle
Newport Daily News
New York Amsterdam News
Norfolk Journal and Guide
Norfolk Virginian
Norfolk-Virginian Pilot
Pittsburgh Courier
Philadelphia Tribune
Presbyterian of the South
Richmond Daily Dispatch
Richmond Free Press
Richmond Planet
Richmond Times
Richmond Times-Dispatch
Southern Workman

Tazewell Church Valley News
Washington Post

Archival Collections

Library of Virginia, Richmond, Virginia
Virginia High School Yearbooks
Virginia State Board of Education

University of Massachusetts
W. E. B Du Bois Collection

Virginia State University, Petersburg, Virginia
Virginia Interscholastic Association Papers

Virginia Union University, Richmond Virginia
Virginia Union Athletic Department Collection
Colored Intercollegiate Athletic Association Papers
Henry Boyd Hucles Jr. Collection
Virginia Interscholastic Athletic League Papers
Virginia Union Yearbook Collection

Other Primary Source Documents

About the Black College Football Hall of Fame, Black College Hall of Fame (website). Undated.

About Black Fives Foundation, Black Fives Foundation (website). Undated.

All Time CIAA Men's Basketball Champions, list found in CIAA (website). Undated.

And 1's Legendary History. And 1 (website). Undated.

"Carlisle's 1955 Integrated Team," Kentucky African American Database (website). Undated.

CIAA Championships by School, chart found in "HBCU Football Championship History," NCAA (website). February 4, 2022.

CIAA Hall of Fame Profile for Dave Robbins of Virginia Union University. CIAA (website). Undated.

Composite and Characteristics for Urban and Rural Districts of Virginia, 1910 and 1920, U.S. Census for the Commonwealth of Virginia, Census.gov (website).

Fall 2020 Enrollment at Highland Springs High School in Henrico County, Virginia, statistics found in Virginia Department of Education School Quality Profiles (website). Undated.

Flannery, Mary Ellen. "HBCUs as Economic Engines of Upward Mobility," National Education Association (website). December 12, 2018.

Hall of Fame Profile for Sonny Hill, Philadelphia Sports Hall of Fame (website). Undated.

History of the Prairie View Interscholastic League. Prairie View Interscholastic League Coaches Association (website). Undated.

Kelly, Matt, et al. "First steps in Identifying Academic Migration using Memento and Qasi-Canonicalization," National Science Foundation (website). Undated.

Profile for Charles H. Williams, Virginia Sports Hall of Fame (website). Undated.

Profile of Gideon Smith for the Hampton Athletic Hall of Fame, Hampton Pirates Hall of Fame (website). 2009.

Profile of Gideon E. Smith. Jim Crow Museum of Racist Memorabilia, Ferris State University (website). September 2016.

Profile for Marcellus Spencer "Boo" Williams, Library of Virginia: Virginia Changemakers (website). Undated.

Rashad, Kenn. "Division 1 HBCU Revenue Rankings." HBCU Sports (website). July 3, 2018.

Savage, Howard J., et al. "American College Athletics," Report by the Carnegie Foundation for the Advancement of Teaching, 1929, chapter VII.

The Lion. 1940 Lincoln University Student Yearbook, 50.

VIA Heritage Association. "Awards Banquet and Planning Meeting." *VIA Story* (website), July 1, 2018.

VIA Heritage Association. "Inaugural Meeting for Virginia Interscholastic Association Story Website." *VIA Story* (website). September 30, 2017.

VIA Heritage Association Hall of Fame 2018 Press Release. VIA Heritage (website). January 28, 2018.

Walker, Thomas Calhoun. *Lawyer Walker of Gloucester*. Williamsburg, VA: College of William and Mary Special Collection, undated.

Secondary Sources

"African-American College Athletes: Debunking the Myth of the Dumb Jock." *Journal of Blacks in Higher Education* 35 (Spring 2002): 36–40.

Aiello, Thomas. *Bayou Classic: The Grambling-Southern Football Rivalry*. Baton Rouge: Louisiana State University Press, 2010.

———. *Hoops: A Cultural History of Basketball in America*. New York: Rowman & Littlefield, 2021.

———. *The Kings of Casino Park: Black Baseball in the Lost Season of 1932*. Tuscaloosa: University of Alabama Press, 2011.

Alderson, William T. "The Freedmen's Bureau and Negro Education in Virginia." *North Carolina Historical Review* 29, no.1 (January 1952): 64–90.

Alexander, Fred M. *Education for the Needs of the Negro in Virginia*. Washington, DC: Southern Education Foundation, 1943.

Allen, Henry Lee. "The Mobility of Black Collegiate Faculty Revisited: Whatever Happened to the 'Brain Drain'?" *Journal of Negro Education* 60, no. 1 (Winter 1991): 97–109.

Allen, Walter R., et al. "Historically Black Colleges and Universities: Honoring the Past, Engaging the Present, Touching the Future," *Journal of Negro Education* 76, no. 3 (Summer 2007): 263–80.

Anderson, James D. *The Education of Blacks in the South, 1860–1935*. Chapel Hill: University of North Carolina Press, 1988.

Archer, S. H. "Football in Negro Colleges." *Voice of the Negro* 3, no. 3 (March 1906): 198–205.

Arnson, Eric. *Brotherhoods of Color: Black Railroad Workers and the Struggle for Racial Equality*. Cambridge, MA: Harvard University Press.

Arsenault, Raymond. *Arthur Ashe: A Life*. New York: Simon & Schuster, 2018.

Ashe, Arthur, and Arnold Rampersad. *Days of Grace: A Memoir*. New York: Knopf, 1993.

Austin, Brad. *Democratic Sports: Men's and Women's College Athletics During the Great Depression*. Fayetteville: University of Arkansas Press, 2015.

Ayers, Edward L. *The Promise of the New South: Life After Reconstruction*. Oxford, UK: Oxford University Press, 1992.

Baker, S. Zebulon. "'On the Opposite Side of the Fence': The University of Kentucky and the Racial Desegregation of the Southeastern Conference." *Register of the Kentucky Historical Society* 115, no. 4 (Autumn 2017): 561–610.

Baker, Scott. "Testing Equality: The National Teacher Examination and the NAACP's Legal Campaign to Equalize Teachers' Salaries in the South, 1936–63." *History of Education Quarterly* 35, no.1 (Spring 1995): 49–64.

Bass, Amy. "State of the Field: Sports History and the 'Cultural Turn.'" *Journal of American History* 101, no. 1 (June 2014): 148–72.

Baradaran, Mehrsa. *The Color of Money: Black Banks and the Racial Wealth Gap*. Cambridge, MA: Harvard University Press, 2017.

"Black Teams, White Coaches: Racial Inequality in Coaching of College Sports." *Journal of Blacks in Higher Education* 63 (Spring 2009): 36–37.

Beamon, Krystal. "'I'm a Baller': Athletic Identity Foreclosure among African-American Former Student Athletes." *Journal of African American Studies* 16, no. 2 (June 2012): 195–208.

———. "Racism and Stereotyping on Campus: Experiences of African American Male Student Athletes." *Journal of Negro Education* 83, no. 2 (Spring 2014): 121–34.

Beezer, Bruce. "Black Teachers' Salaries and the Federal Courts Before *Brown v. Board of Education*: One Beginning for Equity." *Journal of Negro Education* 55, no. 2 (Spring 1986): 200–213.

Bell, Andrew McIlwaine. *The Origins of Southern College Football: How An Ivy League Game Became a Dixie Tradition*. Baton Rouge: Louisiana State University Press, 2020.

Bell, Daryl. "No One Can Deny the Coaching Greatness of the White Shadow." AndScape (website) (then known as the Undefeated), October 13, 2016.

Bernard, Luther L. "The Teaching of Sociology in Southern Colleges and Universities." *American Journal of Sociology* 23, no. 4 (January 1918): 491–515.

Bey, Leon Wright. "Impact of Desegregation on Selected Aspects of the Athletic Programs of Traditionally Black Institutions in the Central Intercollegiate Athletic Association." PhD diss., Temple University, 1985.

Biondi, Martha. *The Black Revolution on Campus*. Berkeley: University of California Press, 2014.

Bosenberg, Eva. "Who's Afraid of Shaq Attaq? Constructions of Black Masculinity and the NBA," *American Studies* 43, no. 4 (1998): 681–91.

Boykin, Leander L. "The Status and Trends of Differentials Between White and

Negro Teachers' Salaries in the Southern States, 1900–1946," *Journal of Negro Education* 18, no. 1 (Winter 1949): 40–47.

Breen, T. H. "Horses and Gentlemen: The Cultural Significance of Gambling Among the Gentry of Virginia." *William and Mary Quarterly* 34, no. 2 (April 1977): 239–57.

Briggs, Gabriel A. *The New Negro in the Old South*. New Brunswick, NJ: Rutgers University Press, 2015.

Brooks, Clayton McClure. *The Uplift Generation: Cooperation Across the Color-line in Early Twentieth Century Virginia*. Charlottesville: University of Virginia Press, 2017.

Brooks, Lyman Beecher. *Upward Bound: A History of Norfolk State University*. Washington, DC: Howard University Press, 1983.

Brooks, Scott N. "City of Basketball Love: Philadelphia and the Nurturing of Black Males' Hoop Dreams." *Journal of African American History* 96, no. 4 (Fall 2011): 522–36.

———. "High School Basketball Needs Its Own Commission" (opinion). Global Sports Matters: Arizona State University Global Sport Institute (website). May 17, 2018.

Brooks, Scott N., and Dexter Blackman. "African Americans and the History of Sports—New Perspectives," *Journal of African American History* 96, no. 4 (October 2011): 441–47.

Brown, Bruce Alain. "Justice, Patience, Reason: The Writings of Virginius Dabney on Matters of Race." MA thesis at the College of William and Mary, 1987.

Brown, Tamara L., et al., eds. *African American Fraternities and Sororities: The Legacy and the Vision*. Lexington: University of Kentucky Press, 2010.

Brundage, W. Fitzhugh. *Lynching in the New South: Georgia and Virginia, 1800–1930*. Urbana: University of Illinois Press, 1993.

Bundgaard, Axel. *Muscle and Manliness: The Rise of Sport in American Boarding Schools*. Syracuse, NY: Syracuse University Press, 2005.

Bynum, Cornelius L. "The New Negro and Social Democracy during the Harlem Renaissance, 1917–37." *Journal of the Gilded Age and Progressive Era* 10, no. 1 (January 2011): 89–112.

Campanelli, Lou, and Dave Newsome. *Dare to Dream: How James Madison University Became Coed and Shocked the Basketball World*. Charlottesville: University of Virginia Press, 2015.

Cardon, Nathan. "The South's "New Negroes" and African American Visions of Progress at the Atlanta and Nashville International Expositions, 1895–1897." *Journal of Southern History* 80, no. 2 (May 2014): 287–396.

Chalk, Ocania. *Black College Sport*. New York: Dodd, Mead & Company, 1976.

Chansky, Art. *Game Changers: Dean Smith, Charlie Scott, and the Era That Transformed a Southern College Town*. Chapel Hill: University of North Carolina Press, 2018.

Childress, Autumn. "Soul of RVA: A Look Inside VUU's Dominant Basketball Program and Coach Behind Team's Success," ABC 8 News (website), April 7, 2016.

Chiles, Marvin. "Down Where the South Begins: Black Richmond Activism Before the Modern Civil Rights Movement, 1899–1930." *Journal of African American History* 105, no. 1 (Winter 2020): 56–82.

———. "Our Metropolitan Separations: The Case for Metropolitan Public Schools in the Commonwealth of Virginia." *Journal of Race and Policy* 16, no. 1 (Winter 2022): 59–80.

———. "A Period of Misunderstanding: Reforming Jim Crow in Richmond, Virginia." *Virginia Magazine of History and Biography* 129, no. 3 (Fall 2021): 244–78.

Chiles, Nick. "HBCUs Graduate More Poor Students Than White Colleges." NPR (website). March 1, 2017.

Coit, Jonathan S. "'Our Changed Attitude': Armed Defense and the New Negro in the 1919 Chicago Race Riot." *Journal of the Gilded Age and Progressive Era* 11, no. 2 (April 2012): 225–27.

Daugherity, Brian J. *Keep on Keeping On: The NAACP and the Implementation of Brown v. Board of Education in Virginia*. Charlottesville: University of Virginia Press, 2016.

Davis, Amari Rose. "New Directions in African American Sports History: A Field of One's Own." *Journal of African American History* 96, no. 1 (Fall 2021): 183–88.

"DC Assault Co-Founder Curtis Malone Released from Prison." NBC Sports (website). May 13, 2020.

Demas, Lane. *Integrating the Gridiron: Black Civil Rights and American College Football*. New Brunswick, NJ: Rutgers University Press, 2010.

Doyle, Leo Andrew. "Causes Won, Not Lost: Football and Southern Culture, 1892–1983." PhD diss., Emory University, 1998.

"Dr. Chaoqun Ni Awarded Grant to Study Faculty Mobility at Historically Black Colleges and Universities (HBCUs)." The Information School at the University of Wisconsin (website). October 6, 2021.

Edds, Margaret. *We Face the Dawn: Oliver Hill, Spottswood Robinson, and the Legal Team That Dismantled Jim Crow*. Charlottesville: University of Virginia Press, 2018.

Editorial Comment, "Eight Years of Rating of Negro Schools and Colleges by the Southern Association: An Evaluation," *Journal of Negro Education* 8, no. 1 (January 1939): 1–8.

Edwards, Harry. *Revolt of the Black Athlete: 50th Anniversary Edition*. Urbana: University of Illinois Press, 2017.

Eliot, Charles W. "College Football," *Journal of Education* 61, no. 7 (February 1905): 171–72.

Ellsworth, Scott. *The Secret Game: A Wartime Story for Courage, Change, and Basketball's Lost Triumph*. New York: Little, Brown and Company, 2015.

Emmons, Caroline. "Not a Single Battle but Rather a Real War: The Fight to Equalize Teachers' Salaries in Florida in the 1930s and 1940s." *Florida Historical Quarterly* 81, no. 4 (Spring 2003): 418–35.

Engs, Robert F. *Freedom's First Generation: Black Hampton, Virginia, 1861–1890*. New York: Fordham University Press, 1979.

Eskridge, Sara K. "Virginia's Pupil Placement Board and the Practical Applications of Massive Resistance, 1956–1966." *Virginia Magazine of History & Biography* 118, no. 3 (June 2010): 246–76.

Fairclough, Adam. *Teaching Equality: Black Schools in the Age of Jim Crow.* Athens: University of Georgia Press, 2001.

Field, Ann Alexander. *Race Man: The Rise and Fall of "Fighting Editor" John Mitchell, Jr.* Charlottesville: University of Virginia Press, 2002.

Fink, Rob. *Football at Historically Black Colleges and Universities in Texas.* College Station: Texas A&M University Press, 2019.

Fishwick, Marshall W. "The Negro in Twentieth Century Virginia." *Negro History Bulletin* 12, no. 8 (May 1949): 182–84.

Foster, O. D. "In Southern Universities." *Christian Education* 8, no. 6 (March 1925): 265–66.

Frazier, E. Franklin. *Black Bourgeoisie.* New York: Free Press, 1957.

Frederickson, Kari. *Dixiecrat Revolt and the End of the Solid South, 1932–1968.* Chapel Hill: University of North Carolina Press, 2001.

Freedman, David. "African-American Schooling in the South Prior to 1861." *Journal of Negro History* 84, no. 1 (Winter 1999): 1–47.

Freedman, Samuel G. *Breaking the Line: The Season in Black College Football That Transformed the Sport and Changed the Course of Civil Rights.* New York: Simon & Schuster, 2014.

Gaines, Kevin. *Uplifting the Race: Black Leadership, Politics, and Culture in the Twentieth Century.* Chapel Hill: University of North Carolina Press, 1996.

Gaither, Stephen, J. "HBCU One Step Closer to Bringing Home National Title." HBCU Gameday (website). March 20, 2022.

Gates, Henry Louis, Jr. "The Trope of a New Negro and the Reconstruction of the Image of the Black," *Representation* 24 (Autumn 1988), 131–38.

Gates, Robbins L. *The Making of Massive Resistance: Virginia's Politics of Public School Desegregation, 1954–1956.* Chapel Hill: University of North Carolina Press, 1964.

Gavins, Raymond. *Perils and Prospects of Southern Black Leadership: Gordon Blaine Hancock, 1884–1970.* Durham, NC: Duke University Press, 1977.

Gems, Gerald R. "Blocked Shot: The Development of Basketball in the African-American Community of Chicago." *Journal of Sport History* 22, no. 2 (Summer 1995): 135–48.

George, Nelson. *Elevating the Game: Black Men and Basketball.* New York: Harper Collins Publishing, 1995.

Glier, Ray. "Historically Black College Football Programs Struggling to Keep Up." *Al Jazeera America* (website). January 24, 2014.

Gosse, Van. *The First Reconstruction: Black Politics in America from Revolution to Civil War.* Chapel Hill: University of North Carolina Press, 2021.

Goudsouzian, Aram. "House of Cards: Leisure, Freedom, Authority, Revolution, and the Diary of Landon Carter." *Journal of Sport History* 49, no. 1 (Spring 2022): 1–19.

Grant, Keneshia N. *The Great Migration and the Democratic Party: Black Voters and the Realignment of American Politics in the 20th Century*. Philadelphia: Temple University Press, 2020.

Green, Dan S., and Earl Smith. "W.E.B. DuBois and the Concepts of Race and Class." *Phylon* 44, no. 4 (4th Quarter, 1983): 262–72.

Greenberg, Cheryl Lynn. *To Ask for an Equal Chance: African Americans in the Great Depression*. New York: Rowman & Littlefield Publishers, 2010.

Grundman, Adolph H. "Northern Baptists and the Founding of Virginia Union University: The Perils of Paternalism." *Journal of Negro History* 63, no. 1 (January 1978): 26–41.

Grundy, Pamela. *Learning to Win: Sports, Education, Social Change in Twentieth Century North Carolina*. Chapel Hill: University of North Carolina, 2001.

Grundy, Pamela, and Susan Shackelford. *Shattering the Glass: The Remarkable History of Women's Basketball*. New York: New Press, 2005.

Gudmestad, Robert H. "Baseball, the Lost Cause, and the New South in Richmond, Virginia, 1883–1890," *Virginia Magazine of History and Biography* 106, no. 3 (Summer 1998): 267–300.

Gulick, Luther Hasley. "Organized Play." *Journal of Education* 71, no. 14 (April 1910): 370–71.

———. "Team Games and Civic Loyalty." *School Review* 14, no. 9 (November 1906): 676–78.

Guthrie, James. "50 Years Later, Black High School Athletic League's Legacy Endures." *Daily Press* (VA) (website). February 17, 2018.

Hale, Jon. "'The Development of Power Is the Main Business of the School': The Agency of Southern Black Teacher Associations from Jim Crow Through Desegregation." *Journal of Negro Education* 87, no. 4 (Fall 2018): 444–59.

———. "'The Fight Was Instilled in Us': High School Activism and The Civil Rights Movement in Charleston." *South Carolina Historical Magazine* 114, no. 1 (January 2013): 4–28.

Hall, Eric Allen. *Arthur Ashe: Tennis and Justice in the Civil Rights Era*. Baltimore, MD: Johns Hopkins University Press, 2016.

Hamilton, Tikia K. "The Cost of Integration: The Contentious Career of Garnet C. Wilkinson." *Washington History* 30, no. 1 (Spring 2018): 50–60.

Handbook of the Virginia High School Literary and Athletic League, 1921–1923. Charlottesville: University of Virginia, 1923.

Hartmann, Douglas. *Race, Culture, and Revolt of the Black Athlete: The 1968 Olympic Protests and Their Aftermath*. Chicago: University of Chicago Press, 2004.

Harris, Carl V. "Stability and Change in Discrimination against Black Public Schools: Birmingham, Alabama, 1871–1931." *Journal of Southern History* 51, no. 3 (August 1985): 375–416.

Harris, Lashawn. "Running with the Reds: African American Women and the Communist Party during the Great Depression." *Journal of African American History* 94, no. 1 (Winter 2009): 21–43.

Harrison, Carlton Keith. "'Eagles Don't Fly with Sparrows': Self-Determination Theory, African American Male Scholar-Athletes and Peer Group Influences on Motivation." *Journal of Negro Education* 84, no. 1 (Winter 2015): 80–93.

Haun, John W., et al. *The 25th Edition of the Virginia High School League Record Book*. Charlottesville: Virginia High School League, April 2022.

Hawkins, Billy, et al. *The Athletic Experience at Historically Black Colleges and Universities: Past, Present, and Persistence*. New York: Rowman & Littlefield, 2015.

———. "The Black Student Athlete: The Colonized Black Body." *Journal of African American Men* 1, no. 3 (Winter 1995/96): 23–35.

———. *The New Plantation: Black Athletes, College Sports, and Predominantly White NCAA Institutions*. London: Palgrave MacMillan, 2010.

Hawkins, Stacy. "Reverse Integration: Centering HBCUs in the Fight for Education Equality." *Journal of Law and Social Change* 24, no. 3 (2021): 351–410.

Hayter, Julian Maxwell. *The Dream Is Lost: Race, Voting Rights, and the Politics of Race in Richmond, Virginia*. Lexington: University of Kentucky Press, 2017.

Haywood, D'Weston. *Let Us Make Men: The Twentieth Century Black Press and a Manly Vision for Racial Advancement*. Chapel Hill: University of North Carolina Press, 2017.

Heineman, Ronald L. *Depression and New Deal in Virginia: The Enduring Dominion* (Charlottesville: University of Virginia Press, 1983)

———. *Harry Byrd of Virginia*. Charlottesville: University of Virginia Press. 1996.

Henderson, Edwin Bancroft. *The Negro in Sports*. Washington, DC: Associated Publishers, 1939.

Henderson, Edwin B., and Garnet C. Wilkinson, eds. *Official Handbook: Interscholastic Athletic Association of Middle Atlantic States*. New York: American Sports Publishing Company, 1912.

Higginbothahm, Evelyn Brooks. *Righteous Discontent: The Women's Movement in the Black Baptist Church, 1880–1920*. Cambridge, MA: Harvard University Press, 1994.

Hinton, Milton W. "Minority Athletes Are Not Just for Schools' Show and Tell" (opinion). NJ (website). May 6, 2018.

Holcomb, Todd. "Notebook: 50th Anniversary of First Integrated Game." *Atlanta Journal and Constitution* (website). September 2, 2016.

Holloway, Pippa. *Sexuality, Politics, and Social Control in Virginia, 1920–1945*. Chapel Hill: University of North Carolina Press, 2006.

Holmes, Dwight Oliver. Wendell *The Evolution of the Negro College*. New York: Columbia University Press, 1934.

Hoose, Phillip. *Attucks!: How Crispus Attucks Basketball Broke Racial Barriers and Jolted the World*. New York: Farrar, Straus and Giroux, 2018.

Horton, Adrian. "The Scheme." *Guardian* (website), March 31, 2020.

Howard, Josh. "A Good Base Ball Club Is a Splendid Advertisement to a Town: Baseball and the New South in Clifton Forge, Virginia." *Virginia Magazine of History and Biography* 124, no. 3 (2016): 186–215.

Hughes, Jed. "College Athletic Recruiting: AAU Basketball Corruption and Illegal Recruiting." *Bleacher Report* (website). July 10, 2012.

Hurd, Michael. *Black College Football, 1892–1992: One Hundred Years of History, Education, and Pride*. Virginia Beach, VA: Donning Co., Publishing, 1993.

———. *Thursday Night Lights: The Story of Black High School Football in Texas*. Austin: University of Texas Press, 2017.

Hustwit, William P. *James J. Kilpatrick: Salesman for Segregation*. Chapel Hill: University of North Carolina Press, 2013.

Hutton, Frankie. *The Early Black Press in America, 1827–1860*. Westport, CT: Greenwood Press, 1993.

Ingrassia, B. M. "Public Influence Inside the College Walls: Progressive Era Universities, Social Scientists, and Intercollegiate Football Reform." *Journal of Gilded Age and Progressive Era* 10, no. 1 (January 2011): 59–88.

Jacobus, Robert. *Black Man in the Middle: Stories from the Integration of Texas Football*. College Station: Texas A&M University Press, 2019.

Jackson, Luther P. *A History of the Virginia Teachers Association*. Norfolk, VA: Guide Publishing, 1937.

Jeffries, Hassan Kwame. "Fields of Play: The Mediums through Which Black Athletes Engaged in Sports in Jim Crow Georgia." *Journal of Negro History* 86, no. 3 (Summer 2001): 264–75.

Jeter, Fred. "Highland Springs Wins State Football Title Again." *Richmond Free Press* (website). December 13, 2018.

"Joe Taylor Named to the College FB Hall of Fame." *Hampton University News* (website). January 7, 2019.

Johnson, Charles W. "V for Virginia: The Commonwealth Goes to War." *Virginia Magazine of History and Biography* 100, no. 3 (July 1992): 365–98.

Jones, Daniel J., et al. "When the Mirage Fades: Black Boys Encountering Antiblackness in a Predominantly White Catholic High School." *Race, Ethnicity, and Education* 22, no. 7 (July 2020): 958–77.

Jones, Oliver S. "Morality in College Athletics." *North American Review* 160, no. 462 (May 1895): 638–40.

Jordan, William G. *Black Newspapers & America's War for Democracy, 1914–1920*. Chapel Hill: University of North Carolina Press. 2001.

Joseph, Andrew. "An Animated Lebron Helped Coach His Son's AAU Team to a National Championship." *USA Today* (website). July 22, 2018.

Judge-Stasiak, Angela. "Special Admission: How College Sports Recruitment Favors White, Suburban Athletes." *International Journal of Educational Integrity* 18, no.1 (December 2022): 1–4.

Junot, Jim. "Barco-Stevens Hall: 80 Years of History." *Virginia Union Sports News* (website). May 1, 2019.

———. "The Forgotten Champion." *Virginia Union University Athletic News* (website). Undated.

———. "The Story of Henry Hucles." *Virginia Union University Athletic News* (website). December 14, 2010.

Kaliss, Gregory J. "Un-Civil Discourse: Charlie Scott, the Integration of College Basketball, and the 'Progressive Mystique,'" *Journal of Sport History* 35, no. 1 (Spring 2008): 98–117.

Katz, Milton S. *Breaking Through: John B. McLendon, Basketball Legend and Civil Rights Pioneer*. Fayetteville: University of Arkansas Press, 2010.

Kemper, Kurt Edward. *Before March Madness: The Wars for the Soul of College Basketball*. Urbana: University of Illinois Press, 2020.

Kirk, John A. "The NAACP Campaign for Teachers' Salary Equalization: African American Women Educators and the Early Civil Rights Struggle." *Journal of African American History* 94, no. 4 (Fall 2009): 520–32.

Kiracofe, Edgar S. "An Historical Study of Athletics and Physical Education in the Standard Four-Year Colleges in Virginia." *Secondary Education in Virginia: University of Virginia Record* XVL, no. 9 (March 1932): 12–40.

Lake, Robert W. *The New Suburbanites: Race and Housing in the Suburbs*. New York: Taylor & Francis Publishing, 2012.

Lamb, Chris. "'I Never Want to Take Another Trip Like This One': Jackie Robinson's Journey to Integrate Baseball." *Journal of Sport History* 24, no. 2 (Summer 1997): 177–91.

Lamon, Lester C. "Black Public Education in the South, 1861–1920: By Whom, for Whom and Under Whose Control?" *Journal of Thought* 18, no. 3 (Fall 1983): 76–90.

Lanctot, Neil. *Negro League Baseball: The Rise and Ruin of a Black Institution*. Philadelphia: University of Pennsylvania Press, 2004.

Landsbury, Jennifer H. *A Spectacular Leap: Black Women Athletes in Twentieth-Century America*. Fayetteville: University of Arkansas Press, 2014.

Lapchick, Richard. "College Grad Rates Slide." ESPN (website). December 23, 2020.

Lassiter, Matthew D., and Andrew B. Lewis, eds. *The Moderates' Dilemma: Massive Resistance to School Desegregation in Virginia*. Charlottesville: University of Virginia Press, 1998.

Leavell, Ullin Whitney. *Philanthropy in Negro Education*. Nashville, TN: George Peabody College for Teachers, 1930.

Leidholdt, Alexander S. *Standing Before the Shouting Mob: Lenoir Chambers and Virginia's Massive Resistance to Public School Integration*. Tuscaloosa: University of Alabama Press, 1997.

Leloudis, James L., II. "School Reforms in the New South: The Women's Association for the Betterment of Public Schools in North Carolina, 1902–1919." *Journal of American History* 69, no. 4 (March 1983): 886–909.

Lewis, Earl. *In Their Own Interest: Race, Class and Power in Twentieth Century Norfolk*. Berkeley: University of California Press, 1991.

Lewis, Guy M. "Theodore Roosevelt's Role in the 1905 Football Controversy." *Research Quarterly* 40, no. 4 (Winter 1967): 717–24.

Link, William A. *A Hard Country and Lonely Place: Schooling, Society, and*

Reform in Rural Virginia, 1870–1920. Chapel Hill: University of North Carolina Press, 2018.

Ligeon, Charlene Butts. *Fearless: How a Poor Virginia Seamstress Took on Jim Crow, Beat the Poll Tax and Changed Her City Forever*. Bellevue, NE: Smallwood Charlotte Press, 2018.

Lincoln, C. Eric, and Lawrence H. Mamiya. *The Black Church in the African American Experience*. Durham, NC: Duke University Press, 1990.

Littlejohn, Jeffrey E., and Charles H. Ford. *Elusive Equality: Desegregation and Resegregation in Norfolk's Public Schools*. Charlottesville: University of Virginia Press, 2012.

Locke, Alain L. "Enter the New Negro." *Survey Graphic*: National Humanities Center (March 1925): 1–6.

———, ed. *The New Negro: An Interpretation*. New York: Albert and Charles Boni, Inc., 1925.

Lomax, Michael E. "The African American Experience in Professional Football." *Journal of Social History* 33, no. 1 (Autumn 1999): 163–78.

Lovett, Bobby L. *America's Historically Black Colleges: A Narrative History, 1837–2009*. Macon, GA: Mercer University Press, 2011. 199–203.

Mangan, J. A. *Athleticism in the Victorian and Edwardian Public School: The Emergence and Consolidation of an Educational Ideology*. New York: Routledge, Taylor, and Francis, 1981.

Marlowe, Gertrude Woodruff. *A Right Worthy Grand Mission: Maggie Lena Walker and The Quest for Black Economic Empowerment*. Washington, DC: Howard University Press, 2003.

Martin, Charles H. *Benching Jim Crow: The Rise and Fall of the Color Line in Southern College Sports, 1890–1980*. Chapel Hill: University of North Carolina Press, 2010.

McKinney, Charles W., Jr. "Multiple Fronts: The Struggle for Black Educational and Political Equality in Wilson, North Carolina, 1941–1953." *North Carolina Historical Review* 88, no. 1 (January 2011): 1–39.

McNamara, John. *The Capital of Basketball: A History of DC Area High School Hoops*. Washington, DC: Georgetown University Press, 2019.

McTaggart, Ursula. "Writing Baseball into History: The *Pittsburgh Courier*, Integration, and Baseball in a War of Position." *American Studies* 47, no. 1 (Spring 2006): 113–32.

Mennell, James. "The Service of Football Program of World War I: Its Impact on the Popularity of the Game." *Journal of Sports History* 16, no. 3 (Winter 1989): 248.

Meyers, Christopher C. "Unrelenting War on Football: The Death of Richard Von Gammon and the Attempt to Ban Football in Georgia." *Georgia Historical Quarterly* 93, no. 4 (Winter 2009): 388–407.

Miller, James W. *Integrated: The Lincoln Institute and Vanished Tradition*. Lexington: University of Kentucky Press, 2017.

Miller, Patrick B. "The Manly, the Moral, and the Proficient: College Sport in the New South." *Journal of Sports History* 24, no. 3 (Fall 1997): 285–316.

———. "Muscular Assimilation: Sport and the Paradoxes of Racial Reform."

In Charles K. Ross, ed., *Race and Sport: The Struggle for Equality On and Off the Field*, 146–82 (Jackson: University Press of Mississippi, 2004).

Milton, George F. "Note on the Recent Industrial Crisis at the South." *Sewanee Review* 2, no. 2 (February 1894): 227–38.

Mitchell, Michele. *Righteous Propagation: African Americans the Politics of Racial Destiny After Reconstruction*. Chapel Hill: University of North Carolina Press, 2004.

"Money Woes, Declining Talent Plague HBCU Football." *USA Today* (website). May 26, 2014.

Moore, Jacqueline M. *Booker T. Washington, W. E. B. Du Bois, and the Struggle for Racial Uplift*. Wilmington, DE: Rowman & Littlefield, 2003.

Moore, James T. "Black Militancy in Readjuster Virginia, 1879–1883." *Journal of Southern History* 41, no. 2 (May 1975): 167–86.

Money, Tony. *Manly and Muscular Diversions: Public Schools in the Nineteenth-Century Sporting Revival*. London: Bristol Classic Press, 2001.

Morris, Eddie W. "The Contemporary Negro College and the Brain Drain." *Journal of Negro Education* 41, no. 4 (Autumn 1972): 309–19.

Mosley, Kyle T. "Deion Sanders: Confident HBCUs Can Compete Against FBS Programs." *Sports Illustrated* (website). September 18, 2021.

Muse, Benjamin. *Virginia's Massive Resistance*. Bloomington: University of Indiana Press, 1961.

Naison, Mark. *Communists in Harlem During the Depression: The Origins and Impact of America's Black Left*. Urbana: University of Illinois Press, 1983.

Nargiso, Brianna. "Why HBCUs Athletic Programs Have Not Reached Top Tier Status." Howard University News Service (website). undated.

Nathan, Daniel A., ed. *Rooting for the Home Team: Sports, Community, and Identity*. Urbana: University of Illinois Press, 2013.

Newman, Henry "Zipp." *The Impact of Southern College Football*. Kearney, NE: Morris Publishing Company, 1969.

Newman, Roberta J., and Joel Nathan Rosen. *Black Baseball, Black Business: Race Enterprise and the Fate of the Segregated Dollar*. Jackson: University Press of Mississippi, 2015.

O'Donnell, Ricky. "The NCAA Is Wrong about Grassroots Basketball." SB Nation (website). September 12, 2018.

O'Kelly, Charlotte G. "Black Newspapers and the Black Protest Movement: Their Historical Relationship, 1827–1945." *Phylon* 43, no. 1 (1st Qtr., 1982): 1–14.

Orfield, Gary. *Dismantling Desegregation: The Quiet Reversal of Brown v. Board of Education*. New York: Free Press, 2001.

Orfield, Gary and Erica Frankenberg. *Educational Delusions?: Why Choice Can Deepen Inequality and How to Make Schools Fair*. Berkeley: University of California Press, 2013.

Oriard, Michard. "Football Town Under Friday Night Lights: High School Football and American Dreams," pp.68–79 Nathan, Daniel A., ed.

Rooting for the Home Team: Sport, Community, and Identity. Urbana: University of Illinois Press. 2013.

———. *King Football: Sport and Spectacle in the Golden Age of Radio and Newsreels, Movies, and Magazines, the Weeklies and the Daily Press*. Chapel Hill: University of North Carolina Press, 2001, 24–39.

———. *Reading Football: How the Popular Press Created an American Spectacle*. Chapel Hill: University of North Carolina Press. 2000.

Ownby, Ted. *Subduing Satan: Religion, Recreation, and Manhood in the Rural South, 1865–1920*. Chapel Hill: University of North Carolina Press, 2014.

Parcel, Toby L., and Andrew J. Taylor. *The End of Consensus: Diversity Neighborhoods and the Politics of Public School Assignments*. Chapel Hill: University of North Carolina Press, 2015.

Park, Roberta J. "From Football to Rugby—and Back: The University of California-Stanford Response to the 'Football Crisis of 1905.'" *Journal of Sports History* 11, no. 3 (Winter 1984): 5–40.

Parriss, Wendell A. "Integration of Athletics in the District of Columbia Public High Schools." *Negro History Bulletin* 19, no. 1 (October 1955): 14–15.

Picott, J. Rupert. "Desegregation of Higher Education in Virginia." *Journal of Negro Education* 27, no. 3 (Summer 1958): 324–31.

Pincham, Linda B. "A League of Willing Workers: The Impact of Northern Philanthropy, Virginia Estelle Randolph and the Jeanes Teachers in Early Twentieth-Century Virginia." *Journal of Negro Education* 74, no. 2 (Spring 2005): 112–23.

"Physical Education." *Massachusetts Teacher* 3, no. 11 (November 1850): 342–48.

Pogge, Paul. "Full Court Press: Problems Plaguing Youth Basketball in the United States and an Aggressive Plan to Attack Them." *University of Denver Sports and Entertainment Law* (website).

Pratt, Robert A. *The Color of Their Skin: Education and Race in Richmond, Virginia, 1954–89*. Charlottesville: University of Virginia Press, 1992.

Pruter, Robert. *The Rise of American High School Sports and the Search for Control, 1880–1930*. Syracuse, NY: Syracuse University Press, 2013.

Pryor, Dante. "Changing the Narrative About HBCU Athletes." Saturday Blitz (website). May 21, 2021.

Rabinowitz, Howard N. "Half a Loaf: The Shift from White to Black Teachers in the Negro Schools of the Urban South, 1865–1890." *Journal of Southern History* 40, no. 4 (November 1974): 565–94.

Rael, Patrick. *Black Identity & Black Protest in the Antebellum North*. Chapel Hill: University of North Carolina Press, 2002.

Randolph, Adah L. Ward. "It Is Better to Light a Candle Than Curse the Darkness: Ethel Thompson Overby and Democratic Schooling in Richmond, Virginia, 1910–1958." *Journal of American Educational Studies Association* 48, no. 3 (May 2012): 220–43.

Reavis, Ralph. "Virginia Seminary: A Tangible Symbol of Opposition to White

Paternalism and Commitment to Self-Reliance." PhD diss., University of Virginia, 1989.

Reed, Adolph L., Jr. "W.E.B. Dubois: A Perspective on the Bases of His Political Thought." *Political Theory* 13, no. 3 (August 1985): 431–56.

Reynolds, Jesse A. *History of WPA Recreation*. Washington, DC: Works Progress Administration, 1947.

Rhoden, William C. *Forty Million Dollar Slaves: The Rise, Fall, and Redemption of the Black Athlete*. New York: Crown Publishing Group, 2006.

Ribowski, Mark. *A Complete History of the Negro Leagues, 1884 to 1955*. New York: Birch Lane Press, 1995.

Richardson, Archie G. *The Development of Negro Education in Virginia, 1831–1970*. Richmond, VA: Phi Delta Kappa, 1976.

Richardson, Jeanita W., and J. John Harris II. "Brown and Historically Black Colleges and Universities (HBCUs): A Paradox of Desegregation Policy." *Journal of Negro Education* 73, no. 3 (Summer 2004): 365–78.

Robertson, Sean. "Highland Springs Wins Class 5 State Football Championship After Victory Over Maury," *CBS News 6* (website). December 11, 2022.

Roe, Donald. "From Desegregation to Resegregation: The Crisis in the District of Columbia Public School System, 1954–1962." *Black History Bulletin* 67, no. 1/4 (January–December 2004): 18–25.

Rosa, Andrew J. "New Negroes on Campus: St. Clair Drake and the Culture of Education, Reform, and Rebellion at Hampton Institute." *History of Education Quarterly* 53, no. 3 (August 2013): 203–32.

Ross, Charles K., ed. *Race and Sport: The Struggle for Equality On and Off the Field*. Jackson: University Press of Mississippi, 2004.

———. *Outside the Lines: African Americans and the Integration of the National Football League*. New York: New York University Press, 2001.

Ross, Marlon B. *Manning the Race: Reforming Black Men in the Jim Crow Era*. New York: New York University Press, 2004.

Rudwick, Elliot M. "W. E. B. Du Bois in the Role of Crisis Editor." *Journal of Negro History* 43, no. 3 (July 1958): 214–40.

Russell, James S. "Rural Economic Progress of the Negro in Virginia." *Journal of Negro History* 11, no. 4 (October 1926): 556–62.

Ryan, James E. *Five Miles Away, A World Apart: One City, Two Schools, and the Story of Educational Opportunity in Modern America*. Oxford, UK: Oxford University Press, 2016.

Scamardo, Peter L., II. "Legend Reflects on How Corpus Christi Led Way to Integrate High School Football in Texas." *Corpus Cristi Caller Times* (website). November 25, 2019.

Schlabach, Mark. "Feds Drop Charges Against AAU Basketball Program Director." *ABC News* (website). February 14, 2018.

Schmidt, Raymond. *Shaping College Football: The Transformation of an American Sport, 1919–1930*. Syracuse, NY: Syracuse University Press, 2007.

Schultz, Jaime. "Contesting the Master Narrative: The Arthur Ashe Statue and

Monument Avenue in Richmond, Virginia." *International Journal of the History of Sport* 28, no. 8–9 (May 2011): 1235–51.

Seigel-Hawley, Genevieve. *When the Fences Come Down: Twenty-First Century Lessons from Metropolitan School Desegregation*. Chapel Hill: University of North Carolina Press, 2016.

Shampe, Clay, and Thomas R. Garrett. *Baseball in Portsmouth, Virginia*. Charleston, SC: Arcadia Publishing, 2004.

Shircliffe, Barbara J. "Rethinking *Turner v. Keefe*: The Parallel Mobilization of African-American and White Teachers in Tampa, Florida, 1936–1946." *History of Education Quarterly* 52, no. 1 (February 2012): 99–136.

Singleton Gregory Holmes. "Birth, Rebirth, and the "New Negro" of the 1920s." *Phylon* 43, no. 1 (1st Qtr., 1982): 29–45.

Smith, Hoke. "The Resources and Development of the South." *North American Review* 159, no. 453 (August 1894): 129–36.

Smith, J. Douglas. *Managing White Supremacy: Race, Politics, and Citizenship in Jim Crow Virginia*. Chapel Hill: University of North Carolina Press, 2002.

Smith, Ronald A. "Harvard and Columbia and a Reconsideration of the 1905–6 Football Crisis." *Journal of Sports History* 8, no. 3 (Winter 1981): 5–19.

———. *Play-By-Play: Radio, Television, and Big-Time College Sport*. Baltimore, MD: Johns Hopkins University Press, 2001.

———. "The William and Mary Athletic Scandal of 1951: Governance and the Battle for Academic and Athletic Integrity." *Journal of Sport History* 34, no. 3 (Fall 2007): 353–73.

Smith, Martin P., et al. "The Historical Hypocrisy of the Black Student-Athlete." *Race, Gender & Class* 21, no. 1/2 (2013): 220–35.

Snell, David Kingsley. *The Baron and the Bear: Rupp's Runts, Haskins's Miners, and the Season That Changed Basketball Forever*. Lincoln: University of Nebraska Press, 2016.

Soares, Leigh Alexandra. "A Bold Promise: Black Readjusters and the Founding of Virginia State University." MA thesis, Duke University, 2010.

Solomon, Mark. *The Cry Was Unity: Communists and African Americans, 1917–1936*. Jackson: University Press of Mississippi, 1998.

Spearman, Karhan. The Future of HBCU Football, Daily Dot (website). October 6, 2021.

Spivey, Donald. *Racism, Activism, and Integrity in College Football: The Bates Must Play Movement*. Durham, NC: Carolina Academic Publishing, 2021.

Springer, Shira. "HBCUs and Their Role in Disrupting the College Sports Cartel." WBUR (website). October 13, 2017.

Stark, Douglas. *Breaking Barriers: A History of Integration in Professional Basketball*. Washington, DC: Rowman & Littlefield, 2018.

Stewart, Peter C. *American Sports and the Great War: College, Military and Professional Athletics, 1916–1919*. Jefferson, NC: McFarland & Company Press, 2021.

———. *Early Professional Baseball in Hampton Roads, A History, 1884–1928.* Jefferson, NC: McFarland & Company Press, 2010.

Stewart, Peter, and Thomas R. Garrett. *The Legacy Renewed, Football and Foreman Field: Norfolk Division—Old Dominion University.* Kitty Hawk, NC: Outer Banks Press, 2009.

Struna, Nancy L. "The Formalizing of Sport and the Formation of an Elite: The Chesapeake Gentry, 1650–1720s." *Journal of Sports History* 13, no. 3 (Winter 1986): 212–34.

Suggs, H. Lewis. "Black Strategy and Ideology in the Segregation Era: P. B. Young and the *Norfolk Journal and Guide*, 1910–1954." *Virginia Magazine of History and Biography* 91, no. 2 (April 1983): 161–90.

———. *P. B. Young, Newspaperman: Race, Politics, and Journalism in the New South.* Charlottesville: University of Virginia Press, 1989.

———. "P. B. Young of the *Norfolk Journal and Guide*: A Booker T. Washington Militant, 1904–1928," *Journal of Negro History* 64, no. 4 (Autumn 1979): 365–76.

Suggs, H. Lewis, ed. *The Black Press in the South, 1865–1979.* Westport, CT: Greenwood Press, 1983.

Summers, Martin. *Manliness and Its Discontents: The Black Middle Class and the Transformation of Masculinity, 1900–1930.* Chapel Hill: University of North Carolina Press, 2004.

Surdam, David George. *Wins, Losses, and Empty Seats: How Baseball Outlasted the Great Depression.* Lincoln: University of Nebraska Press, 2011.

Swain, Martha H. "The Harrison Education Bills, 1936–1941." *Mississippi Quarterly* 31, no. 1 (Winter 1977): 119–31.

Sweeney, James R., ed. *Race, Reason, and Massive Resistance: The Diary of David J. Mays, 1954–1959.* Athens: University of Georgia Press, 2008.

———. "Southern Strategies." *Virginia Magazine of History and Biography* 106, no. 2 (Spring 1998): 165–200.

Taylor, Kay Ann. "Mary S. Peake and Charlotte L. Forten: Black Teachers During the Civil War and Reconstruction." *Journal of Negro Education* 74, no. 2 (Spring 2005): 124–37.

Taylor, Keeanga Yamahtta. *Race for Profit: How Banks and the Real Estate Industry Undermined Black Homeownership.* Chapel Hill: University of North Carolina Press, 2019.

Thompson, C. H. "Editorial Comment: The Harrison-Black-Fletcher Bill Makes Its Debut." *Journal of Negro Education* 6, no. 2 (April 1937): 129–33.

———. "The History of the National Basketball Tournament for Black High Schools." PhD diss., Louisiana State University, 1980.

Thomas, Damion L. *Globetrotting: African American Athletes and Cold War Politics.* Urbana: University of Illinois Press, 2017.

Thomas, David Y. "Political Science in Southern Universities," *Sewanee Review* 16, no. 4 (October 1908): 466–71.

Thomas, Niklas, and Till Neuhas. "Shut Up and Dribble: Fractured Race Relations in the NBA in Times of (Perceived) Corporate Crisis." *Jam It! Fractured States of America* 6 (May 2022): 132–54.

Thornbrough, Emma Lou. "American Negro Newspapers, 1880–1914." *Business History Review* 40, no. 4 (Winter 1966): 467–90.

Thorp, Daniel B. *Facing Freedom: An African American Community in Virginia From Reconstruction to Jim Crow.* Charlottesville: University of Virginia Press, 2017.

Thurman, Francis Ashton. "The History of Saint Paul's College, Lawrenceville, Virginia, 1888–1959." PhD diss., Howard University, 1979.

Titus, Jill Ogline. *Brown's Battleground: Students, Segregationists, and the Struggle for Justice in Prince Edward County, Virginia.* Chapel Hill: University of North Carolina Press, 2011.

Tomas, J. Douglas. *Football U: Spectator Sports in the Life of the American University.* Ann Arbor: University of Michigan Press, 2003.

Toppin, Edgar Allen. *Loyal Sons and Daughters: Virginia State University, 1882 to 1992.* New York: Pictorial Heritage Publishing, Co., 1992.

———. "Walter White and the Atlanta NAACP's Fight for Equal Schools." *History of Education Quarterly* 7, no. 1 (Spring 1967): 3–21.

Trahan, Kevin. "Should Grambling State, Southern, and Other HBCUs Drop out of Division 1 Football?" Vice (website). May 12, 2016.

Trotter, Joe William, Jr. *From a Raw Deal to a New Deal?: African Americans, 1929–1945.* New York: Oxford University Press, 1996.

Tynes, Tyler. "The Golden Age of Black College Football Lost to Integration." The Ringer (website). September 19, 2019.

Valkeakari, Tuire. "New Negro Men, World War I, and African American Masculinity in Guy Johnson's 'Standing at the Scratch Line.'" *MELUS* 39, no. 4 (Winter 2014): 50–68.

Verbrugge, Martha H., and Drew Yingling. "The Politics of Play: The Struggle over Racial Segregation and Public Recreation in Washington, D.C., 1945–1950." *Washington History* 27, no. 2 (Fall 2015): 56–69.

Virginia Writer's Project. *The Negro in Virginia.* New York: Hastings House, 1940.

Walker, Curtis H. "The Social Sciences in Southern Colleges and Universities." *Social Forces* 7, no. 2 (December 1928): 230–34.

Wallerstein, Peter. *Blue Laws and Black Codes: Conflicts, Courts, and Change in Twentieth Century Virginia.* Charlottesville: University of Virginia Press, 2004.

———. *Race, Sex, and the Freedom to Marry: Loving v. Virginia.* Lawrence: University of Kansas Press, 2014.

Watson, John Brown. "Football in Southern Negro Football." *Voice of the Negro* 4, no. 4 (May 1907): 165–66.

Watterson, John Sayle. *College Football: History, Spectacle, Controversy.* Baltimore, MD: Johns Hopkins University Press, 2000.

———. "The Death of Archer Christian: College President and the Reform of College Football." *Journal of Sports History* 22, no. 3 (Summer 1995): 149–67.

———. "Football at the University of Virginia, 1951–1961: A Perfect Gridiron Storm." *Journal of Sport History* 34, no. 3 (Fall 2007): 375–87.

———. "The Gridiron Crisis of 1905: Was it Really a Crisis." *Journal of Sports History* 27, no. 2 (Summer 2000): 291–98.

———. "Political Football: Theodore Roosevelt, Woodrow Wilson and the Gridiron Reform Movement." *Presidential Studies Quarterly* 25, no. 3 (Summer 1995): 555–64.

Wennersten, John R. "The Black School Teacher in Maryland, 1930's." *Negro History Bulletin* 38, no. 1 (April/May 1975): 370–73.

Wetzel, Dan. "Former AAU Basketball Coach Says Those Wrapped Up in College Basketball Scandal Will Flip for Feds." Yahoo News (website). September 26, 2017.

White, Derrick. *Blood, Sweat, and Tears: Jake Gathers, Florida A&M, and the History of Black College Football.* Chapel Hill: University of North Carolina Press, 2019.

Wiggins, David K. "Edwin Bancroft Henderson: Physical Educator, Civil Rights Activist, and Chronicler of African American Athletes." *Research Quarterly for Exercise and Sport* 70, no. 2 (June 1999): 91–112.

———. "'The Future of College Athletics Is at Stake:' Black Athletes and Racial Turmoil on Three Predominantly White University Campuses, 1968–1972." *Journal of Sport History* 15, no. 3 (Winter 1988): 304–33.

———. *Glory Bound: Black Athletes in a White America.* Syracuse, NY: Syracuse University Press, 1997.

———. "'With All Deliberate Speed': High School Sports, Race, and *Brown v. Board of Education.*" *Journal of Sports History* 37, no. 3 (Fall 2010): 329–46.

Wiggins, David K., and Ryan Swanson, eds. *Separate Games: African American Sport Behind the Walls of Segregation.* Fayetteville: University of Arkansas Press, 2016.

Wilkerson, Doxey A. "The Negro School Movement in Virginia: From 'Equalization' to 'Integration.'" *Journal of Negro Education* 29, no. 1 (Winter 1960): 17–29.

Williams, Chad L. "Vanguards of the New Negro: African American Veterans and Post-World War I Racial Militancy." *Journal of African American History* 92, no. 3 (Summer 2007): 347–70.

Winsboro, Irvin D. S., and Abel A. Bartley. "Race, Education, and Regionalism: The Long and Troubling History of School Desegregation in the Sunshine State." *Florida Historical Quarterly* 92, no. 4 (Spring 2014): 714–45.

Woldoff, Rachel A. *White Flight/Black Flight: The Dynamics of Racial Change in an American Neighborhood.* Ithaca, NY: Cornell University Press, 2011.

Woodruff, Fuzzy. *A History of Southern Football, 1890–1928.* Walter M. Brown Publishing, 1928.

Woodward, C. Vann. *Origins of the New South, 1877–1913.* Baton Rouge: Louisiana State University Press, 1951.

Wright, Dianne Swann. *Claiming Family and Freedom in the New South.* Charlottesville: University of Virginia Press, 2002.

Wright, Joshua. "Be Like Mike?: The Black Athlete's Dilemma." *Spectrum: A Journal on Black Men* 4, no. 2 (Spring 2016): 1–19.

Wynes, Charles E. *Race Relations in Virginia*. Lanham, MD: Rowman & Littlefield, 1971.

Young, A. S. "Doc." Negro Firsts in Sports. Chicago: Johnson Publishing Co., 1963.

Yusuf, Omer. "Team Penny Captures Second Straight AAU National Title." *Commercial Appeal* (Memphis, TN) (website). July 13, 2015.

Zimbalist, Andrew. *Unpaid Professionals: Commercialism and Conflict in Big-Time College Sports*. Princeton, NJ: Princeton University Press, 1999.

Index

Page numbers in italics refer to figures